WORLD DESIGN

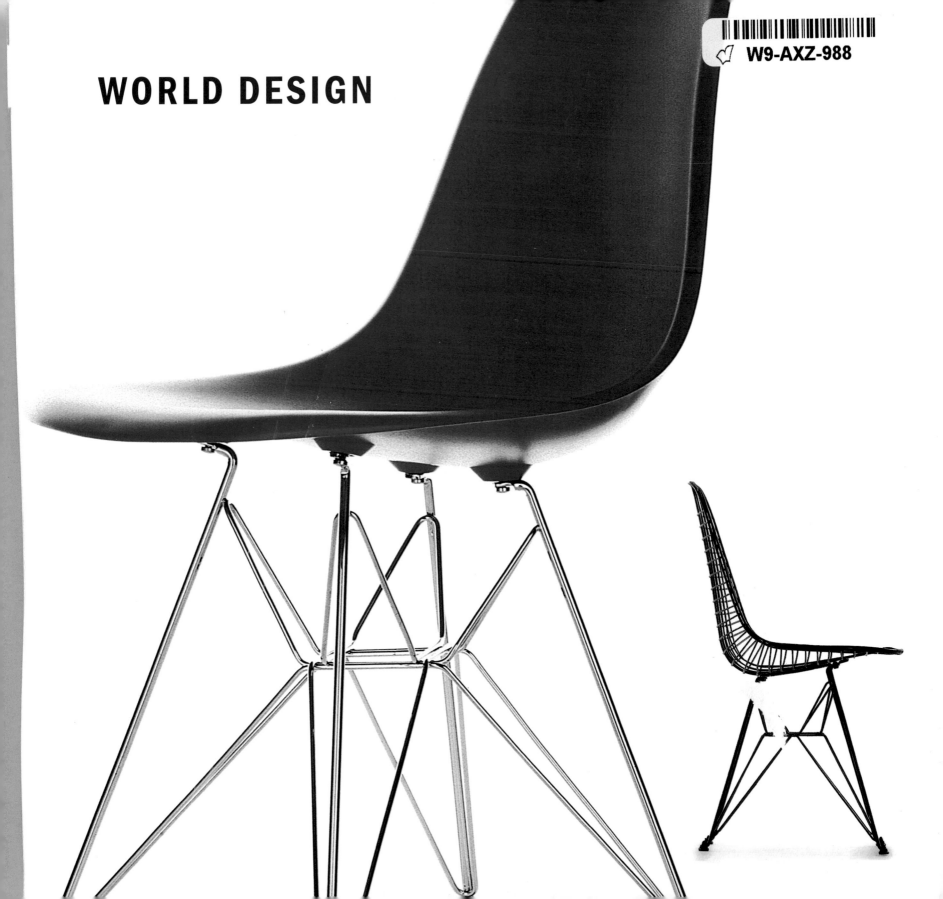

WORLD DESIGN

The Best in Classic and Contemporary Furniture, Fashion, Graphics and More

Uta Abendroth   Karin Beate Phillips   Christian Pixis   Volkard Steinbach   Bernd Polster (Editor)

CHRONICLE BOOKS

SAN FRANCISCO

First published in the United States in 2000 by
Chronicle Books
Text copyright © 1999 by Howard Buch Produktion
Bonn, Germany

Concept and realization:
Howard Buch Produktion
Editor: Bernd Polster
Art director: Olaf Meyer

Cover design: Jeremy Stout

English translation © 1999 by Pavilion Books Limited

Library of Congress Cataloging-in-Publication Data
available.

Half-title page:
Charles Eames, Ray Eames,
Plastic chair, 1959; Wire chair, 1961
Title page:
Battista Pinin Farina,
Cisitalia coupé, 1947;
Ron Arad,
Europa steel sofa, 1994

ISBN 0-8118-2624-4
Printed in Italy.

10 9 8 7 6 5 4 3 2 1

Chronicle Books
85 Second Street
San Francisco, California 94105

www.chroniclebooks.com

Charles Rennie Mackintosh
Willow chair, 1904

Yves Saint Laurent
Mondrian dress, 1966

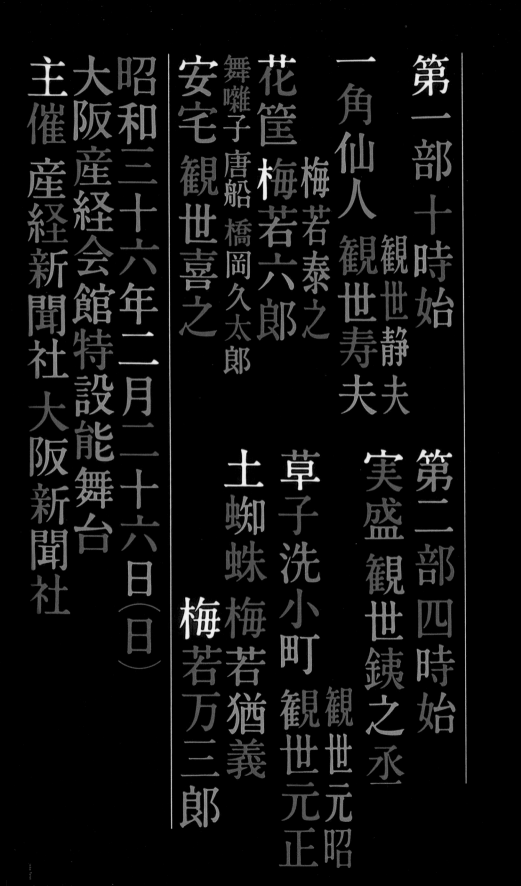

第八回産経観世能

第一部 十時始

一角仙人 観世寿夫
観世静夫

花筐 梅若六郎
梅若泰之

安宅 観世喜之
観世喜之

舞囃子 唐船 橋岡久太郎

第二部 四時始

実盛 観世銕之丞

草子洗小町 観世元昭
観世元正

土蜘蛛 梅若万三郎
梅若猶義

昭和三十六年二月二十六日(日)
大阪産経会館特設能舞台
主催 産経新聞社 大阪新聞社

Ikko Tanaka
Theater poster, 1961

Hans Gugelot, Dieter Rams
Braun *SK4 Phonosuper*
radiogram, 1956

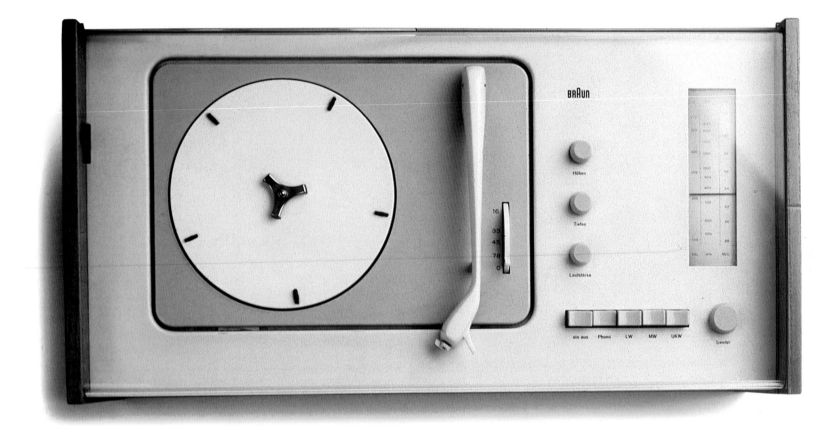

Contents

George Nelson
Model 4755 wall clock, 1947

" In modern society, the father may be a stonemason, the mother a teacher and the daughter a movie star. The modern dwelling must be built to meet all these requirements. **Alvar Aalto** From now on the tendency of our age should follow a manner of design appropriate to machine production. **Peter Behrens** There is no urban form which has not failed or is not in the process of failing. **Andrea Branzi** I wanted every spread you opened to be a poster. **Neville Brody** One cannot communicate anything. **David Carson** Every object is a message that demands an answer. The fact that it is produced in tens of thousands is very stimulating because it brings you in contact with the whole world. **Anna Castelli Ferrieri** Video has recorded the movie. Taped music has become more real than live performance. Advertising has sublimated the product. **Nigel Coates** Affluence offers the kind of freedom I am deeply suspicious of. It offers freedom from restraint, and it is virtually impossible to do something without restraints. **Charles Eames** Basically it is a matter of making our customers successful. **Hartmut Esslinger** In America I brazenly sell my jeans for fifty dollars. If you think about it, fifty bucks isn't a hell of a lot to pay for a lovely ass. **Elio Fiorucci** It is unimportant what style we use, baroque or tubular steel. What modernism has given us is freedom. **Josef Frank** The white spaces inside a letter are more important than its external outline. **Adrian Frutiger** The Bauhaus fights imitation, inferior craftsmanship and artistic dilettantism. **Walter Gropius** Lighting is like driving a car. The requirements are the same. **Poul Henningsen** I believe that finished products and industrial design make people more neighborly. In small things the status symbol disappears. **Arne Jacobsen** I am influenced by the world that says I influence it. **Kenzo Takada** Everything begins with the cut. **Calvin Klein** Poetic insight will remain fundamental to the exaltation of the individual. **Jack Lenor Larsen** My clothing is anti-fashion. I like things that will age, that will look better next year. **Ralph Lauren** Decoration is disguise. **Le Corbusier** Design is the art that combines consumer needs with the possibilities of industrial production. **Olavi Lindén** Ugliness sells badly. **Raymond F. Loewy** Less is more. **Ludwig Mies van der Rohe**

The first rule for a designer is to find the right customer. **Massimo Morozzi**   Apart from the desire to produce beautiful things, the leading passion of my life has been hatred of modern civilization. **William Morris**   It is a marketing ploy of huge dimensions, calculated to sell a product by covering it with a skin which smells of design. No one finds this smell as bad as the designer, whose good intentions are sliced in two and sprayed matte black. **Jasper Morrison**   I am deeply suspicious of the still-popular version of the "designer genius" who designs a flower vase today and an airplane tomorrow. **Alexander Neumeister**   A failed experiment can be more important than a trivial design. **Verner Panton**   There will be no postmodern design. **Pentagon**   Art has become enamored of industry and industry has become part of an intellectual phenomenon. **Gio Ponti**   Showing off with design has become fashionable. **Andrée Putman**   All a designer can do is to anticipate a mood before people realize that they are bored. It is simply a question of getting bored first. **Mary Quant** I want to make things that recede into the background. **Dieter Rams**   Our chairs, tables and cupboards will be abstract-real sculptures in the interiors of the future. **Gerrit Rietveld**   We don't expect everyone to become expert designers. That is neither possible nor desirable. We cannot all become accountants, but we can learn to read a balance sheet. **Gordon Russell**   Having an idea is something that cannot be learned anywhere. **Richard Sapper**   The accusation that all cars look alike has existed for ages. I believe that there is a strong tendency to invalidate it. **Peter Schreyer**   For fifty years function has been considered an established concept when in fact it has never been fully understood. **Borek Sipek**   I am not taken in by good form. **Ettore Sottsass**   Design does not really interest me. **Philippe Starck**   Where there is already a hole one must not drill another one. **Stiletto** Less is bore. **Robert Venturi**   Sex is fashion. **Vivienne Westwood**   Good taste is ` not a substitute for knowledge. **Frank Lloyd Wright**

"

Aino **Aalto** Alvar Aalto Eero Aarnio Otl Aicher Werner Aisslinger Franco Albini Ron Arad Junichi Arai

Michio Arai Archizoom Giorgio Armani Gunnar Asplund Sergio Asti Antonia Astori Gae Aulenti Hiroshi

Awatsuji Jonathan Barnbrook Saul Bass Herbert Bayer Martine Bedin Peter Behrens Mario Bellini Maria

Benktzon Morris Fuller Benton Sigvard Bernadotte Lucian Bernhard Harry Bertoia Nuccio Bertone

Flaminio Bertoni Max Bill Cini Boeri Jonas Bohlin Kay Bojesen Osvaldo Borsani Mario Botta Marianne

Brandt Andrea Branzi Wilhelm Braun-Feldweg Marcel Breuer Neville Brody Julian Brown Carlo Bugatti

Rido Busse Erberto Carboni David Carson Louis Cartier A.M. Cassandre Jean-Charles de Castelbajac

Anna Castelli Ferrieri Achille Castiglioni Coco Chanel Pierre Chareau Antonio Citterio Claesson, Koivisto,

Rune Nigel Coates Wells Coates Luigi Colani Joe Colombo Terence Conran Hans Coray Nick Crosbie

Björn Dahlström Lucienne Day Robin Day Michele De Lucchi De Pas, D'Urbino, Lomazzi Paolo Deganello

Christian Dell Christian Dior Nanna Ditzel Tom Dixon Christopher Dresser Henry Dreyfuss Gert Dumbar

James Dyson Charles Eames, Ray Eames Harley Earl Egon Eiermann Kenji Ekuan Hartmut Esslinger

Battista Pinin Farina Edward Fella Adele Fendi Salvatore Ferragamo Gianfranco Ferré Marco Ferreri

Elio Fiorucci Willy Fleckhaus Piero Fornasetti Norman Foster Kaj Franck Josef Frank Gianfranco Frattini

Adrian Frutiger Shigeo Fukuda Olivier Gagnère John Galliano Niels Gammelgaard Elizabeth Garouste,

Mattia Bonetti Gatti, Paolini, Teodoro Antoni Gaudí Jean-Paul Gaultier Frank O. Gehry Romeo Gigli

Stefano Giovannoni Giorgetto Giugiaro Hubert de Givenchy Milton Glaser Kenneth Grange Michael Graves

Eileen Gray Konstantin Grcic Walter Gropius Hans Gugelot Tricia Guild Alfredo Walter Häberli, Christophe

Marchand Edward Hald Niels Jørgen Haugesen Rolf Heide Poul Henningsen Josef Hoffmann Hans Hollein

Knud Holscher Fujiwo Ishimoto Alec Issigonis Arne Jacobsen Grete Jalk Georg Jensen Jacob Jensen

Hella Jongerius Finn Juhl Yusaku Kamekura Mitsuo Katsui Edward McKnight Kauffer Katsuo Kawasaki

Isamu Kenmochi Kenzo Takada Perry A. King, Santiago Miranda Toshiyuki Kita Poul Kjaerholm Calvin

Klein Kaare Klint Florence Knoll Henning Koppel Ferdinand Kramer Yrjö Kukkapuro Shiro Kuramata

Masayuki Kurokawa Christian Lacroix Karl Lagerfeld René Lalique Jack Lenor Larsen Ralph Lauren Le

Corbusier Alain Le Quernec David Lewis Christian Liaigre Börge Lindau Olavi Lindén Stefan Lindfors

Vicke Lindstrand   El Lissitzky   Raymond F. Loewy   Adolf Loos   Ross Lovegrove   Ingeborg Lundin   Claus Luthe   Charles Rennie Mackintosh   Vico Magistretti   Erik Magnussen   John Makepeace   Robert Mallet-Stevens   Peter Maly   Angelo Mangiarotti   Enzo Mari   Maurice Marinot   Javier Mariscal   Michael Marriott   Bruno Mathsson   Robert Sebastian Matta   Herbert Matter   Ingo Maurer   J Mays   Sergio Mazza   Warren McArthur   Alexander McQueen   Alberto Meda   David Mellor   Alessandro Mendini   Grethe Meyer   Ludwig Mies van der Rohe   Issey Miyake   Børge Mogensen   Bill Moggeridge   László Moholy-Nagy   Carlo Mollino   Claude Montana   Hiroshi Morishima   Massimo Morozzi   William Morris   Jasper Morrison   Franco Moschino   Alex Moulton   Pascal Mourgue   Thierry Mugler   Bruno Munari   George Nelson   Alexander Neumeister   Mark Newson   Bruno Ninaber van Eyben   Marcello Nizzoli   Isamu Noguchi   Jean Henri Nouvel   Eliot Noyes   Antti Nurmesniemi   Vuokko Nurmesniemi   Sinya Okayama   Vaughan Oliver   Peter Opsvik   Verner Panton   Jorge Pensi   Pentagon   Charlotte Perriand   Gaetano Pesce   Roberto Pezzetta   Christophe Pillet   Warren Platner   Paul Poiret   Gio Ponti   Ferdinand A. Porsche   Carl Pott   Jean Prouvé   Andrée Putman   Mary Quant   Paco Rabanne   Ernest Race   Ingegerd Råman   Dieter Rams   Paul Rand   Prospero Rasulo   Jamie Reid   Paul Renner   Richard Riemerschmid   Gerrit Rietveld   Jens Risom   Paolo Rizzatto   Alexander Rodtschenko   Johan Rohde   Aldo Rossi   Jacques- Émile Ruhlmann   Gordon Russell   Eero Saarinen   Eliel Saarinen   Lino Sabattini   Bruno Sacco   Marc Sadler   Yves Saint Laurent   Roberto Sambonet   Thomas Sandell   Denis Santachiara   Richard Sapper   Gino Sarfatti   Timo Sarpaneva   Sixten Sason   Peter Saville   William Sawaya   Carlo Scarpa   Peter Schmidt   Peter Schreyer   Ben Shahn   Shounsai Shono   Dieter Sieger   Borek Sípek   Paul Smith   Ettore Sottsass   Mart Stam   Philippe Starck   Stiletto   Giotto Stoppino   Studio 65   Gerald Summers   Superstudio   Kazuhide Takahama   Roger Tallon   Ikko Tanaka   Walter Dorwin Teague   Giuseppe Terragni   Mats Theselius   Michael Thonet   Matteo Thun   Kurt Thut   Louis Comfort Tiffany   Tomato   Earl S. Tupper   Oscar Tusquets Blanca   Masanori Umeda   Valentino   Gino Valle   Valvomo   Henry van de Velde   Rudy Vanderlans   Paolo Venini   Robert Venturi   Gianni Versace   Lella Vignelli, Massimo Vignelli   Arnout Visser   Burkhard Vogtherr   Wilhelm Wagenfeld   Otto Wagner   Marcel Wanders   Kem Weber   Josiah Wedgwood   Hans J. Wegner   Daniel Weil   Vivienne Westwood   Stefan Wewerka   Why Not   Tapio Wirkkala   Frank Lloyd Wright   Russel Wright   Yohji Yamamoto   Sori Yanagi   Tadanori Yokoo   Marco **Zanuso**

Aino **Aalto**

1894–1949 **Finland**

Beautiful glass for all. The ribbed, cone-shaped glasses opening out towards the top helped to bring contemporary Finnish glass design to international notice. Dating from 1932, Aino Aalto's *Bölgeblick* range consisted of ordinary household goods made of pressed glass, originally produced by the Iittala glass factory and continuing in production for several years. This popular set was not simply inexpensive and very extensive —it included carafes and brandy glasses—but it also had a magnificent clarity. Ingeniously, the ribbing served to conceal any initial deficiencies in quality. Aino Aalto, born Aino Marsio, was an architect who married the as yet unknown Alvar Aalto in 1924, when both of them were living in the country. Aino played an important part in her husband's success. In fact, it is never quite clear who designed what. Certainly, without Aino, who managed the jointly owned Artek company, Alvar's products would not have been sold throughout the world.

1 *Bölgeblick* jug, 1932
2 *Bölgeblick* glass, 1932

1

2

Alvar **Aalto** 1898–1976 **Finland**

Functionalism in birch. Aalto became famous for the Finnish pavilion he designed for the New York World's Fair of 1939, which was described as a "symphony in wood." In the late 1920s the architect Alvar Aalto was designing the very modernist sanatorium in Paimio, near Turku, and as a perfectionist who thought his buildings through to the smallest detail, he also made sure that the furniture was right. He did not want the sick to sit on the cold, metal chairs that were then the symbol of modernism. Instead, Aalto used wood, a traditional material he had been experimenting with for many years. Thin wooden sheets were glued together in layers. From these laminates he made curved flexible elements on which he mounted plywood bent into an S-shape for the seat and back. Aalto used Finnish birch in this way for the *Paimio* armchair, thus creating a new type of furniture. Alvar Aalto's designs were quite different from the "international style" that was current at the time. Their shapes were organic—forms which became known as "Aalto waves"—already heralding the kidney-shaped tables of the 1950s; they made use of a natural material, and their function was related to the human form. Aalto furniture is still produced today by Artek, the company co-founded by Aalto in 1935. One of its greatest commercial successes has been the first cantilever armchair made of wood, the Scandinavian answer to the Bauhaus. Although Aalto's furniture was never mass-produced, many will be familiar with the *No. 60* stool.

2

1

1 Dish, 1936
2 *Savoy* vase, 1936
3 *43* chaise longue, 1936
4 *331* ceiling light, 1954
5 *Paimio* armchair, 1931

4

5

3

Eero **Aarnio** b. 1932 **Finland**

The breakdown of design conventions. Aarnio designed a plastic ball inside which one could withdraw, whose unusual appearance led to its appearance in several science fiction films. Eero Aarnio was a young furniture maker from Helsinki who became a sought-after designer of international renown in the early 1960s as a result of this plastic *Ball* chair. It was Aarnio's first experiment with synthetic materials and it became an immediate success. *Ball* was not only a quiet place for turbulent times but also a manifesto for individual self-rule. Above all, however, Aarnio had also questioned the tradition of furniture design with this strict, geometric shape. *Ball* was the craziest seat of all time, an innovative concept that led to new body postures and ways of communicating. In the years that followed, the "newcomer" from Finland continued to experiment with other modern materials such as fiberglass, nylon, steel and foam rubber, while overturning many conventions. Chairs such as the *Pastilli*, *Bubble* and *Tomato* are classics of the pop era and they are enjoying renewed popularity, after a period in which they were pushed into the background by ecological awareness.

1

1 *Ball* chair, 1963
2 *Delfin* tables, 1993
3 *Pastilli* armchair, 1967
4 *Screw* table, 1991
5 *Bubble* chair, 1968
6 *Formular* armchair, 1998

3

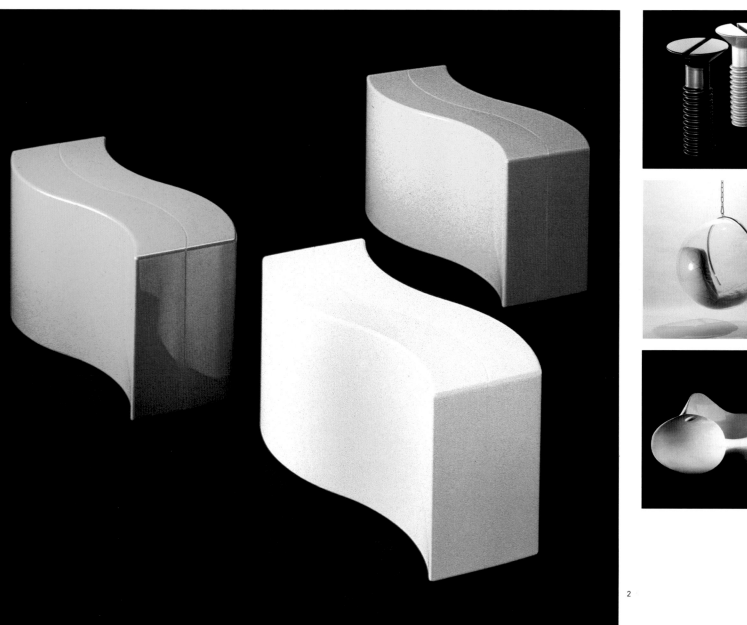

2

4

5

6

Otl **Aicher**

1922–91 **Germany**

The man who changed the world by changing typefaces. Otl Aicher's lettering for the airline Lufthansa literally went round the world, and he has undoubtedly had a great influence on the craft of visual communication. His many creations are distinguished by their clarity and restraint, exemplified by the internationally understandable system of pictograms which he originally developed for the 1972 Munich Olympic games. Following World War II, Aicher gave up his art studies after a few terms in order to set up as an independent designer. He and his late wife Inge Scholl—whose siblings were murdered by the Nazis for being members of the resistance—were among the founders of the Ulm School of Design, one of the most important and influential post-1945 design initiatives, which Aicher saw as an important part of the democratic rebuilding of Germany. Together with Max Bill he had a lasting influence on the development of design. Much of Otl Aicher's work was for design-oriented firms such as Braun, Erco and FSB, but he was also retained by large companies like BMW and the Dresdner Bank. His rational, holistic approach typically resulted in a complete renewal of the client's corporate identity. Shortly before his death he developed a typeface which he named after the village where he lived: *Rotis* (1988).

1 Logo, 1969
2 Logo, 1976
3 *Rotis* typeface, 1988
4 Logo for the 1972 Olympic Games
5 Pictograms for the 1972 Olympic Games

1 *Endless Shelf* shelving unit, 1994
2 *Soft Cell* chair, 1997

Werner **Aisslinger** b. 1964 **Germany**

Systems with ideas. With his basket chair *Juli* (1996, for Cappellini) Aisslinger paid tribute to the "organic design" of the 1940s and 1950s. This surprisingly refreshing retro object was immediately acquired by the Museum of Modern Art for inclusion in its permanent collection, an honor not often granted to furniture designers from Germany; the previous one had been Richard Sapper in 1964. Werner Aisslinger benefited greatly from periods of apprenticeship with renowned furniture designers. In London he worked with Ron Arad and Jasper Morrison, while back in Germany he worked with Andreas Brandolini before taking part in various projects for Michele De Lucchi in Milan in the early 1990s. Shortly after he began as an independent designer, he had a breakthrough with the shelving unit *Endless Shelf* (1994, for Porro). Extendable in all directions, this was extremely popular and led to a wider range of work: he has, for instance, developed showroom concepts for Mercedes Benz and for the telephone company E-plus. His *Soft Cell* seating furniture (1999) is strikingly innovative, made from a transparent gel which until recently was mainly used in medicine.

Franco **Albini**

1905–77 **Italy**

The perfectionist. The ideals of the
Bauhaus provided a model for the
architect and furniture designer Franco
Albini. Once hailed by Alessandro
Mendini as "the greatest master of
modern architecture in Italy," Albini was a
champion of rationalist architecture and a
designer of rigorously simple chairs. But
while chairs like the *Luisa* (1954, for
Poggi) or the *Fiorenza* armchair (1956, for
Arflex) are reminiscent of the German
example, their lines also reveal an Italian
element, a certain fluidity, which softens
the frequently dogmatic approach of
Bauhaus design. Franco Albini had a
weakness for sophisticated solutions; for
instance, for the 1940 Milan Triennale he
designed an "afternoon room" for a villa
which boasted stairs suspended from
steel cables and a tree growing through
the floor, as well as a pair of armchairs
which hung from the ceiling like the seats
of a double chairlift—the very symbol of
free suspension. A transparent radio
designed in 1938 was never produced. On
the other hand, one of his projects,
carried out with his partner Franca Helg
and graphic designer Bob Noorda, still
dominates the cityscape of Milan: the
subway stations of Line 1.

1

1 *LB 7* bookshelves, 1957
2 *Cavalletto* table, 1951
3 *Luisa* chair, 1954
4 *PL 19* armchair (with Franca Helg), 1957

Ron **Arad** b. 1951 **Israel and Great Britain**

From collector of rejects to cult figure. The shelves, bookcases, chairs, sofas and tables created by London-based Israeli Ron Arad look more like sculptural objects than furniture. Recognized as one of the most creative representative designers of the 1980s, the artist is now part of the "Design Establishment." This was not always to be predicted. After studying art at the Jerusalem Academy for two years, Arad came to London in 1973 to study architecture and went on to work in an architect's office. It was only in 1981 that the adopted Londoner turned to furniture making. Using reject materials from high-tech industry such as tubes, coupling boxes and joints, he began to weld together his aluminum and steel objects. Today Arad's works are often made in two versions, the original from steel, and the mass production made from synthetics or other soft materials. Originally made from steel strip, the plastic version of the "spring" bookshelf/support *Bookworm* (1994, Kartell) became a resounding commercial success. Ron Arad is now involved in important large-scale projects such as the interior decoration of the Opera house in Tel Aviv. He is a much sought-after designer, especially in Italy where famous names such as Moroso, Sawaya & Moroni, Poltronova, Kartell and Fiam Italia vie for his services.

2

1

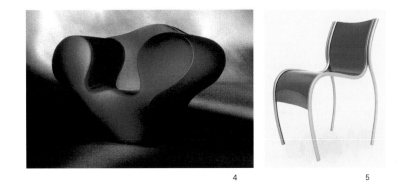

1 Bookshelf, 1993
2 *A Suitable Case* chair, 1994
3 *After Spring / Before Summer* table, 1992
4 *Soft Big Easy* armchair, 1989
5 *Fantastic Plastic Elastic* chair, 1998

4   5

Junichi **Arai** b. 1932 Japan

Inspirations from the printer's workshop. The 36 patents registered by textile designer Junichi Arai speak for themselves and mark him out as one of the most productive artists in his field, and a man who is also known for introducing new manufacturing processes. Arai's passion for fabrics and their versatility did not come about by chance and indeed it started almost in the cradle; he was brought up in a family of weavers in the ancient textile center of Kiryu. He started his career in the family business and completed his training in one of his father's kimono factories. However, he soon abandoned the traditional Japanese approach. As early as the mid-1950s he began to experiment with modern weaves such as metal yarns and chemically modified fibers. Two decades later he was one of the first to realize the computer's great potential in the design of fabrics and also in the field of production. An example was his manufacture of quadruple-printed fabric with varying patterns. Since the 1980s Arai has also experimented with techniques outside those traditionally used in the textile trade, such as thermal printing processes. He became even more famous when Japanese fashion designers Issey Miyake and Rei Kawakubo discovered him and used his fabrics in their collections.

1 Fabric, 1992
2 Bag, 1998
3 Fabric, 1997

2

3

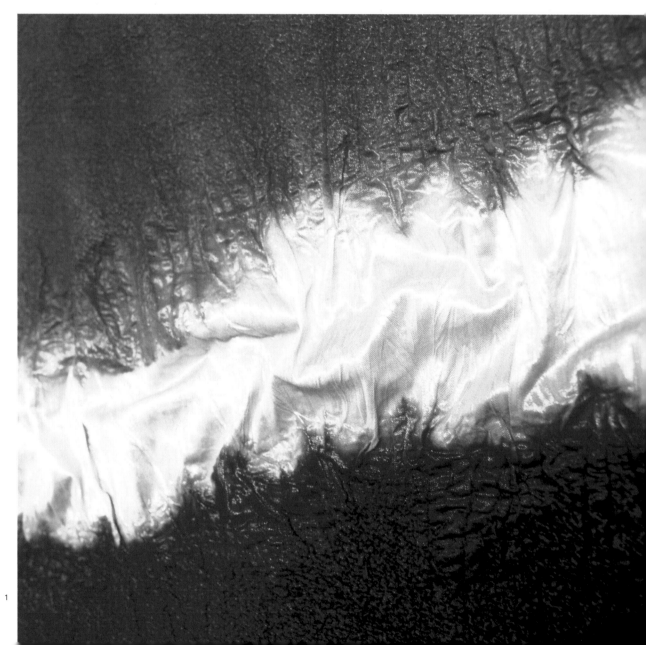

1

Michio **Arai** b. 1938 **Japan**

Snazzy helmets. Motorbike enthusiasts are familiar with the elegant, futuristic helmets designed by Michio Arai that are among the best available on the international market. The family business was founded by his father Hirotake Arai in 1950, and it was the first Japanese company to manufacture motorbike helmets from fiberglass and molded expanded plastic. Michio Arai has been in charge of the company since 1986. He studied engineering at Keio University in Tokyo and at the Indiana Institute of Technology in Fort Wayne. From 1963 onward he has had a substantial influence on the technological development and product design of the company, and he has registered some 20 patents for his innovations. A semi-professional participant in car and motorcycle racing, he is always searching for the greatest wearing and driving comfort in his helmets, even at high speeds, combined with the maximum possible security and perfect vision.

1

1 Motorbike helmet, 1999
2 Motocross helmet, 1978

2

Archizoom Founded 1966 **Italy**

Uncomfortable objects. In protest against politics, industry, consumption, fashion and the role of design as a status symbol, Andrea Branzi, Gilberto Coretti, Paolo Deganello, Massimo Morozzi, and Dario and Lucia Bartolini founded Archizoom Associates in Florence in 1966. The model for the rebels and initiators of the Radical Design movement in Italy was the architects' group "Archigram," founded in 1961. Although the few Archizoom designs that were produced, such as the *Safari* chair (1968) or the *Superonda* sofa (1970, both produced for Poltronova), now fetch extremely high prices among collectors, the real objective of the group was to be provocative about form and content. With their radical, ironic approach they came to represent the very concept of "Anti-design." At the 1968 Milan Triennale they opened "the center for eclectic conspiracy" with the *Mies* chair. This deliberately uncomfortable, almost unusable chair caricatured the constructional characteristics of an armchair designed by the architect Mies van der Rohe, making a mockery of functionalism. Archizoom was dissolved in 1974 but its ideas—without the political motivation—were taken up and developed further by Alchymia and Memphis.

Mies chair, 1969

Giorgio **Armani**

b. 1934 **Italy**

An extremist in his sense of nobility. Giorgio Armani has said that "Wrapping one's body in a valuable fabric is the most sensual thing in the world," and he has built a fashion empire on this philosophy. It is a fact that Armani only uses the best fabrics in his designs, which never look over the top; they always appear simple and wearable, almost basic, and invariably aristocratic. Unlike many of his colleagues he does not like to dress up women and yet does so. In the 1980s, his broad-shouldered, power business dressing spread far and wide, well beyond the boundaries of Wall Street. The fashion career of this purist designer was quite circuitous. Armani studied medicine after completing his secondary education, but moved from the university lecture theater to the display windows of La Rinascente in Milan. There he progressed from window dresser to the rank of men's fashion buyer. He began his career as a designer in the mid-1960s at Nino Cerruti. In 1970 he opened his own studio and worked as a freelance fashion designer for several companies. Five years later, he set up the Milan-based company Giorgio Armani S.p.A with his then partner Sergio Galeotti. Armani has always remained faithful to his love of fine fabrics and pure style, shown off by a perfect cut and soft lines.

1   Spring collection, 1992
2   Spring collection, 2000

Gunnar **Asplund** 1885–1940 **Sweden**

Classicism from the North. In ancient Greece there were benches on which people could recline at the table. Perhaps this was Gunnar Asplund's inspiration when in the mid-1920s he designed a chaise longue that allowed a relaxed sitting position similar to the recumbent position so popular in antiquity, a piece of furniture of great formal elegance. Asplund was Sweden's greatest twentieth-century architect and a strong influence on Scandinavian architecture and design. Although he became seriously involved with modern materials like tubular steel, he never abandoned his love of classicism. This is evident in the public buildings that he designed in Stockholm, parts of which he adorned with white paper Chinese lanterns hanging from the ceiling. Gunnar Asplund belonged to the Svenska Sljödföreningen circle, the well-known group of Swedish designers who stood for "more beautiful everyday objects" and for whom he designed the pioneering, controversial Stockholm exhibition of 1930 that heralded the arrival of modernism in Scandinavia.

1   *AV* ceiling light, 1926
2   *GA-2* chair, 1930
3   *GA-1* chair, 1930

2

3

1

Sergio **Asti** b. 1926 Italy

Specialist in fine accessories. Marble, ceramic, glass: Asti has a particular penchant for these valuable materials which have been used in Italy for centuries. This versatile architect, furniture and product designer is a specialist in the design of distinguished domestic objects, including vases, tableware, household fittings and lights. His creations have organic, partly streamlined contoured forms combining harmoniously with function, and with them Asti has put his stamp on fine Italian design since the mid-fifties. In the late 1950s the so-called Neo-Liberty movement was formed, meeting the dominant functionalism with stylistic elements of the Jugendstil. Asti contributed two designs, the *Bertoli* wooden table and the *Marco* vase. Today the architect and designer is still involved in the production of objects and exhibition architecture.

1   Soda siphon, 1955
2   *Boca* cutlery, 1975

1

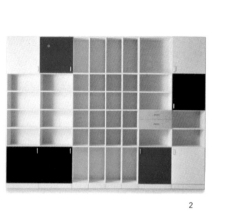

1 *Pantos* storage system, 1993
2 *Oikos I* storage system, 1972

Antonia **Astori** b. 1942 **Italy**

The business woman of system furniture. Antonia Astori is known all over the world for designing corporate offices and fair exhibits. The exhibition architect and furniture designer also has an international reputation for her company Driade and the system furniture she designs for it. She started the company in 1968 with her brother Enrico Astori and his wife Adelaide Acerbi. Since then Driade has worked with international designers including Achille Castiglioni, Philippe Starck, Borek Sipek, Ross Lovegrove, Alfredo Häberli and Paola Navona to produce its collections, which are seen as a barometer of fashion and a point of reference for new design. Antonia Astori is not involved in the administration and development of Driade's visual communication, but rather contributes to the expansion of markets with her own designs. For over thirty years she has been concentrating on one theme in particular: system furniture. With *Driade I* (1968), *Oikos I* (1972), *Bric* (1977, with Enzo Mari), *Oikos II* (1980), *Kaos* (1986) and *Pantos* (1993), she has created elements which can be used equally as furniture for the kitchen, bathroom, bedroom and living room.

Gae **Aulenti**

b. 1927 **Italy**

The grand old lady of architecture.
Gae Aulenti is one of the most important
architects of the twentieth century and
has contributed much to the development
of architectural theory in post-war Italy.
But she is better known to the public for
her lights and glass tables, designs that
often arose as part of architectural
assignments. An example is the flower-
shaped *Pipistrello* light designed by
Aulenti for Olivetti's Paris offices. The
Pipistrello light quickly became a classic
and in 1967 it began to be mass-produced
by Martinelli Luce. Her most important
exhibition project was *Italy: The New
Domestic Landscape*, which was held at
the Museum of Modern Art, New York in
1972. This survey of the latest Italian
design showed south-European projects
for future utopias in which plastic was the
dominant material. The title of the
exhibition gave its name to the design
trend of the 1970s: foam plastic used to
create domestic landscapes for cozy
togetherness made up of individual
armchairs, chairs and sofas. But Aulenti's
greatest influence has been in the field of
architecture and interior design. In the
1980s she converted the Gare d'Orsay in
Paris into a museum and renovated the
Musée d'Art Moderne in the Centre
Pompidou. She also designed showrooms
for Olivetti and Fiat, and was responsible
for redesigning the Palazzo Grassi in
Venice and the Catalan Museum in
Barcelona.

1

1 *Pipistrello* light, 1967
2 *Tour* table, 1993
3 *April* chair, 1972

2   3

Hiroshi **Awatsuji** b. 1929 **Japan**

The fabric designer. The main characteristic of Hiroshi Awatsuji's textile designs is over-sized motifs. He started his career working for Kanegafuchi (now Kanebo) and Kenjiro Oishi, then in 1958 he set up his own workshop. In 1963 he began designing fabrics for Fujie. The motifs designed by Awatsuji for his fabrics—a bicycle, a banana tree, a cup—were evidently very different from traditional Japanese patterns. Nevertheless, some of his creations are reminiscent of the raked, sandy surfaces in the gardens of Zen temples. In 1970 Awatsuji was asked to design the carpets and curtains for two pavilions at the Osaka Expo. This soon led to further commissions from banks, hotels and other companies. In 1988 he founded his own production company which designed and produced textiles, as well as tableware with a variety of black and white patterns.

1 *AWA* crockery, 1988
2 *Spectacular* fabric, 1988

1

2

Jonathan **Barnbrook** b. 1966 **Great Britain**

Britannia's creative strength. When Damien Hirst opened the theme restaurant called *Pharmacy* in London in 1998, it was clear that Jonathan Barnbrook had contributed to the menu. The year before he had designed the concept book on the controversial and celebrated installation artist, a magnificently visual work bursting with ideas. The two men belong to the avant-garde of Britain's new creative movement. Jonathan Barnbrook is also involved in making film trailers and commercials. In addition he is particularly interested in mechanically engraved stone plaques, a perfect example of the "made in Britain" communication design that has long ago crossed the traditional boundaries of the discipline. After his studies, he worked first for the Why Not group before he set up on his own in 1990. He has designed a number of typefaces including *Prototype*, *Bastard* (both 1990), *Nylon* (1996) and *Apocalypso* (1997).

1/2 *Cult of Virus* catalog, 1997

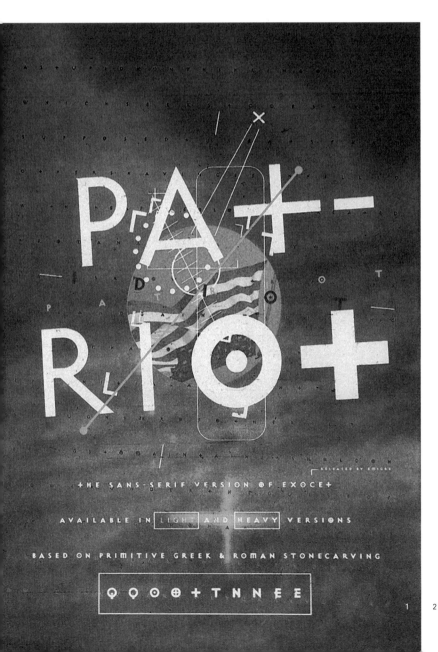

1

2

Saul **Bass** 1920–96 USA

The man with the golden eye. Saul Bass developed the image campaign for Paramount's box-office success *The Man with the Golden Arm*. It was the first complete movie industry media package, covering every detail from posters to the opening titles. His invention of creative opening credits made history with titles such as *Carmen Jones* (1954), *Vertigo* (1958), *The Shining* (1980) and *Casino* (1996). Saul Bass was a graphic artist who studied at Brooklyn College under the Bauhaus-inspired master Gyorgy Kepes. In Hollywood he had an eye for the essential. Alfred Hitchcock appreciated his skills in his classic *Psycho* (1960), and it was Bass who designed the famous shower scene in the film. Saul Bass also worked as a director himself, and he was awarded an Academy Award for his short film *Why Man Creates*. Having set up a design company with Herb Yager in 1978, he worked on corporate image campaigns for which his movie industry experience was very useful. He counted many multinationals among his clients, including United Airlines, Quaker, Bell, AT&T, Warner and Minolta, as well as the 1984 Los Angeles Olympic Games. The graphic artist also became involved in another kind of industry which concentrated on visual identity. He developed a consistent system of visual symbols for his gas stations for Exxon (1980) and BP (1991); they were trailblazing and widely copied.

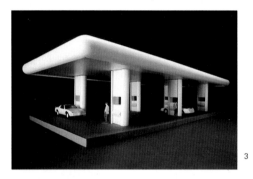

3

4

1 Movie poster, 1960
2 Logo for American Airlines, *c.* 1970
3 Filling station (prototype), 1985
4 Logo, 1978

2

1

THE MAGNIFICENT SEVEN   DIRECTED BY JOHN STURGES

Herbert **Bayer** 1900–85 Austria, Germany and USA

From the Bauhaus to Corporate America. The Bauhaus played a significant role in the broad movement of functionalism, and the exceptional importance it achieved. The graphic designer Herbert Bayer was largely responsible for this. He studied under Johannes Itten in 1921 and later became head of the newly created workshop for printing and advertising. Bayer introduced the DIN standards for all printed matter, he designed books and posters, and he developed *Universa-Type*. He moved to Berlin in 1928, where he worked for an advertising agency and became known for his magical photomontages, such as *Lonely City* (1932). After the Nazis came to power he emigrated to America in the late 1930s. In New York he designed several exhibitions, including the 1938 Bauhaus show at the Museum of Modern Art. Eventually he became art director of the Container Corporation of America, the country's leading packaging enterprise. During his time in the USA, Bayer undertook an ever-widening range of activities. After he moved to Aspen in 1946, he was employed as an architect and teacher, but he also occupied himself with landscape parks and developed the corporate identity of an oil company.

1 Book jacket, 1923

2 Advertising kiosk (design), 1924

1

Martine **Bedin** b. 1957 France

Not typically French. With her *Super* range of lights made from fiberglass and rubber, reminiscent of children's toys on wheels, Martine Bedin created an icon in the Memphis style. This French woman was one of the youngest members of the Memphis group, which in the early 1980s turned against functionalism by creating cheerful, playful objects. Bedin had first studied architecture and design in Paris before going to Italy, where she worked with Adolfo Natalini. Through him she came in contact with Superstudio and later met Ettore Sottsass. For a time the Bordeaux-born artist taught at the Ecole des Beaux-Arts there, commuting between France and Italy. As well as creating furniture and lamps, she designed a collection for the couturier Daniel Hechter (1986) and a range of luggage for Louis Vuitton (1987). Since 1995, Martine Bedin has been running the design department of the Loewe electronics company in Spain, while also designing houses for private clients. Her witty, functional objects do not fit in with typical French design, which is usually more associated with luxury and lavish decoration.

Super light, 1981

Peter **Behrens** 1868–1940 Germany

The first industrial designer. The work of Peter Behrens laid the foundation for endowing industrial design with professional status. Very much in the reforming spirit of his time, he founded *Vereinigten Werkstätten* ("United Workshops") with like-minded artists, an enterprise that manufactured everyday objects such as tableware, jewelry and furniture. In 1900, Behrens built a show house for an artists' colony in Darmstadt, in which he expressed the idea of *Gesamtkunstwerk*, the "total work of art." However, the decisive turning point in his life came in 1907, the year in which Behrens co-founded the *Deutsche Werkbund*. In the same year he was appointed artistic adviser for the electrical company AEG, the first time that so large a company had made such an appointment. Behrens turned the whole company into an expression of *Gesamtkunstwerk*, a synthesis of all the arts, from writing paper to factory interiors. In other words Behrens invented what is now known as "corporate identity." As well as a new logo, he designed many products for AEG such as lamps, fans, kettles, heating appliances and clocks, all of which stand out for their simplicity and well thought-out technical features. Behrens may rightly be called the first modern industrial designer.

1 Desk fan, 1908
2 Kettle, 1913
3 Electric heater, 1911

1

Mario **Bellini**

b. 1935 **Italy**

The jack-of-all-trades. It seems that
anything Mario Bellini touches is a
success. Whether he is designing fountain
pens (1991, for Lamy), teapots (1985/1987,
for Rosenthal), typewriters and calculators
(since 1965, for Olivetti), lamps (1985, for
Erco) or furniture (like the *Cab* chair for
Cassina in 1976 or the *Figura* office chair
in 1984, for Vitra), the objects have all
become classics. Bellini's style combines
precision and emotion and he has
become one of the most important Italian
designers of the last thirty years. Since
1984 Bellini has also turned to
architecture and he is now one of the
most famous international architects in
Asia. But he does not make a big fuss
about his art: "Design is finding and
inventing at the same time," he says, and
he speaks of the logic existing within
objects dictating their arrangement so
that they are ultimately effective. It is
apparent that the Milan-based artist is
very skilled at achieving this with every
one of his projects. Recognition of this
ability was provided in 1987 by his great
coup in being the first living designer
since Charles Eames to be honored with a
one-man exhibition at the Museum of
Modern Art in New York. But this highly
respected and successful man does not
devote himself only to architectural and
design projects: between 1986 and 1991
Bellini was chief editor of the influential
magazine *Domus*, while also accepting
teaching assignments.

3

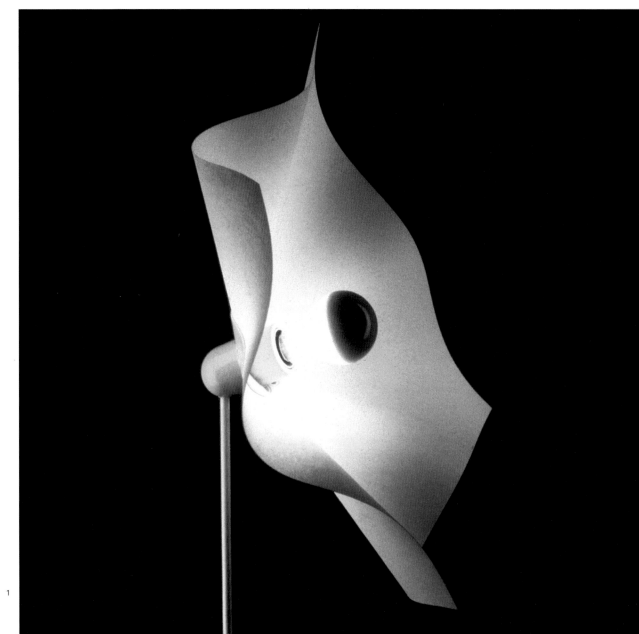

1

4

5

1 Area light, 1974
2 *Divisumma 18* portable printing calculator, 1972
3 *Il colonnato* table, 1977
4 *La Bombole* sofa, 1972
5 *412 Cab* chair, 1976

1 *Beauty* brush and comb, 1997
2 *Ergo* screwdriver, 1986
3 *Ideal* cook's knife, 1974

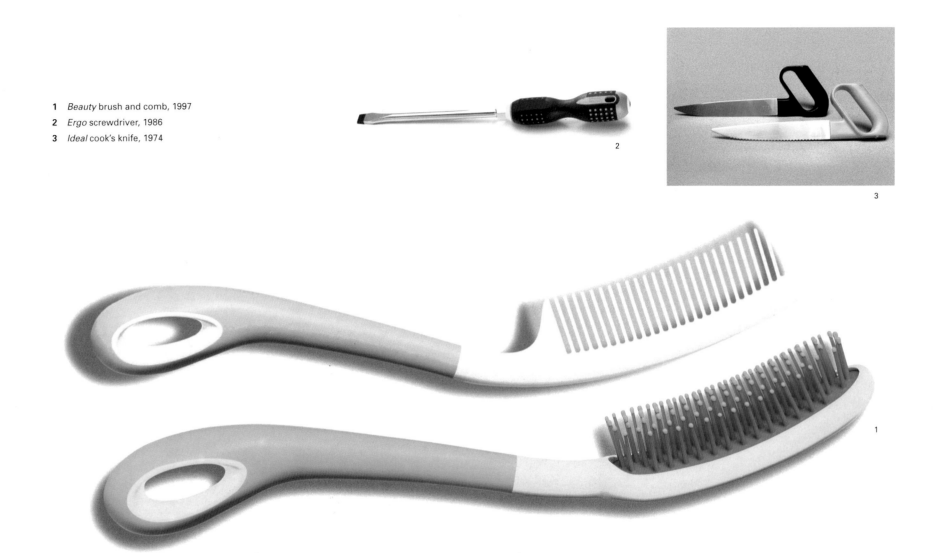

Maria **Benktzon** b. 1946 **Sweden**

Independence for the weak. A champion of ergonomic methods and democratic principles, Maria Benktzon's motto is that "One should concentrate one's attention on areas with unsolved problems." Following this principle, which aims to make every kind of human activity easier by means of optimized equipment, she has among other things created a completely new kind of cutlery: for instance, a cross between a knife and a fork which she called the *Snork*. Benktzon has also—largely with her colleague Sven Eric Juhlin—created a completely new design field: design for the disabled. For many years Benktzon and Juhlin had worked for the Stockholm design studio Ergonomi and at the beginning of the 1970s they developed a new kind of grip for crutches based on clinical studies. This was followed by a large number of other innovative products, for instance cutlery designed for specific diseases such as muscular weakness. Maria Benktzon does not see her work as a purely technical challenge. What motivates her is the desire to make handicapped people independent from others, thereby integrating weaker people into society. The exhibition *Design for Independent Living* organized in 1988 at the Museum of Modern Art in New York made this new design for minorities internationally known.

ABCDEFG

Ng

Morris Fuller **Benton**

1872–1948 **USA**

The power of type. After training as a mechanic and engineer, M. F. Benton went to work for American Type Founders Company (ATF), ultimately becoming its designer-in-chief. ATF was the most important typographical company in the country at the time, employing many famous designers such as Lucian Bernhard. Benton soon became a prolific and creative typeface designer, and in the first decade of the twentieth century he designed a number of very successful sans-serif typefaces including Franklin Gothic (1903) and the newspaper typeface News Gothic (1908), both of which are still widely used today. He developed over 200 typefaces for ATF in all.

ABCDabcdefg
ABCDabcdefg

3

1   *Franklin Gothic* typeface 1903–12
2   *Bureau Empire* typeface, 1937
3   *Franklin Gothic* and *News Gothic* typefaces, 1908

Sigvard **Bernadotte**

b. 1907 **Sweden**

Noble industrial ware. A set of cutlery for the Danish silversmith Georg Jensen (1939), a stereo set for Philips (1968), a video telephone for Ericsson (1971): the list of Sigvard Bernadotte's clients is long and international. He was among the first of Europe's industrial designers to apply the motto "beauty for all" to the new consumer goods of the postwar years. Bernadotte was born the son of King Gustave VI of Sweden. Early in life this Swedish aristocrat showed an interest in arts and crafts, theater and motion pictures, eventually going to Hollywood where he became an assistant director. Impressed by America and its consumer society, in 1950 he and the Danish designer Acton Bjorn founded a studio for industrial design in Copenhagen, the first in Scandinavia. They produced numerous products for well-known companies, such as tableware for airplanes commissioned by SAS (1966) and the *Beolit* portable radio for Bang and Olufsen (1964). The designer-prince was particularly popular with housewives on account of the modern kitchen equipment he designed in the 1950s, among which were the very practical *Margarethe* range of plastic dishes and a whisk for Esge that became a kitchen classic.

1 *Zauberstab* mixer, 1997
2 *Beolit 500* radio, 1964
3 *Margarethe* plastic bowls, 1950

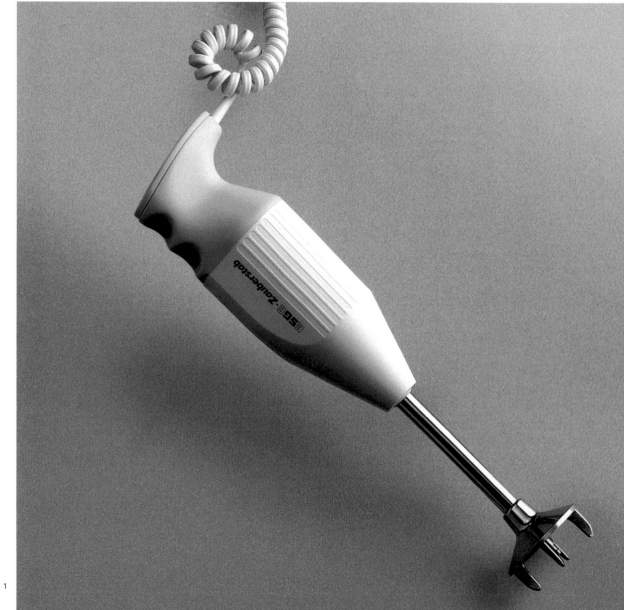

2

1

Lucian **Bernhard** 1883–1972 **Germany and USA**

A sign of the times. Lucian Bernhard went to art college in Berlin and Munich but gave up after a short time. His career really took off in 1905 when he won a poster competition organized by the match manufacturers Priester. In the same year, the self-taught designer whose real name was Emil Kahn decided to use the pseudonym Lucian Bernhard. His strengths lay in abstract forms, contrasting colors (with a strong preference for black), and dramatic symbolism, exemplified in his work for the spark-plug manufacturer Bosch. He was also very knowledgeable about typefaces and designed several himself, including *Antiqua* (1911), *Fraktur* (1913) and *Cursive* (1925). In 1910 Bernhard was co-founder of the magazine *Das Plakat* ("The Poster"). During the First World War he designed numerous typographical propaganda posters for the German troops. Appointed the first professor of poster design at the Berlin Academy of Art, Bernhard took advantage of a tour of the United States to gain a professional foothold there. His work with American Type Founders Company was particularly successful and he designed the *Gothic* (1930) and *Tango* (1933) typefaces for them.

1 Advertising poster, c. 1910 **2** Advertising poster, 1908

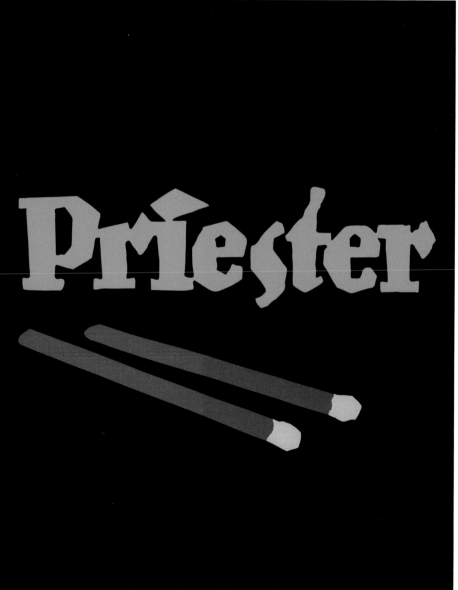

Harry **Bertoia**

1915–78 **Italy and USA**

Form and wire mesh. The Italian artist, university lecturer and furniture designer Harry Bertoia had been living in the United States for 15 years when, with a unique stroke of genius, he designed the patented *Diamond Chair* from wire mesh for Knoll International in 1952. Innovative, comfortable and unusually beautiful, it is amazingly strong in spite of its delicate filigree appearance. Bearing the hallmark of the highly skilled sculptor and graphic artist, this chair has been an exciting model for generations of young, up-and-coming artists. The same is true of his *Bird* chair (1952), a high-backed chair developed from the *Diamond Chair* that truly looks like a bird with spread wings. Like Charles and Ray Eames (with whom he briefly worked), Bertoia was an inventor of form while also enriching furniture design by his introduction of a new material: he turned industrial wire mesh into a design icon.

1 *Diamond* armchair, 1952
2 *Diamond* range of chairs and armchairs, 1952

2

1

Nuccio **Bertone** 1914–97 **Italy**

Objects of desire. Nuccio Bertone was, after Pininfarina and with his pupil Giorgetto Giugiaro, one of the most important Italian car designers. He succeeded in turning the car into a cult object. The secret of his success was to give a mass-produced model the look of a competition car, with a streamlined body and a slim silhouette. In 1912 his father, Giovanni Bertone, had opened a workshop in Turin for the construction of car bodies. Nuccio joined the family firm in 1934 and transformed the business into an international company that developed the Fiat 2800 Cabriolet. The great breakthrough came in 1954 with the Alfa Romeo *Giulietta Sprint*. The original plan was for only 500 to be built, but it actually continued to be produced for 13 years without any changes. With his belief that a car must appeal to the emotions of the buyer, Nuccio Bertone always achieved his objective. Since 1950 the Bertone studio has developed over 60 important prototypes and 40 production cars, including the legendary Lamborghini *Miura* (1966), the Ferrari *Dino 308* (1973), the Citroën *BX* (1982) and the convertible versions of the Opel *Kadett* (1987), the Opel *Astra* and the Fiat *Punto* (1994).

1 Alfa Romeo *Giulietta Sprint,* 1954

2 Lamborghini *Countach,* 1975

2

1

Flaminio **Bertoni** 1903–64 **Italy and France**

The car as sculpture. The model that Flaminio Bertoni thought was his best was also his most controversial. The Citroën *Ami 6* (1961) with its boxy body and its distinctive backward-tilted rear window (designed to remain clear of snow and rain) never achieved the popularity of its predecessor, the *2CV* (1939). That inexpensive multi-purpose vehicle was current for nearly half a century and became a cult, with its strong, unmistakable form that was uncompromisingly functional for its time. Flaminio Bertoni was an artist and sculptor from Varese with an interest in nature and astronomy, and he joined Citroën in 1932. He hardly ever sketched his designs; he preferred to visualize his ideas through models, quite crude sculptures that he created quickly. This spontaneity was probably the reason for the amazingly original lines of the *DS 19*. This elegant sedan was the sensation of the 1955 Paris Motor Show, and many rated it the most successful car of the 1950s, partly because of its many technical innovations (the long hood was made of aluminum and the roof of synthetic material), and also because of its breathtaking appearance. Bertoni's aerodynamic masterpiece became a design classic.

1

1 Citroën *DS19,* 1955
2 Citroën *2CV,* 1948

2

46

Max **Bill** 1908–94 **Switzerland and Germany**

A persistent simplifier. The work of this architect, graphic artist, designer, theoretician and publicist was wide-ranging, including such varied creations as a three-legged table for Züricher Wohnbedarf AG (1950), wall clocks and wristwatches for Junghans, the Swiss pavilion at the 1936 and 1951 Milan Triennales, and the buildings of the Ulm Academy of Design (whose principal he was between 1951 and 1956). His contribution to modern design rests mainly on his tenacious pursuit of the ideas developed by the Bauhaus, where he studied in the late 1920s. Whether designing door handles, stools or lamps, or producing paintings and sculptures, the champion of "good form" never strayed from the path of pure functionalism. His products are permeated with the spirit of his mentors Josef Albers, László Moholy-Nagy, Piet Mondrian, Paul Klee and Walter Gropius, but the model pupil also developed his own ideas. In 1949 he published a manifesto against an excessively narrow interpretation of utility design. Max Bill believed that beauty was not just the result of a successful construction, but that it had a value in itself.

2

1 *Ulmer* stool, 1950
2 Wall clock, 1963

1

Cini **Boeri** b. 1924 **Italy**

Theory and practice of living. Cini Boeri belongs to a minority, being one of the few women who have put their mark on Italian architecture and design. She became widely known for her designs in the 1960s and 1970s, the period when the development of new materials such as synthetics propelled Italian design into the limelight. Her *Serpentone* snake seat, produced by Arflex in 1971, played a major part in this; the malleable rubber piece of furniture that could be produced in any desired length became synonymous with comfortable lounging by all devotees of sit-ins. Boeri worked in Marco Zanuso's studio between 1952 and 1963 and then set up her own studio at the age of thirty-nine, developing a versatile range of activities. She designs furniture for the house and the office, as well as fittings such as lamps and door handles. In addition to this, her architectural projects include private and public commissions, showroom design, and a prefabricated house. But Cini Boeri is not only concerned with practice; she is also deeply involved with the theory of living, a subject about which she has written books, and she is a professor at the University of California at Berkeley and the Milan Polytechnic.

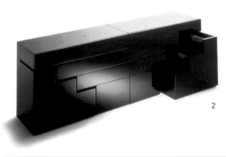

1 *Bobo* chair, 1967
2 *Steps* container system, 1982
3 *Strips* armchair, 1979

2   3

1   Concrete chair, 1980
2   *Zink* shelves, 1984
3   *Larv* halogen lamp, 1990

Jonas **Bohlin**

b. 1953 **Sweden**

Poetry and function. Jonas Bohlin treads the narrow line between art and design. Believers in the concept of utility are completely disconcerted by his furniture and lamps that look remarkably like sculptures and whose purpose is not immediately obvious, such as his *Nonting* sofa, a mattress-wedge that can also be placed upright. Jonas Bohlin frequently uses harsh materials that are not common in design. His almost unmovable concrete chair presented to a dumbfounded public in 1980 caused a terrible scandal in Sweden's traditional furniture industry and gave him his reputation as an *enfant terrible* of design. Subsequently, while the Källemo concrete chair was marketed as a cult object, Jonas Bohlin was awarded the highly regarded Georg Jensen Prize and invited to join the illustrious Swedish Academy of Arts. At the beginning of the 1990s he rowed from Stockholm to Paris with a few designer friends, a "happening" he recorded in a book. He also designed the *Liv* collection of furniture to commemorate the event. In spite of the unusual nature of his ideas, on closer examination it becomes apparent that Bohlin's designs are functional and effective; for example, the zigzag-shaped newspaper stand *Zink* (1984) that can be used from both sides, or the *Larv* halogen lamp that sits on a leather stocking, and which can be bent and hung up.

1

Kay **Bojesen** 1886–1958 **Denmark**

The road away from ornament. Six years of training with the fashionable firm of Georg Jensen were sufficient for silversmith Kay Bojesen. In 1913 he set up on his own and developed his personal style from what he had learned from the master. Bojesen achieved the renunciation of form. The steel cutlery designed in 1938 became famous, an example of elegant simplicity in which all the pointed ends had been rounded off; it was also made in silver. This stylish tableware was awarded a prize at the Milan Triennale, and with it the dominance of hammered silver from the House of Jensen was brought to an end. Bojesen had founded an ornament-free tradition and is seen as a pioneer of functionalism, or at least of its Danish version, in that the rounded forms of his designs were in strong contrast with the cold right angles of the Bauhaus. In 1931 he helped to found *Den Permanente*, the gallery and store that was Europe's first design showroom, and there he surprised the public with well-designed wooden toys for children. His trains, spider monkeys and soldiers made "Uncle Bojesen" famous all over the world in the 1950s.

1 Toy elephant, c. 1930
2 Toy monkey, 1951
3 Cutlery, 1938

Osvaldo **Borsani** 1911–85 Italy

Technical masterstrokes. With his brother Fulgenzio, Osvaldo Borsani founded the Tecno company in 1953. The name itself described the company's program and the first pieces of furniture, the *P40* chaise longue and the *D70* folding sofa, were technically advanced creations. The footrests, seat and back of the chaise longue could be adjusted and arranged in 486 different positions, which was a record in itself. The Milan-based architect and furniture designer enjoyed such technical subtleties, seeing design as the solution of technical challenges. For many years Borsani was the company's only designer and the designs he created were based on this principle which shaped Tecno's image. It was only in the mid-1980s that other designers such as Gae Aulenti and Norman Foster started working for the company, which in the meantime was managed by Paolo and Valeria Borsani. It is now known as a specialist in the field of furniture for offices and public buildings.

1 *P40* chaise longue, 1955
2 *D70* sofa, 1954

1

Mario **Botta** b. 1943 **Switzerland**

VIP designs. Mario Botta has long overtaken his mentors Carlo Scraper and Louis Kahn as far as fame is concerned. He has been a visiting professor in Lausanne and at Yale, he has been awarded the most important architecture prizes, and the Museum of Modern Art has honored him with a solo exhibition. But this much-fêted designer is also the subject of controversy. His admirers praise his rational-organic forms of expression, but others accuse him of disfiguring the environment. His characteristic approach is described by himself as "a marvel of geometry created by light." What is certain is that Botta's architecture leaves no one indifferent, and this is true also of his mass-produced furniture: chairs, tables and lamps that he has been creating since 1982 for Alias and Artemide and which can be seen as expressive interpretations of functionalism. The *Quinta* chair is an excellent example of this: a radical, minimalist, coolly elegant object made from steel tubes whose seat consists of perforated metal plates and high cantilevered armrests that are connected to the back.

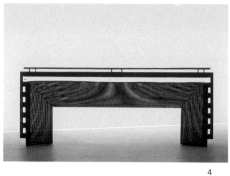

4

1/2 *Quarta* chair, 1984

3   *Seconda* chair, 1982

4   *Tesi* table, 1986

5   *Quinta* chair, 1986

5

3

Marianne **Brandt** 1893–1983 **Germany**

A classic Bauhaus designer. The painter and sculptor Marianne Brandt was one of the female Bauhaus designers who, unexpectedly for the time, were active in the field of metalwork. She ran the Bauhaus metalwork department very successfully, she herself specializing in the design of elegant metal objects. The controlled functionality and simple lines of her ashtrays, sugar bowls and cream jugs reflected the ideals of her mentor László Moholy-Nagy and became part of the image of the Bauhaus. How very modern Brandt's designs were is reflected in the fact that her coffee set and tea service, designed in 1924, are still produced by Alessi today. Besides tableware, she also created new designs for lights, some with aluminum reflectors. After the Bauhaus closed, little was heard of her until 1949 when she started teaching again, this time at the State College for Arts and Crafts in Dresden and later at the Institute for Applied Arts in East Berlin. She did not return to metalwork but she experimented instead with leather and ceramics, before devoting herself once more to painting and sculpture in the 1950s.

1

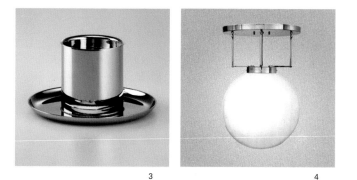

3

4

5

2

1902–81 **Hungary, Germany and USA**

A chair on runners. The Hungarian-born Marcel Breuer began his studies at the Bauhaus in 1920, one of the first pupils at this new workshop for original, functional products. He began to teach there in 1925. Although he ran the woodwork department, it was another material that made him famous. He is recognized as one of the pioneering furniture designers of the twentieth century because of his experiments with steel tubing, a material which until then was used only in bicycles and heating systems. The *Wassily* tubular steel armchair designed by him in 1925 is still produced today by Knoll. The name was given to it in the 1960s by the Italian manufacturer Gavina, after Wassily Kandinsky, who had one of the innovative armchairs in his office. The construction of canvas or leather strips suspended on steel tubes was the first chair of its kind, a classic and a symbol of modernism that became the prototype for a whole series of products, as well as the subject of countless patent controversies. Breuer designed many other pieces of tubular steel furniture, including a cantilevered sofa and a glass-topped table (both 1931). He moved to Berlin in 1928 but left Nazi Germany in the mid-1930s, settling first in London where he designed laminate and plywood furniture manufactured by Isokon. He then moved to the United States at the invitation of Walter Gropius, teaching at Harvard University before becoming an architect. He worked on prestigious projects such as the UNESCO buildings in Paris and the Whitney Museum in New York (1966).

3

4

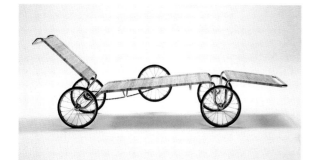

1 *Wassily* chair, 1925
2 *S 285* desk, c. 1930
3 Radiogram, 1936
4 Chair (for Isokon), 1936
5 *F 41* chaise longue, 1930
6 *Laccio* table and chair, 1926

5

6

2

Neville **Brody** b. 1957 **Great Britain**

Typography as creative impact. Brody reacted with exuberant analogies to the minimalist graphic design style of the 1970s and 1980s. He designed record sleeves for independent labels including Al McDowell's Rocking Russian Company, Stiff Records and Fetish Records; with their exciting mixture of artwork and typography, his sleeves matched the provocative potential of the music they contained. As art director of the avant-garde magazine *The Face* (1981–86), Brody celebrated the visual possibilities of typography as an independent identity for the publication, and this led eventually to the development of an innovative typeface that was characteristic of the decade: *Typeface Six* (1986). He has since designed other new typefaces for Linotype, Adobe, and FontFont, as well as publishing some widely respected books. He has worked for a wide range of magazines, including the London magazine *City Limits* (1983–87), the political magazine *New Socialist*, the men's magazine *Arena* (1987), and the interactive typography magazine *Fuse* (since 1990). In 1988 this graphic rebel was honored by the Victoria and Albert Museum with his own retrospective exhibition.

3

S A BCDEFGHI

4

b cdefghij

5

6

1

7

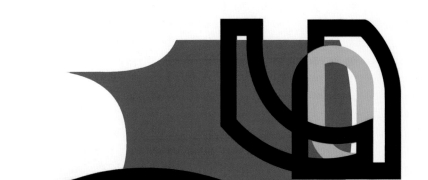

2

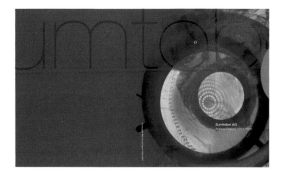

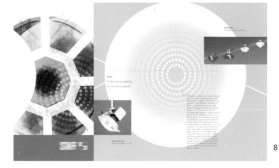

8

9

Julian **Brown** b. 1955 **Great Britain**

Playful and useful. Julian Brown's specialties are fun but functional too. Based in Bath, England, he follows his motto "We need objects that make us laugh," creating cheerful, colorful objects such as the *Vercingetorix* alarm clock (1993, for Rexite). No less confusing is the *Attila* can-crusher (1996 for Rexite) which crushes beer or Coke cans into aluminum puck-like discs. This can be seen as a Brown contribution to help save the environment: "Recycling is a serious business," says Brown, "but it must be fun. That is the only way to ensure that it will be done." But Julian Brown is far from being a technophobic environmentalist, and for sixteen years he has been building a motorcycle made from glass fiber. After studying at Leicester Polytechnic and the Royal College of Art in London he worked for Porsche Design, designing spectacles for Carrera. Between 1986 and 1990 he worked with Ross Lovegrove, designing furniture for clients such as Knoll International, tennis rackets for Puma and luggage for Louis Vuitton. The range of materials used was vast: briar wood, leather, titanium, ceramic, plastics and plastic-coated materials. Since 1990, Julian Brown has been working independently.

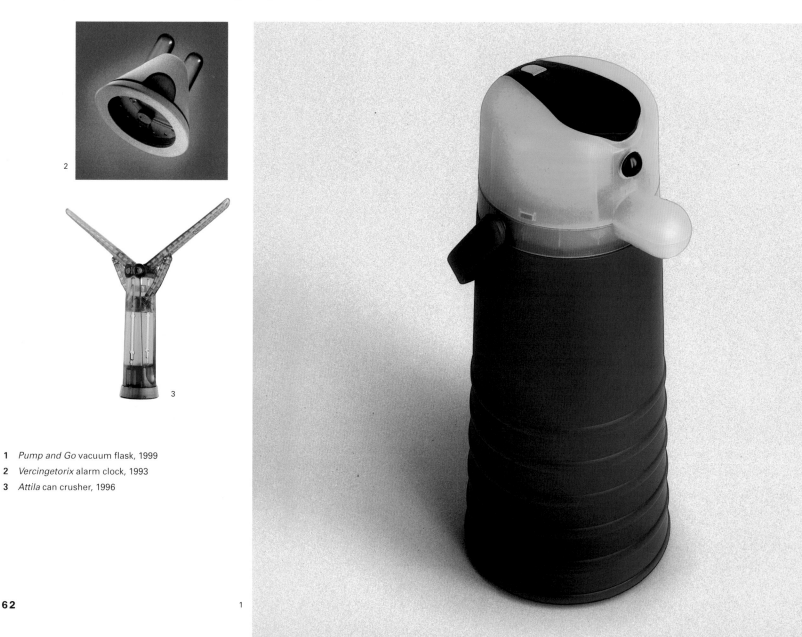

1 *Pump and Go* vacuum flask, 1999
2 *Vercingetorix* alarm clock, 1993
3 *Attila* can crusher, 1996

1

Carlo **Bugatti**

1856–1940 **Italy**

Artistic craftsmanship. For many people the name Bugatti is synonymous with sports and racing cars, made by the racing driver and car designer Ettore Bugatti, who was the son of the cabinetmaker Carlo Bugatti. This artistic Milanese craftsman astonished his contemporaries with his decorative furniture, which revealed strong oriental and African influences. As decoration he used tassels made from raffia or fabric, filigree wood carvings, floral patterns and heraldic motifs. Carlo Bugatti's furniture was much sought after by high society in the late nineteenth and early twentieth centuries when exoticism was all the rage. This is clearly illustrated by the so-called "snail-room" in Turin, dating from 1902, where the furniture is covered with parchment, brightly painted in red and gold. Carlo Bugatti gave up cabinet-making when he moved to Paris in 1904, working there first as a silversmith and subsequently as a painter.

1 *Turin* chair, 1902
2 Table, c. 1900

Rido **Busse** b. 1934 **Germany**

School of Germany. Rido Busse has conceived more than products: in 1977 he founded the Plagarius award, a negative distinction given for the particularly brazen stealing of an idea. This was followed a year later by the Longlife Design Award for products that retained their market validity for longer than eight years. Both prizes reflect Busse's work philosophy, which dictates that a product must be genuinely new, sensual and long-lasting. He was deeply influenced by his studies at the legendary Ulm Design School and his success is clearly reflected in the long list of major clients who have commissioned work from him. These include German companies such as AEG, Bosch and Zeiss, as well as international companies like IBM and Kodak. Rido Busse has become one of the most famous German industrial designers because so many companies appreciate the functional rectilinearity of his designs and his professional guidance. He was responsible for changing the appearance of German streets in the 1990s with his new generation of telephone boxes, designed for German Telekom.

2

3

1 Mixing bowl, 1960
2 *2000* saw, 1994
3 *Viking* lawn mower, 1996

1

Erberto **Carboni** 1899-1984 **Italy**

The high art of communications. The graphic artist and furniture designer Erberto Carboni had the rare ability to produce graphic representations of abstract concepts. In the 1920s and 1930s his postcards and calendars for the pasta manufacturer Barilla were already sought-after collector's pieces. Whether advertising penne, spaghetti or ravioli, Carboni's pasta advertisements such as "Con pasta Barilla è sempre domenica!" ("With Barilla pasta it is always Sunday!") achieved cult status, even in the postwar years. He created simple, modern graphics with loose noodles often shown on a blue background. The red and white trademark was also his creation. Erberto Carboni coined the term "atomico" to define the isolation of certain elements in the dynamic design concept. Besides important clients like Agib, Campari and the RAI, Carboni also worked for the legendary advertising and design department of the typewriter manufacturer Olivetti, which was set up in the 1930s. During the 1950s he was an important contributor to the success of the Milan-based graphic studio Boggeri. In 1996 Carboni's *Delfino* armchair was among the 1950s and 1960s seating classics exhibited by the furniture manufacturer Arflex at the Cologne Furniture Fair.

1   *Barilla* advertising poster, 1952
2   *Delfino* armchair, 1954
3   Packaging for *Barilla*, 1956

la pasta del buon appetito

Barilla

casa fondata a Parma nel 1877 per la produzione delle paste alimentari

1

2

3

David **Carson** b. 1957 USA

Apocalypse of communication. Many claim that David Carson "ruins layouts and tortures characters." The photographer Albert Watson, on the other hand, sees him as an artist who "uses characters like a painter uses color," while to musician David Byrne his style is "like rock and roll." What is certain is that graphic artist David Carson revolutionized visual communication in the 1990s and altered visual perception forever with his unconventional use of typography and page design. Carson is a semi-professional surfer and he worked on various surf magazines before becoming art director of the magazine *Beach Culture* in 1989. Only six issues appeared, but they won a total of 150 design awards. This prompted the publisher of the music magazine *Ray Gun* to offer Carson a job (he worked for three years on this ultra-hip magazine), and he was also approached by major youth-orientated companies like Nike and Levi Strauss. Carson's status as cult figure was finally confirmed by the anthology in which his work could be seen properly for the first time. Its title was *The End of Print*.

The End of Print book, Bangert Verlag, 1995

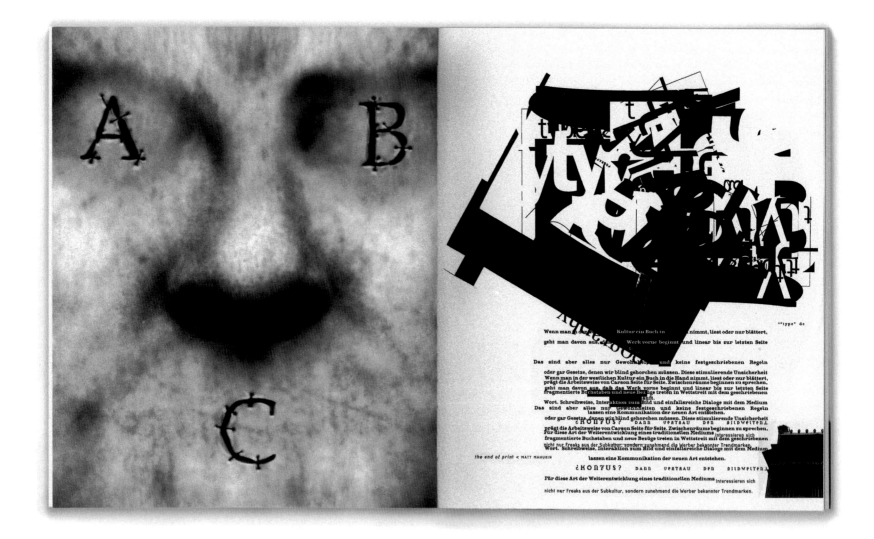

Louis **Cartier** 1875–1942 **France**

Virtual re-inventor of the watch. When Rudolf Valentino played in his last film *The Son of the Sheikh* in 1926, he was sporting a Cartier *Tank* on his wrist. Louis Cartier had created this watch in 1917 in honor of General Pershing's armored corps. It was launched on the market in 1922 and is still a best-seller today. The House of Cartier was founded in Paris in 1847, and in 1898 the founder's son Alfred took his own son Louis into partnership, as Alfred Cartier et Fils. The House designed precious jewelry for many of the crowned heads of Europe, and Louis Cartier extended the range by adding new items. These included a small object which would play a decisive part in the history of the company: the first wristwatch with a leather strap, which he designed in 1904 for his friend, the Brazilian aviator Alberto Santos-Dumont. Louis Cartier thereby laid the foundation of Cartier's lasting success, and the winding crown with sapphire cabochon has become as distinctive a mark as the entwined C of the House's logo.

1 *Santos* watch, 1998
2 *Tank Basculante* watch, 1999
3 The first *Tank* watch, 1922

Jean-Charles de **Castelbajac** b. 1949 **Morocco and France**

The great improviser. The fashion designer Jean-Charles de Castelbajac has retained the childlike gift of being able to improvise playfully with whatever is at hand, a talent that is reflected in all his designs, whether for fashion, furniture or interior design. One of his coats consisted of 39 white teddy bears, while his fabrics may be decorated by a combination of kindergarten drawings and modern art. He has used absorbent gauze and sacking as fabrics in his collections as well as bedsheets or car-seat covers. Castelbajac was born in Casablanca and originally studied law, but by 1968 he had already created his first designs for Ko & Co, a company owned by his mother. He launched his first collections in 1969 before finally creating his own label and opening several boutiques in Paris, New York and Tokyo. With his loud, daring designs he soon became the darling of pop musicians such as Rod Stewart and Elton John. Since the 1980s Jean-Charles de Castelbajac has also designed furniture (e.g. for Ligne Roset), bed linen, jewelry and even chocolate.

1 Glove, 2000
2 Spring collection, 1999
3 Bag, 2000
4 *27 j. d'amour* carpet, 1999
5 Lighting, 1999
6 Spring-summer collection, 1999

5

6

Anna **Castelli Ferrieri** b. 1920 **Italy**

The plastics designer. There is hardly any task that this Milan designer could not take on. Anna Castelli Ferrieri is an architect as well as a designer, lecturer, town planner, and journalist (in the 1950s Anna Castelli Ferrieri was editor-in-chief of *Casabella Costruzioni* and editor of the magazine *Architectural Digest*). Her importance as a central figure of Italian design in the 1960s and 1970s is particularly based on the part she played in her husband's company, Kartell. As well as designing its office building she was its art director, design consultant, and designer, playing a fundamental role in creating the image of the company. Anna Castelli Ferrieri set new standards in colorful plastics design with her pieces, many of which are still current today, for example her sweeping *7450* salad servers and the bowls *7125–28* (dating from 1976 for Kartell). In addition Anna Castelli Ferrieri was a founding member, and president from 1969 to 1971, of ADI (Associazione per il Disegno Industriale, "Association for Industrial Design"). She has taught at the Domus Academy in Milan since 1987.

2

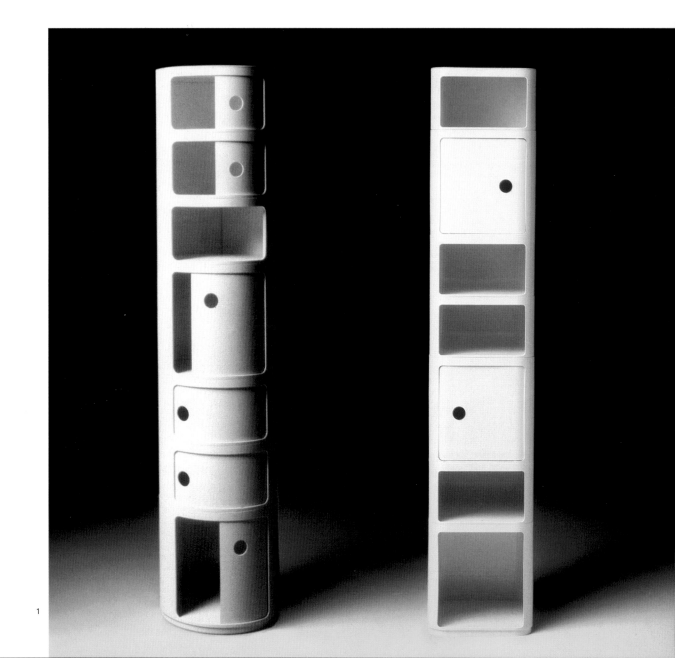

1

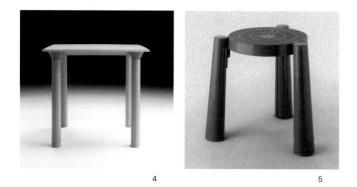

4

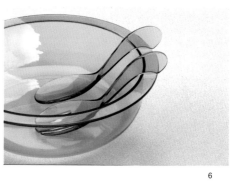

5

1　*4966/67* round storage module and
　4970/84 square storage module, 1967
2　*4822/26* bar stool, 1979
3　*4310* table, 1983
4　Table, 1983
5　*4810* stool, 1987
6　Salad bowl and servers, 1976

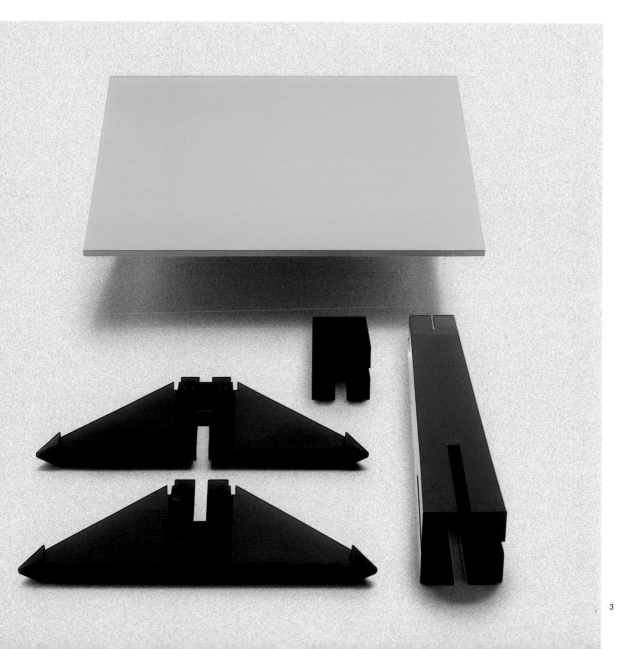

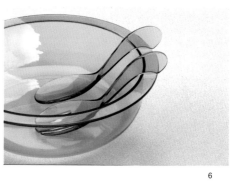

6

3

Achille **Castiglioni** b. 1918 **Italy**

Pre-eminence. Italian design would not be the same without Achille Castiglioni. He is one of the most prominent, playful and elegant designers of the postwar period. But with great modesty he himself says that he owes his success to his brothers Livio (1911–79) and Pier Giacomo (1913–68) with whom he worked for 24 years from 1944. Achille Castiglioni loves technical subtleties, playing with everyday things and changing their use. At the end of the creative process objects of perfect, refined function and stunning appearance emerge. Examples are the *Sella* stool using a bicycle saddle, the *Cumano* folding bistro table that can be hung on the wall, and the *Mezzadro* tractor seat (all produced by Zanotta since the seventies). The luminous vision of this brilliant Italian designer confirms his love of moving parts and folding mechanisms, a fact that is particularly evident in his lights. The *Parantesi* adjustable metal sail lights (1971, with Pio Manzù), the *Frisbi* (1978) inspired by a frisbee, and *Toio*, one of the first halogen ceiling lights (1962, all for Flos) are just a few examples of his brilliance. Castiglioni has been awarded the Compasso d'Oro seven times and has designed everything from exhibitions to cutlery, furniture, lights, radios and watches.

1

2

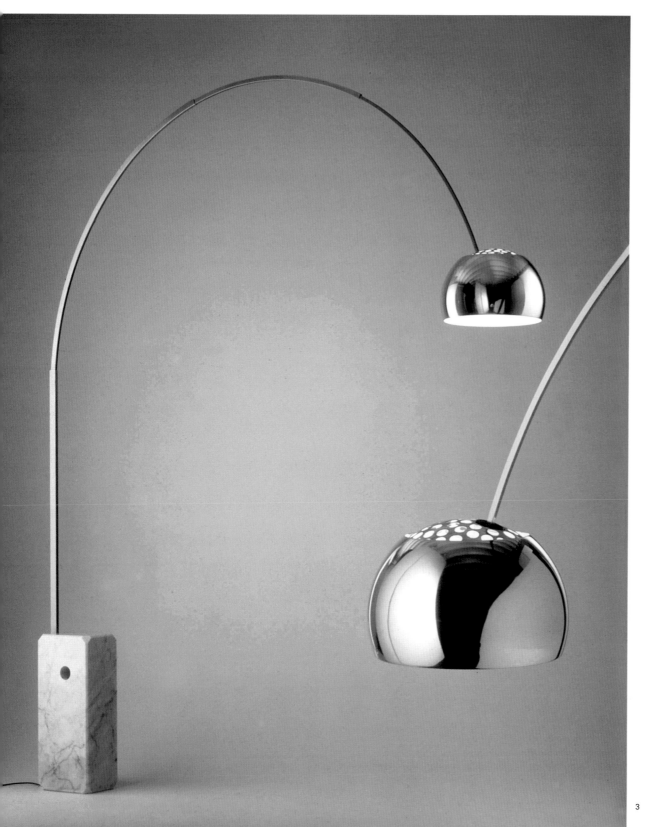

1 *Primate* easy chair, 1970
2 *Mezzadro* tractor seat stool, 1957
3 *Arco* standard lamp, 1962
4 *Sella* bicycle saddle stool, 1958
5 *Fuchsia* ceiling light, 1996
6 *Servomuto* table, 1975

4

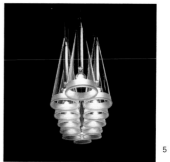

5

6

3

Coco **Chanel** 1883–1971 **France**

From orphan to fashion millionairess. Coco Chanel's story reads like a modern fairytale. Born Gabrielle Chanel, she was one of twelve children; her mother died when she was still very young, her father could not cope, and she was therefore sent an orphanage where she spent fifteen years. When she finished school she found a job in a fashion house and soon made a name for herself as a talented milliner. She called herself "Coco" after the title of a song and quickly forgot her origins and started to move in rather select circles. At the beginning of the century Coco Chanel lived with British millionaire Boy Capel and he made it possible for her to open a boutique in the Paris fashion quarter. Her simple, sporty-elegant style was in stark contrast with the fashion of the time and it was a great success. Coco Chanel claimed that "a woman without perfume is a woman without a past," and in 1921 she launched Chanel *No. 5*, the perfume which would bring her great wealth.

1   Bag, 1955
2   *No. 5* perfume, 1921

1

2

Pierre **Chareau** 1883–1950 **France**

Promoter of the modern. Pierre Chareau was among the masters of Art Deco, the fashionable modern style that was extremely famous in France in the 1920s and 1930s. The architect and designer Chareau came from the south of France and he started his career as a graphic artist in the Paris branch of the English furniture company Waring & Gillow. Shortly before World War I he set up his own studio for interior design, creating whole interiors and very functional pieces of furniture with soft lines, mostly using fine, rare hardwoods, and strongly influenced by Josef Hoffmann and the Wiener Werkstätte. Pierre Chareau also believed in the harmonious blending of architecture, craftsmanship and art. In 1919 he met a Paris doctor, Jean Dalsace, for whom he designed a town house, La Maison de Verre (1932), whose design was based on the modern concepts of architecture. At the beginning of World War II, Pierre Chareau emigrated to the United States where he worked increasingly with metal and tubular steel, turning away from Art Deco as Jacques-Émile Ruhlmann and Eileen Gray had done before.

1 *T* stool, 1927
2 *Table éventail*, c. 1930

1

2

77

Antonio **Citterio**

b. 1950 **Italy**

Timeless modern domestic objects.
There is no such thing as a typical,
immediately recognizable Citterio design.
This is because the man who is hailed as
one of the most important young
designers in Italy pays the greatest
attention to the use of the most modern
techniques and materials, but he does not
feel committed to any particular form
when he designs an object—unless the
almost Japanese reticence of his designs
qualifies as form. Nor has Antonio Citterio
ever joined any particular avant-garde
association. But there is no doubt that this
native of northern Italy has design in his
blood. He was born in the Mecca of
furniture, Meda, north of Milan, and grew
up surrounded by the names of famous
companies such as Cassina and Flos. In
1973, even before he graduated as an
architect from the Polytechnic in Milan, he
set up a studio with Paolo Nava. During
that period he produced his first designs
for B&B. In 1981 he finally opened his
own studio. Since then he has created
modern, timeless furniture and lights,
often in collaboration with Glen Oliver
Löw. These include the *Ad hoc* office
furniture program and the *AC Program*
office chair system (both for Vitra), and
the *Lastra* lights (1998 for Flos) which are
reminiscent of a gigantic printed circuit
serving as a power distributor, which is
normally concealed.

1

3

4

5

2

6

1 *T-Chair* office chair, 1990
2 *Mobil* storage system, 1996
3 *ABC* chair, 1998
4 *Elettra* lighting system (with Glen Oliver Löw), 1993
5 *Visasoft* chair (with Glen Oliver Löw), 1990
6 Cutlery from the *Tools* range, 1988

Claesson, Koivisto, Rune

founded 1993 **Sweden**

Northern revival. It is very unusual for a budding designer to succeed in producing an unmistakable chair while still studying, but Marten Claesson, the youngest partner in the Claesson Koivisto Rune studio, achieved this remarkable feat. The chair was the light, elegant *Maxply*, made of plywood. Its strong affinity with Scandinavian classics is intentional, as it is with the other designs of the trio. These three successful young designers have worked for well-known companies such as Artek and in 1999 had nine pieces of furniture in production. They see themselves as champions fighting the "visual din" of today, returning to the approach of their forefathers, and above all to the deeply rooted Scandinavian ethos of simplicity. Ola Rune's *Cleopatra* chair would have given Bruno Mathsson great pleasure, and *Bowie*, the bench he developed with Eero Koivisto, is a homage to Alvar Aalto.

1   *Cleopatra* chair, 1994
2   *Camp* wall clock, 1995
3   *Maxply 0* chair, 1995

2

3

1

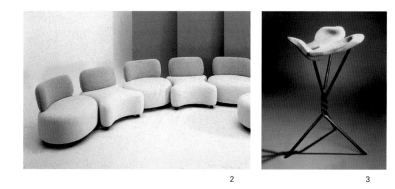

2   3

Nigel **Coates**

b. 1949 **Great Britain**

On a constructive collision course.

Nigel Coates developed the concept of "Narrative Architecture Today," or "NATO," which attacked the sterile, inflexible town planning of the present. A freestyle architect, designer and professor at the London Royal College of Art, he is a man of many talents with a great sense of fun in his approach to work. He is especially famous for his constructive collisions: images, shapes and objects of various periods and time zones are blended into a new, individualistic, incomparable style which is somehow typically English. A partner of the Branson Coates architectural office since 1985, he gave free rein to his inspiration in the mid-1980s when he designed a series of crazily extravagant bars in Tokyo, such as *Cafe Bongo* and *Bohemia Jazz Club*. His trend-setting interior designs for Jigsaw, the British chain of fashion boutiques, and for the fashion designers Katherine Hamnett and Jasper Conran, have integrated unexpected elements of street culture into ambitious architectural concepts. Besides designing furniture for companies such as SCP, Alessi, Arredaesse and Poltronova, the respected professor also enjoys the atmosphere of international show business, designing scenery for theaters and television productions commissioned by clients all over the world.

1   Vase, 1995

2   Seating, 1990

3   *Genius* stool, 1988

Wells **Coates**

1895–1958 **Canada and Great Britain**

Design for all. The Canadian-born architect and designer Wells Coates was one of the most important representatives of the modern movement in England in the 1930s. An architect, engineer and journalist, he turned to design because he was convinced of the latter's influence on society. For him it was the means of putting humanitarian ideas into practice. He experimented with inexpensive materials such as plywood, and this prompted the entrepreneur Jack Pritchard to entrust him with the design of the interior fittings for the acclaimed apartments known as the *Lawn Road Flats* in north London. This collaboration led to the setting up of the Isokon company (1932), which later also produced designs by Marcel Breuer and Walter Gropius. Among Coates's most famous designs were his radios for the E. K. Cole company. These radios were extremely economical in production and material costs, especially the *AD 65* round Bakelite radio (1934). They were Great Britain's first really modern industrial design concept.

Ekco AD 65 radio, 1934

Luigi **Colani** b. 1928 **Germany**

Colani the original. Luigi Colani may no longer be much in demand in Germany, but in Japan he is a highly sought-after designer and consultant. His futuristic chair *Polyeor* (1970, for Cor) was made from glass-fiber reinforced polyester resin. It was an early experiment in synthetic materials with an open-worked, organically shaped seat balanced as if floating on a single leg that ends in a broad, flat foot. A lover of dream women, exotic cars and flowing forms of every kind, the visionary designer Luigi Colani became a darling of the media for a time, a precursor of the designer cult of the 1980s. He has produced exciting versions of countless objects, while his rich retro-style anticipated the bio-design of the 1990s. His work is always full of surprises: although the ball-shaped kitchen, the motorcycle without a tank, and the beak-shaped car never progressed beyond the drawing board, other designs like the *Drop* streamlined tea set (for Rosenthal) and the Colani computer mouse for Sicos have remained very popular.

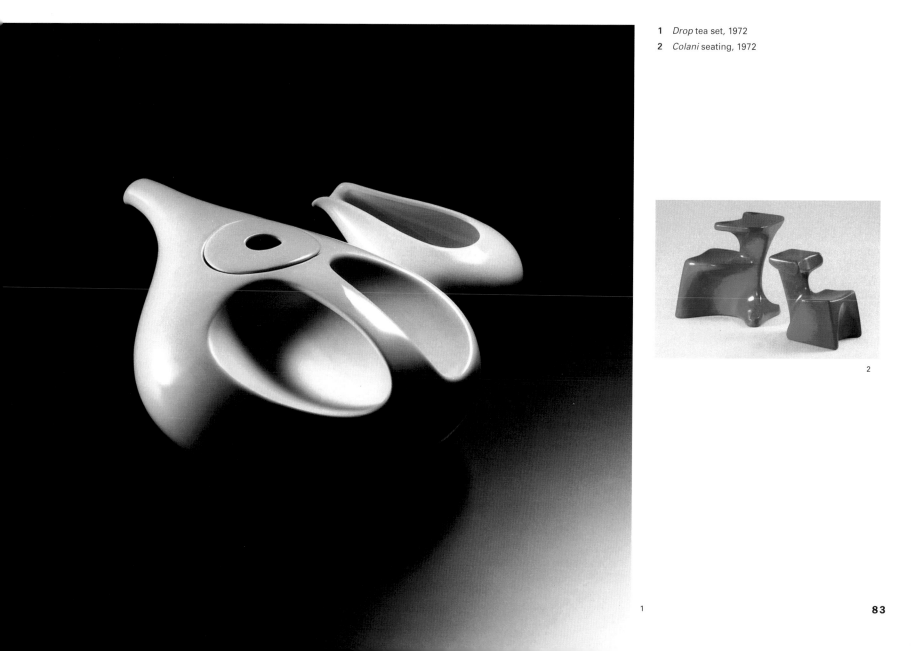

1   *Drop* tea set, 1972
2   *Colani* seating, 1972

2

1

Joe **Colombo**

1930–71 **Italy**

A foundation of subversion and plastics. Joe Colombo was active in Italian design for only ten years, yet his influence was enormous. The painter and sculptor was passionately interested in the most innovative material at the time, plastic. He played with it and whenever possible he incorporated the manufacturing process into the form. For instance, the hole in the back of the plastic chair *4867* (1968, for Kartell) was created by its withdrawal from the mould. The 1960s were revolutionary in many ways and formed the ideal basis for his visions of changing society through design and technology. With his lights and furniture reminiscent of small robots (*Spider*, 1965 for O Luce and *Vademecum*, 1968 for Kartell), or loosely assembled tunnel tubes (*Tubo* chair, 1969 for Flexform), the self-taught designer reacted against traditional domestic design forms and the culture of classical furniture. His premature death soon turned him into a cult designer—deservedly so, since his skillful use of plastics influenced many designers and their projects.

2

1

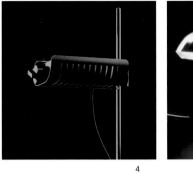

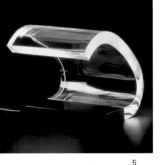

4   5

1 *Tubo* armchair, 1969
2 *Sistema Addizionale* seating system, 1967
3 *Elda* armchair, 1963
4 *626* standard lamp, 1972
5 *281* light, 1962
6 *4867* chair, 1967

6

3

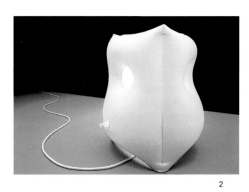

2

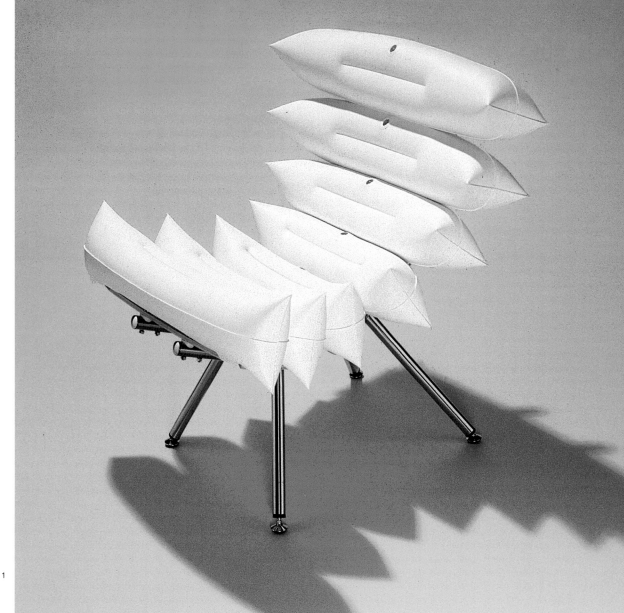

1

1 Chair, 1997

2 Table light, 1997

3 *Pod Bag* (with Craig Morrison), 1998

Nick **Crosbie** b. 1971 **Great Britain**

All hot air. Even as a student Nick Crosbie was experimenting with inflatable objects. After completing his training in 1995, he joined Michael and Mark Sodeau, who had studied with him, to produce clever inflatables, design accessories for the house that called for a lot of air and little money. The shrewd trio, known as Inflate, invented a fashion by giving objects a new softness. Instead of copying the inflatable furniture of the 1960s, Crosbie and his partners apply the principle to everyday objects that they cut out from lightweight PVC. These inflatable objects range from lamps to fruit bowls, egg cups, sofa cushions and postcards, all items that perplex and amuse the public. Crosbie combines his creativity with an outspoken business sense. For instance, he rejected a flattering licensing offer from Alessi, preferring the long-term development of his own brand. In this he has been successful, now having nine people working in his studio for clients such as the BBC, Polygram, Paul Smith, Ford and Sony.

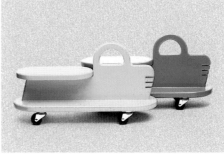

1 *BD 1* chair, 1994
2 Cooking pot from the *Tools* range, 1998
3 Child's ride-on toy, c. 1985

Björn **Dahlström** b. 1957 **Sweden**

Strong profile. The road worker filling the surroundings with a hellish din and shaken to the bone by his pneumatic drill will soon be a thing of the past. The result of years of development, the *Cobra Mk 1* pneumatic drill from the Swedish firm Atlas Copco (1997) vibrates very little and makes only a faint noise when it was operated. But as well as these obvious advantages, the new pneumatic drill is also a beautiful object. It was designed by Björn Dahlström, one of the most promising young Swedish designers. He became known in the mid-1990s particularly for his furniture designs for the CBI company. His first piece was the *BD 1* chair, a curved cuboid that looks like the stroke of a felt-tip pen. This black, minimalist piece of furniture betrays the professional background of its creator: Björn Dahlström started as a commercial artist and cartoonist. Even as a sought-after product designer, he still retains a typographical pithiness and concision.

Lucienne Day

b. 1917 **Great Britain**

Immortal patterns. The textile designer Lucienne Day and her husband the furniture designer Robin Day became famous in the 1950s when they were identified as the representatives of the "contemporary" style. Her original textiles included upholstery fabrics, tablecloths, curtains and rugs, wallpapers and clothes that were sold at Heals in London, one of the best addresses for "good design." One of her best-known fabrics is *Calyx*, which she designed for the Festival of Britain in 1951; she was awarded prizes for it in Italy and the USA, and it has become the archetypal 1950s pattern. This talented artist has also designed porcelain for Rosenthal (1959). In the 1970s she worked as an interior designer and color consultant, developing the technique of silk mosaic, in which tiny pieces of Indian fabrics, sometimes as small as half-an-inch (1 cm) square, are joined together to make a unique, complex design. Lucienne Day's early designs are now experiencing a revival.

1   *Spectators* fabric, 1954
2   *Trig* fabric, c. 1950

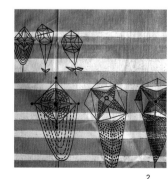

2

1

Robin **Day** b. 1915 **Great Britain**

A man for the good and the unconscious. Robin Day is a monument of British postwar design and his most famous product, the *Polyprop* chair (1962 for Hille) is his most popular creation. The sensational success of the plastic seat with steel tubes which is still used today in Britain's schools and offices made the use of synthetic materials acceptable; until then they had been considered cheap and unpleasant. Produced at a rate of around half a million a year, a total of over 14 million of these minimalist chairs have been sold. Day was an early champion of machine-produced furniture who had studied art and design before opening his own studio in London in 1948 with his wife Lucienne Day, a textile designer. In the same year, Day won his first international award in a competition for inexpensive furniture organized by the Museum of Modern Art. Robin Day was one of the most important representatives of the "Contemporary Style" of the postwar period and the sixties. His designs included simply shaped record players for Pye, as well as work for the Barbican Art Centre and the John Lewis chain store.

1   *Polyprop* chair, 1962
2   Bench, *c.* 1980
3   Seating, *c.* 1965

Michele **De Lucchi**

b. 1951 **Italy**

Countryman goes high-tech.

Although Michele De Lucchi works in
Milan the fuss made there about design
does not suit him, and he spends as
much time as possible in his country
house on Lake Maggiore. Born in Ferrara,
this young architect is now one of the
most highly rated of the young
generation of Italian designers. During his
studies in Florence he founded the Cavert
group (1973–76), which was involved in
experimental architecture. de Lucchi was
a member of Alchymia and a founder
member of Memphis. Since 1979 he has
worked as a design consultant for Olivetti,
being appointed chief designer in 1982.
He has been involved with the Milan
Triennale for 22 years in his capacity of
design guru, promoting the recognition of
design as a form of art. His philosophy is
that whether he is designing notebooks,
telephones or ticket machines, the object
or apparatus must always be easy and
pleasant to use. His architectural projects
are based on the same philosophy of
"service design." In 1990 Michele De
Lucchi, with his partner Nick Bewick,
developed a concept for the design of the
1,200 branches of the Deutsche Bank, and
in 1995 the De Lucchi studio was
commissioned to create a new image for
the German railway system's travel
offices. Meanwhile the *Tolomeo* light (for
Artemide), which he developed with
Giancarlo Fassina in 1987, has achieved
cult status. It was named after the
Italian name of the astronomer Ptolemy
because the desk lamp rotates on its
earthbound axis.

1 *Tolomeo* table light, 1987
2 *First* chair, 1983
3 *Antares* vase, 1993
4 *OFX 1000* fax machine, 1995

2   3   4

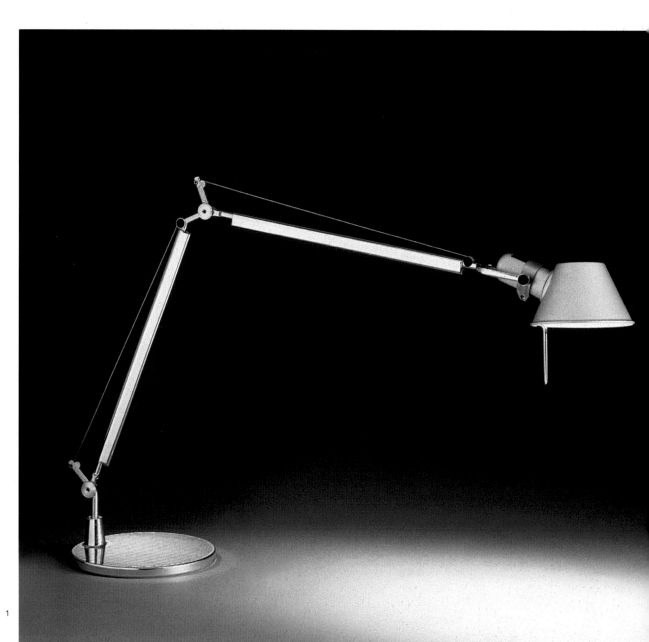

1

De Pas, D'Urbino, Lomazzi founded 1966 **Italy**

Pop veterans. These three architects and designers have worked together and put their stamp on what became known as the "style of enlargement" in pop-art design. Their *Sciangai* wardrobe was reminiscent of a giant Mikado, while the *Joe* chair produced by Poltronova in 1970 was an homage to the baseball player Joe di Maggio and became the symbol of a period. One of their classics is the inflatable *Blow* armchair (produced in 1967, for Zanotta), still much copied today. "We were young, full of life and wanted to break with bourgeois traditions," says Paolo Lomazzi about the designs that he and partners Jonathan De Pas and Donato D'Urbino created in the sixties and seventies. Their furniture is either inflatable or foldable so as to be easily transportable. "We want to make objects that are friendly, cheerful and useful to people" says Lomazzi, describing the studio's philosophy that has remained unchanged since it started. After the death of Jonathan De Pas the studio has been known by the initials DDL. Today, Donato D'Urbino and Paolo Lomazzi design furniture and lighting for famous companies such as Artemide, Driade, Poltronova and Zanotta, but they are also involved in architecture, urban planning and exhibition design at home and abroad, especially in Japan.

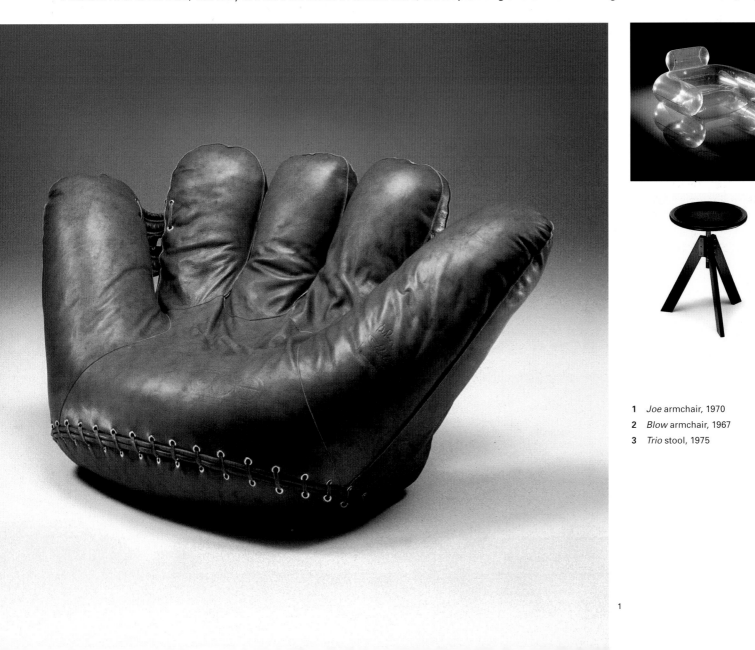

2

3

1 *Joe* armchair, 1970
2 *Blow* armchair, 1967
3 *Trio* stool, 1975

1

Paolo **Deganello** b. 1940 **Italy**

Free-form furniture. Although Paolo Deganello's contribution to design in the 1980s was significant and creative, he steadfastly avoided the limelight. After his architecture studies, this shy designer and journalist worked as a town planner in Calenzano, Florence (1963–72). During this period he was one of the founders of the group Archizoom, with Andrea Branzi, Massimo Morrozi and Gilberto Corretti. Archizoom contributed to the development of Radical Design with its projects that turned against pure functionalism. Deganello, however, always kept a critical distance, in contrast with the members of Memphis and Alchymia. His projects reflect his skeptical attitude towards industry. The characteristically unconventional forms of his furniture, such as his *Regina* chair (1991 for Zanotta), will appeal more to design enthusiasts than to the majority. On the other hand, his *Torso* cushion collection (1982, for Cassina) in which he gives a modern interpretation of the softly curved forms of the 1950s shows that he can also work commercially.

1 *AEO* armchair, 1973
2 *Torso* armchair, 1982
3 *Documenta* chair, 1987

Christian **Dell** 1893–1974 **Germany**

Rationality on the desk. The silversmith Christian Dell was one of the lesser-known Bauhaus designers but also one of the most productive. A pupil of Henry van de Velde, he was head of the metalwork department at the Bauhaus in Weimar, and later returned to Frankfurt. He designed no fewer than 500 lights. The most successful of these was the *i-Dell* desk lamp. It had a parabolic reflector with cylindrical mounting, and a tilting hinge at the base. The *i-Dell* was available in many versions, as a wall light, with a clamp or as twin desk lamps. It was in production for over 60 years and it is still found in many German offices. Even in the 1930s when the Bauhaus designers were still working mainly with wood and metal, Dell was experimenting with the completely new material, plastic.

1 *Classic* light, 1930
2 Light, 1930

Christian **Dior** 1905–57 **France**

Christian of the New Look. Christian Dior originally wanted to study architecture but his father insisted that he should study at the Institut des Sciences Politiques (Institute of Political Science). In 1927 he opened a gallery in Paris with his friend Jacques Bonhan, where he exhibited works by Pablo Picasso and other painters who were friends of his. But art did not bring in money. He had to close the gallery when his father's factory went bankrupt in the world economic crisis of the 1930s. Dior turned to the world of fashion, which he thought of as a stopgap. He started by designing hats before he became famous for his fairytale dresses after World War II. He presented his first collection in 1947 and immediately created a completely new style, the so-called New Look. Wasp waists and very full skirts requiring over twenty yards of material gave women back the feeling of femininity while making them forget the misery of the war. Because Christian Dior firmly believed that fashion must always be different from what preceded it, he began to present two new, innovative collections to the public each year. When the famous couturier died at the age of 52 he left behind a flourishing fashion and perfume empire. The chief designer since 1997 has been the British-born John Galliano.

1 Spring collection, 1995
2 Autumn collection, 1995

1

2

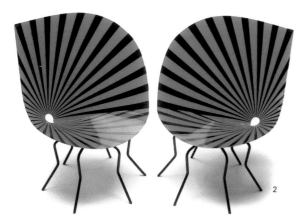

2

Nanna **Ditzel**

b. 1923 **Denmark and Great Britain**

She gave the chair wings. Nanna Ditzel's position is undisputed, both in industry (where she is an important image creator) and with young designers (for whom she is a model of what is still possible in the frequently all too traditional Danish furniture design world). Ditzel studied under Kaare Lint, forming a successful international design partnership with her husband until his death in 1961. She subsequently moved to London where she lived for twenty years. She now lives in Copenhagen again. More than half a century lies between her first design prize, which dates back to 1945, and her most recent creation, the *Tempo* chair (1997, for Fredericia), which was produced using a new adhesive technique. Over this period she has been responsible for many influential designs, whether they be the early furniture such as the famous hanging basket chair (1957, for Bonacina), various textiles, or the jewelry she created for Georg Jensen. But furniture design has always remained her favorite field, and plywood her preferred material whose potential she exploits to the extreme. One of her most exciting pieces is the striped *Butterfly* chair that stands on bent legs, a fashionable counterpoint to Scandinavian functionalism.

1 *Seat for Two* sofa, 1989
2 *Butterfly* chair, 1990

1

97

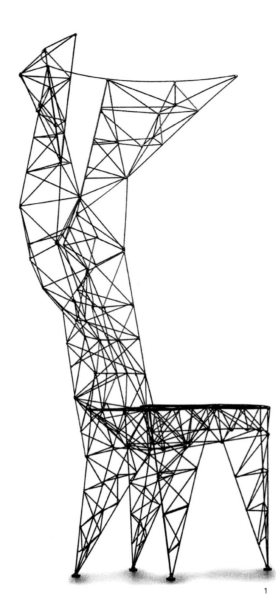

1 *Pylon* chair, 1991
2 *S-Chair*, 1992

Tom **Dixon** b. 1959 **Tunisia and Great Britain**

Freestyle. Tom Dixon is one of the influential pioneers of young British design today. In his Space Gallery in London he has always offered other young designers a presentation platform, rather than promoting only his own designs. Today he is art director for Habitat, one of the largest design-conscious chain stores. He began his design career studying at the Chelsea School of Art in London, while during the 1980s he was a performer in London nightclubs. At some point he began designing sculptural furniture from scrap metal. His experiments with iron, wicker and hard rubber became more a trademark than a particular form of expression. Indeed, although his furniture is usually slender and organic in shape, there is no such thing as a typical Dixon object. The avant-garde designer modestly claims that he has never been commercially successful, but there are a few pieces of furniture such as *Jack*, a chair and a lamp all in one, or the *S-Chair* (1992, for Cappellini), that are "musts" in any serious design collection.

Teapots, c. 1880

Christopher **Dresser** 1834–1904 **Great Britain**

The prodigy. Scottish-born Christopher Dresser was a model pupil at the London School of Design, but his real passion was botany and he studied the subject at several universities. He was in his sixties before he finally set up as a commercial product designer. He had a keen interest in Japanese arts and crafts and wrote several books on the subject of design. There was an interlude of just a year when he worked for the magazine *Furniture Gazette*, during which time he vainly attempted to introduce design reforms. His practical design activities were much more successful and he designed glass, rugs and porcelain for the leading British manufacturers. In his seventies, he became interested in silver and some of his most successful designs are in this metal. Their pure geometry was in strong contrast with the prevailing style, anticipating the modern style. In this they expressed Dresser's principle of "honesty" towards materials, and also the systematic approach that might be expected of the botanist.

Henry **Dreyfuss** 1904–72 USA

The right measure. Henry Dreyfuss was a self-made man who was one of the pioneers of industrial design in America, becoming famous throughout the country like his contemporaries Raymond F. Loewy and Walter Dorwin Teague. Dreyfuss had developed his very own approach to art that had very little to do with his training. After an apprenticeship as scenery designer with Norman Bel Geddes, Henry Dreyfuss set up his own company at the end of the 1920s. *Designing for People* was not only the title of his autobiography published in 1955, it also became his professional motto. Henry Dreyfuss was the pioneer of ergonomics, and his book *The Measure of Man* in which he explained the essential part of anthropomorphic factors in the creative process (published in 1960) was even more successful. Following almost engineering-like principles, he designed many articles of daily use including vacuum cleaners (from 1933, for Hoover), telephones (from 1937, for Bell), agricultural machinery (for John Deere), television sets and cameras, and also locomotives and airplane interiors. Twenty-five years after his tragic suicide, the National Design Museum in New York organized a retrospective of the work of the "Man in the brown suit" as a tribute to him.

2

1

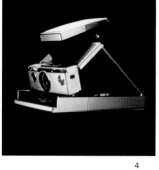

4

5

1 *20th Century Ltd.* locomotive, 1938
2 Thermostat, 1941
3 *Model 500* telephone, 1949
4 *SX-70* Polaroid Land camera, 1972
5 *Model A* tractor, 1937
6 *Princess* telephone, 1959
7 *Trimline* telephone, 1964

6

7

3

3

1 Poster, 1987
2 Signing system (Netherlands Post Office), 1989
3 Corporate identity manuals
   (Netherlands Post Office), 1989

2   1

Gert **Dumbar** b. 1940 Indonesia and Netherlands

A man and his team. Gert Dumbar is one of the most successful graphic artists in Europe but does not like talking about himself. "My success is my team," he modestly declares, and he prefers his name to be simply attached to the Dumbar Studio that he set up in 1977. He studied painting and graphic art at the Academy of Arts in The Hague and attended the Royal College of Art in London during the swinging sixties. On his return to the Netherlands, he built up a graphic design department in the industrial design studio Tel Design. He then set up his own studio with extraordinary success. Besides the usual commissions for the design of posters and signs, he has become especially celebrated in the field of corporate identity. The best-known examples of his work are the corporate images for the Dutch post office and Dutch railways, which broke new ground. His clients also include big multinational companies like IBM, Apple and Philips, as well as august cultural institutions such as the Rijksmuseum in Amsterdam, all of whom appreciate his clear but strongly emotional style.

1 *Dual Cyclone 02*
vacuum cleaner, 1993
2 *Dual Cyclone 04*
vacuum cleaner, 1996

James **Dyson** b. 1947 **Great Britain**

A cyclone sweeps the market. The Dual Cyclone bagless vacuum cleaner (1993) made history as a quantum leap both technically and in its design. It turned its inventor into a multimillionaire. His victory in a near-ruinous lawsuit which preceded production gave this self-made man the status of hero, and he was a champion of the British design community in his fight against the chronic shortsightedness of the world of finance and industry. Once an artist and then a designer, inventor and engineer, Dyson founded his first company in 1975. His first product was a highly maneuverable, stable, plastic wheelbarrow using a ball as its wheel, but the patent for it was stolen from him. Dyson was broke but did not give up. Practically everything about the *Dual Cyclone* vacuum cleaner is new, from its filter and driving technology to its poster-like colors and its marketing strategy. This British vacuum cleaner is already considered a classic in the same vein as Olivetti typewriters or Braun electric razors. In 1996 the London Design Museum devoted a solo exhibition to the "star of the vacuum cleaner."

1

2

Charles **Eames** 1907–78, Ray **Eames** 1912–88 USA

The dream team. The architect Charles Eames and artist Ray Kaiser met at the Cranbrook Academy where Charles Eames taught experimental design. He also worked with Eero Saarinen, with whom he won the "Organic Furniture" competition organized by the Museum of Modern Art in 1940. Charles and Ray married and in 1941 they moved to California where they began to experiment with the forming of laminated wood. Their first mass-produced furniture was launched in 1946 and it led to discovery by George Nelson, the new chief designer at Herman Miller, who decided to include Eames furniture in its program. Among the most important Eames designs are the *LCW* laminated wood chair (1945), the *LCM* chair with tubular steel frame (1946), and the *DCM* and *DCW* dining tables. The leather upholstered *Lounge Chair and Ottoman* (1956) with aluminum frame and separate foot stool is a design classic still in production today. With their technical manufacturing excellence, organic form and comfort, Eames designs are landmarks of modernism. Another of this versatile couple's pioneering creations was the house built from standardized components, their legendary photo archives and their films for IBM and the Indian government.

1 *RAR* chair, 1948–50
2 *ESU* storage system, 1950
3 *EA117* office chair, 1958
4 *670* armchair, 1956
5 *LCW* chair, 1945
6 *ES106* chaise longue, 1968

3

4

5

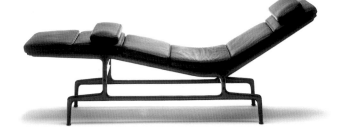

6

Harley **Earl** 1895–1983 **USA**

Cars to look at. In 1926 General Motors set up the "Art and Color Section," the first department in the American automobile industry responsible for the shape and appearance of the cars it produced. The work was called "styling" and the head of the department was Harley Earl, the son of a Los Angeles coachbuilder who had supplied Hollywood stars with cars. Now the style and elegance that had always been reserved for the rich and beautiful would be available to the average customer. Earl was responsible for developing new models every year, starting with the *LaSalle* (1927). His *Cadillac Series 62* (1947) included the first model strongly inspired by aircraft, and it also had a new, special feature: the tail fin, which Earl himself described as a "visible sign of prestige." The 1953 *Chevrolet Corvette* that became a cult car also boasted tail fins. It is known that Earl never made any drawings but he communicated his ideas verbally, in the form of commands. This did not prevent him from introducing innovations into his department. Harley Earl was the first to use clay models (and later Plasticine), and he once even built a full-scale model simply to study how the radiator grille was working.

1

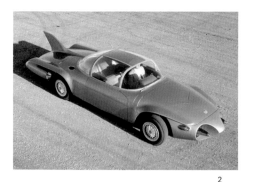

2

3

1 Chevrolet *Corvette*, 1957

2 GM *Firebird II*, 1956

3 Chevrolet *Impala Coupé*, 1956

Egon **Eiermann** 1904–70 Germany

A point of reference. Many of Egon Eiermann's projects have become landmarks, such as the Kaiser Wilhelm memorial church in Berlin (1963) and the Chamber of Deputies in Bonn (1969). Even the few pieces of furniture he designed, usually in connection with his building projects, are also landmarks in the world of design. The *SE18* folding chair (1952 for Wild and Spieth) is a light, inexpensive seat, always available and frequently used for large gatherings in public halls. Today, architects still use another "Eiermann," a supporting structure of crossed bars that can carry a tabletop. Egon Eiermann studied architecture in Berlin in the 1920s before he set up his own studio in 1931. However, he only really became famous after World War II when he went into partnership with Robert Hilgers and taught at the technical college in Karlsruhe. As one of the few architects and designers working during the hectic years of postwar recovery, he emphasized the importance of formal restraint and was very much involved in setting up the German Design Council.

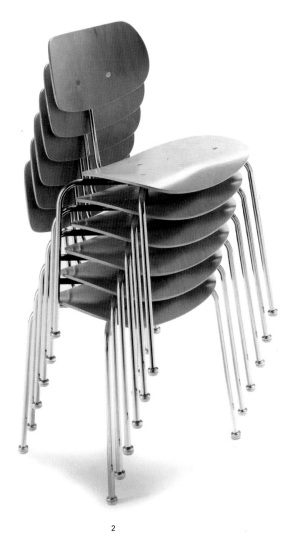

1   *SE18* folding chair, 1952
2   *SE86 su* stacking chair, 1950
3   Stacking stool, 1961

1   2   **107**

Battista Pinin **Farina** 1893–1966 Italy

Dresser of luxury bodies. The name Pininfarina evokes superbly desirable objects such as the Alfa Romeo *Giuletta* Spider (1956), the Ferrari *Testarossa* (1984) and the latest Alfa Romeo *Spider* (1994). The world-famous Italian coachbuilding company was founded in 1930 by Battista Farina. This excellent car body designer was held in such high regard that his nickname "Pinin" became part of the company's name. The elegant profile and rounded shapes of Farina's Cisitalia *Coupé* of 1947 determined the shape of the European automobile of the 1950s. Sergio Farina took over management of the family company in 1959, and in 1995 he was awarded the "Compasso d'Oro" for his achievements because, in the words of the jury, "with his designs for Ferrari he contributed so much to the image of Italy." The company is now run by the third Farina generation. Among its more recent designs are the Peugeot *205* (1983), the Ferrari *F 40* (1987) and the Ferrari *550 Maranello* (1996).

1 Cisitalia *202 Berlinetta*, 1947
2 Ferrari *250 SWB*, 1959
3 Lancia *Aurelia B20*, 1951
4 Ferrari *360 Modena*, 1999

3

4

Edward **Fella** b. 1938 USA

An archetype. Edward Fella has been teaching in California since the late 1980s after completing his studies at the Cranbrook Academy at the age of almost fifty. He often uses torn, faded copies, photocopied many times, which he then skillfully reassembles. Critics claim that aesthetically his work combines the Fluxus and Hippy movements of the rebellious 1960s with the craftsmanship of the traditional "commercial artist." Typical of his work are the sixty or so posters that Fella designed in about 1990 for the Focus Gallery in Detroit, a low-budget commission that allowed him complete freedom. Besides the countless fliers, catalogs and posters, he also created a series of 170 illustrative elements, the "Fella-parts," for *Émigré* magazine. Edward Fella rarely touches computers and instead uses manual techniques that are often quite out of fashion.

1   Poster, 1994
2   Poster, 1993

1

2

Adele **Fendi** 1897–1978 **Italy**

The fur dynasty. Today Fendi is renowned for its modern cutting techniques, its new dyeing and processing methods, and its unusual furs. In the 1920s Edoardo and Adele Fendi owned a small leather and fur shop in central Rome as well as a workshop and a small tailoring business. Business was flourishing and they decided to expand by opening a larger shop. Gradually the five Fendi daughters joined the business, which now consisted of five departments: leatherware, furs, shoes, luggage and fashion. Then three women of the third Fendi generation developed their own "Fendissime" brand, and furniture was added to the range of Fendi products in the early 1990s. Fendi's great breakthrough was in 1962 when Karl Lagerfeld began to work for the family. He invented the famous FF logo and he also revolutionized the processing of fur, turning an expensive garment that was once rigid and heavy into something light and pleasant to wear. Fur had become an item of fashion.

1 *X-Ray* bag, c. 1965
2 Fur coat, 1970
3 *Croissant* bag, 1990
4 *Croissant* bag, 1999

1   2   **113**

Salvatore **Ferragamo** 1898–1960 Italy and USA

Homage to the foot. Arriving in the USA as a poor immigrant and humble cobbler, Salvatore Ferragamo became shoemaker to movie stars and a millionaire. He began making cowboy boots, Egyptian sandals and elegant shoes for the new stars in the early 1920s, just as the motion picture industry was starting to expand, and with his brothers he held the shoe monopoly for the film studios. Ferragamo did not only want to make beautiful shoes; he also wanted to understand the human foot, so he attended anatomy lectures and developed his own revolutionary lasts. Ferragamo returned to Italy at the end of the 1920s. When the League of Nations imposed sanctions on Fascist Italy and raw materials became scarce, he turned the situation to his advantage. Instead of leather, he used substitutes such as metal fibers, felt, cellophane, or wood. Expert craftsmanship and the combination of unusual materials became Ferragamo's trademark, and extraordinary models like the *Invisible Sandals* (1947) turned him into a legend. The wooden models of the feet of Audrey Hepburn, Sophia Loren, Greta Garbo and lesser-known stars have been in his workshop since the 1950s. Today his children run the business, which now also includes bags, towels, ties, fashion and perfume.

2

1

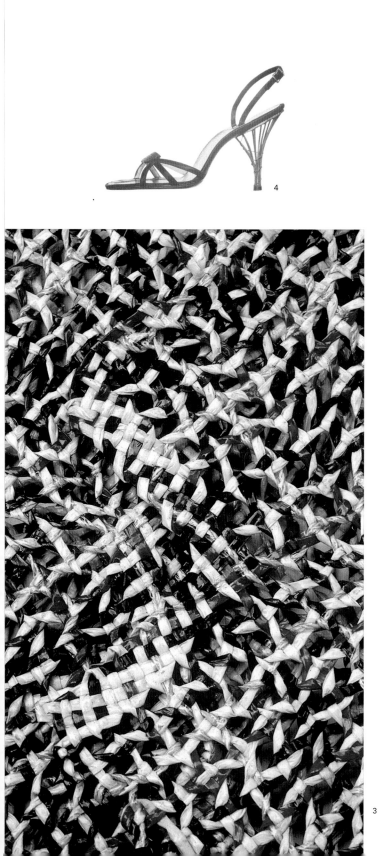

1 Shoe, 1935

2 Shoe, 1941

3 Fabric, 1941

4 *Calipso* sandal, 1956

5 *Liù* slipper, 1945

6 Shoe, 1962

4

5

6

3

1/2 Autumn collection, 1997
3 Spring collection, 1999

Elio **Fiorucci** b. 1935 **Italy**

The stylesurfer. Fiorucci is the name of a man, an international brand name, a sales system and a "look." The architect of this business, artistic and social phenomenon was born in Milan, and in the early 1960s Fiorucci was the shop where the elegant Milanese went to have their clothes and shoes made. When Elio Fiorucci had a pair of colored plastic overshoes illustrated in a fashion magazine, they became a best-seller overnight. Fiorucci has been following this recipe for success ever since. He adapts foreign fashion trends, particularly English and American ones, to the Italian market. This was an eye-opener to Italians at the time, since items such as brightly colored T-shirts made from Lycra and Spandex, or glittering shoes and bags made from fake animal skins, were unknown until then. Today, shock and fun are still part of the Fiorucci philosophy, and jeans are the company's best-selling item. Mad colors and materials are definitely a "must," as is the borrowing from past fashion trends.

willy **Fleckhaus** 1925–83 Germany

Anti-establishment layout. Willy Fleckhaus squashed characters together, he printed text in the margins, he cropped photographs mercilessly, thereby redefining the relationship between text and image. Germany's premier art director invented a clean magazine look using strong contrast. Recognized as one of the most innovative graphic artists of postwar Germany, he started his career as editor of a trade-union magazine. In 1959 he became famous overnight when the new magazine *Twen* was launched. Its new subjects and revolutionary layout reflected the experiment-happy 1960s and Fleckhaus's playful creativity. Ignoring all the traditional graphic conventions, his trademarks were the cover with a black background and a new typographical freedom. He applied this same freedom when he worked as art director for publishers like FAZ and Suhrkamp—he created the legendary "Edition Suhrkamp" in rainbow colors—and as graphic artist for the television channel WDR, which was at the time the largest in Germany.

1 *Twen* magazine, 1964
2 *Twen* magazine, 1960
3 Book jackets for Suhrkamp, from 1959

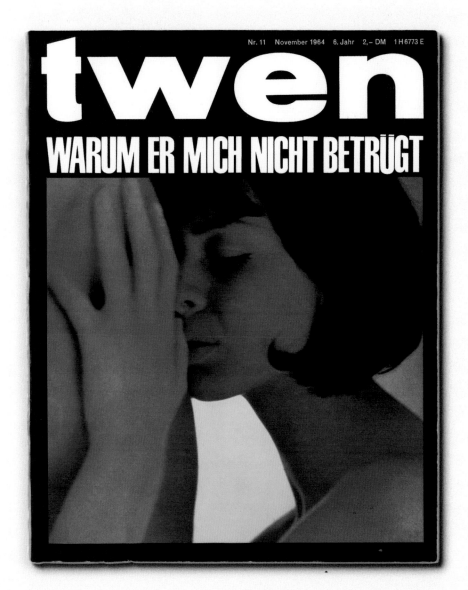

3

2

1

Piero **Fornasetti**

1913–88 **Italy**

The magician. No surface was safe from Piero Fornasetti. He painted furniture, tableware, domestic accessories, textiles and carpets with architectural and fantasy motifs in *trompe-l'œil* style. His inexhaustible, overflowing creativity that contributed to his great success in the 1950s had been his undoing in the 1930s when he was studying art at the Brera Accademia in Milan; after two years he was excluded from the academy because he would not—and could not—conform to the accepted style of the school. His encounter with Gio Ponti in 1940 was a stroke of luck for the self-taught artist. Ponti published many of Fornasetti's works in the magazine *Domus*, and in 1950 they decorated and furnished the casino in San Remo. Today, the famous company in Via Manzoni in Milan is run by Piero's son, Barnaba Fornasetti, and old designs are being produced again in their factory.

1   *Temi e Variazioni* plates, 1954
2   *Quattro Stagioni* table and chairs, c. 1955

2

1

Norman Foster b. 1935 Great Britain

Designs for the world of tomorrow. The design of the new German parliament in Berlin's Reichstag is one of the most prestigious architectural developments of recent times. Norman Foster's project consisted of adding a light inner shell to the existing building. The man who today is building the architectural monuments of tomorrow studied in Manchester before going into apprenticeship with Buckminster Fuller in the United States. Foster is one of the founders of high-tech architecture and his dramatic buildings use modern materials, and take advantage of solar radiation. His product design matches this functional attitude. His *Nomos* range of office furniture (1985 for Tecno) constructed of aluminum, plastic, and steel offered solutions to the new flexible, aesthetically-minded executives. The light system that he developed for the Hong Kong and Shanghai Bank was adopted by Erco (1986). Because his buildings and interiors are so uncompromising and so "un-British," most of his clients are from other countries, with the exception of the Sainsbury Centre for Fine Arts and Stansted Airport.

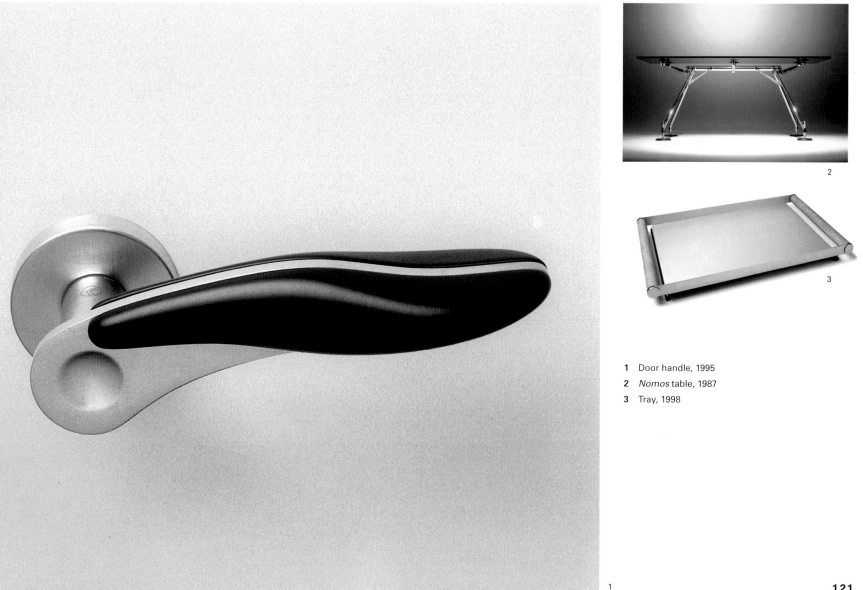

1   Door handle, 1995
2   *Nomos* table, 1987
3   Tray, 1998

Kaj **Franck**

1911–89 **Finland**

3   4

Tableware for everyone. The 1992 exhibition at the Museum of Modern Art devoted to Kaj Franck served to place him in the pantheon of leading product designers, but he has not always been so recognized. During the 1970s his classic designs even stopped being produced and the glass designer and master ceramicist was in danger of falling into oblivion. In the years after World War II he had caused a "revolution on the dining table," as one newspaper described it. As a revolutionary designer with socio-political interests, at first he had great difficulties in carrying out his ideas. Franck was a radical because he preferred the Bauhaus geometry to the new "curvy" style of design. His aim was to develop a new product culture for ordinary people. Franck's plates, bowls and glasses were so practical and his stackable chairs so space-saving that they were true objects for all. His breakthrough came in 1949 with *Kilta* (for Arabia, today *Teema*), an "anti-service" that ignored the European etiquette of the table. This early table-service system in simple forms and colors could be put together and added to according to need. It consists of three dozen pieces that can be combined at will. A total of over 25 million pieces have been sold.

1 Glass, 1955
2 *Kilta* service (now *Teema*), 1949
3 *Prisma* vase, 1954
4 *Kilta* cups, 1949
5 Glasses and jugs, 1955

5

Josef **Frank** 1885–1967 **Austria and Sweden**

Modernist and humanist. The Austrian architect furnished the house he designed for the celebrated Weissenhof development in Stuttgart using cozy upholstered furniture with masses of cushions. This un-modernist act almost caused a scandal at the time. Josef Frank was indeed more interested in the needs of the inhabitants rather than the rigid rules of modern style. In the 1920s he had co-founded the progressive interior design company Haus & Garten and the hope of Austrian architecture had rested on him. But the anti-dogmatist emigrated to Sweden in 1934, and there his name soon became synonymous with what became known as "Swedish Modern," a style particularly popular in America. Frank was then working for the Swedish interior design company Svenskt Tenn, and he was responsible for the design of the Swedish pavilions at the World Fairs of 1937 and 1939. His modern but rather unorthodox style subsequently became a commercial success. Frank's prodigious creativity and exciting designs enhanced this success; he designed some two thousand pieces of furniture, not including lamps, accessories and countless textiles. His famous over-sized sofa covered with a colorful pattern of leaves and flowers (1934) shocked all modernists.

3   4

1

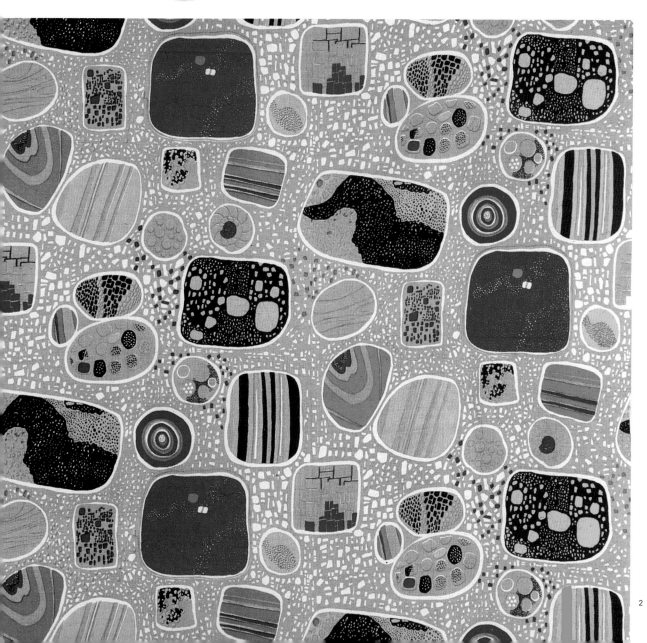

1   Jewel box, 1950

2   *Terrazzo* fabric, 1944

3   Standard lamp, 1939

4   Standard lamp, 1938

5   Sofa, 1934

6   *300* chair, 1925

Gianfranco **Frattini** b. 1926 Italy

Wood and craftsmanship. Gianfranco Frattini is not interested in gimmicks: although he is an industrial designer, he feels very committed to manual traditions of craftsmanship. His elegant, rectilinear wooden tables and writing desks reflect his understanding of natural materials and his love of detail. Spectacular designs like the *Boalum* light snake, made from transparent, flexible synthetic resin which he designed in 1970 with Livio Castiglioni for Artemide, are an exception rather than the rule in his work. Gianfranco Frattini was influenced by Gio Ponti, with whom he worked for a short time before and after his architectural studies in 1953. He himself has had a great influence on Italian design philosophy as cofounder of the Associazone per il Design Industriale (ADI, "Association for Industrial Design") and through his involvement in the managing committee of the Milan Triennale.

2

1 *Boalum* light (with Livio Castiglioni), 1970
2 *Megatron Terra* light, 1979

1

ABCDEFGHIJKLMNOPQRSTUVWXYZ

abcdefghijklmnopqrstuvwxyz

Adrian **Frutiger**

b. 1928 **Switzerland**

Univers-al solutions. In the early 1950s, after working as a typesetter's apprentice in Interlaken and studying in Zurich, Adrian Frutiger accepted the invitation of the leading French typographer Charles Peignot to come to Paris, where he became art director of the type foundry Deberny & Peignot. His first important design *Méridien* (1955) established his reputation in the field, and his typeface *Univers* (1957) brought him worldwide fame. This was a sans-serif typeface distinguished by its simple elegance. The type family included some twenty variations of weight and style, each indicated by a number, and it became the most successful typeface designed since World War II. Also a book designer, calligrapher and sculptor, Frutiger set up his own studio in Paris in 1962. His clients included Linotype AG and IBM, for whom he developed typewriter typefaces. Later he also invented the computer-readable typeface *OCR-B* (1965) that is used throughout the world.

Univers 45	ABCDEFGHIJKLMN
Univers 55	ABCDEFGHIJKLMN
Univers 65	**ABCDEFGHIJKLMN**
Univers 75	**ABCDEFGHIJKLMN**
Univers 47	ABCDEFGHIJKLMN
Univers 57	ABCDEFGHIJKLMN
Univers 67	**ABCDEFGHIJKLMN**

1   *Univers* typeface, 1957
2   *OCR-B* typeface, 1968

Shigeo **Fukuda** b. 1932 **Japan**

Surprisingly light hand. "Every truth has several faces" is one of Shigeo Fukuda's principles. It comes as no surprise that this graphic artist was strongly influenced when young by M. C. Escher's drawings. Fukuda reflects this influence on a much reduced scale in his posters. His abstractions of complex motifs almost become pictograms. His simple and at the same time strongly symbolic designs in which Eastern and Western influences meet and merge remain typical of him. His visual forms of expression are so international that they are equally understood anywhere in the world. After the birth of his daughter, Fukuda turned to other areas of design. For instance, he has designed a toy that was manufactured in the family factory, and countless origami folding shapes; he has also illustrated books and calendars and designed various wooden figures and fittings. Apparently without effort, he moved from designing posters to ambitious projects such as a bridge in the town of Kita-Kyushu and telephone boxes in Shizuoka. Since they are normally entrusted to architects or industrial designers, such projects reflect the faith that clients have in him, and their confidence that they can always expect something unusual.

1 *Rio 92* poster, 1992   **2** *Graphic Design Today* poster, 1990

Olivier **Gagnère** b. 1952 **France**

The success of the self-taught. Although he never attended art school, Olivier Gagnère has secured a place on the international design scene with his unusual vases that appear to be put together from the most varied shapes and parts. After formal training in applied economics, the self-taught designer went to Italy, where he joined the avant-garde Memphis group in 1980. This experience had a lasting influence on the unusual, bold designs on the surfaces of his pieces, which combine artistic and craft techniques. Inspired by the precision of Murano glass and Japanese ceramics, the Paris-born artist started to sell his designs made from metal, glass and earthenware in small numbers at fashionable galleries in Paris. Some are now also mass-produced. Olivier Gagnère was equally successful with the chairs and tables he designed for the Café Marly (1994) in the Grand Louvre in Paris. A year later Artelano publicly launched his collection that combines modern lines and traditional French details.

2

1 *Wild* chair, 1997

2 *Observatoire* screen, 1994

John **Galliano** b. 1960 **Great Britain and France**

Flippant style-mix. John Galliano adores the spectacles he organizes with such amazing virtuosity. Since 1997, the extravert, extravagant Englishman has combined his own flamboyant style with the tradition of the French haute couture House of Dior. The son of Spanish immigrants, he became known as a creative genius in the 1980s for his striking collections with their flippant mixture of pattern, style and period. Russian fairytales and 1940s movie stars influence his designs, as do variations on the parka, Indian-Mexican folk motifs, and Art Deco. He has a marked preference for strong colors. The man who is so good at staging sumptuous fashion shows conquered Paris in 1996 with his creations for Givenchy, and at the age of 37 this eccentric British designer took over from the Italian high-priest of haute couture, Gianfranco Ferré, as chief designer of the glamorous House of Dior founded in 1947.

1 Autumn collection, 1999   **2** Autumn collection, 1989

Niels **Gammelgaard** b. 1944 **Denmark**

The furniture rationalist. From the beginning of his career, first at the Box 25 design office and later with his creative partner Lars Mathiesen at Pelikan Design, this Danish architect and furniture designer has paid attention to the consumers' needs. Whether designing the *Decision* range of sofas (1986), the *Café* range of tables and chairs (1983, both for Fritz Hansen), or the imaginative *Labyrinth* room partitions made from wood, linoleum and fabric, Gammelgaard combines artistic expression and rationality. This approach led him to create ideas for Ikea, for whom his designs include *Ted* (1983), a light, colorful folding chair made from plastic that has sold in millions. His range of products is wide, embracing children's bicycles, bathrooms, furnishings for railway carriages and of course furniture. Gammelgaard sees himself as an industrial designer in the tradition of Arne Jacobsen, very much in contrast with Danish cabinet-making tradition. Characteristic of this is his ability to use his experience derived from the development of a range of products for something completely different.

1

2

1   *Ted* folding chair, 1983

2   *Tribike* children's tricycles, 1980   **131**

Elizabeth **Garouste,** Mattia **Bonetti** b. 1950 **France**, b. 1953 **Switzerland**

The rehabilitation of decoration. The furniture of Elizabeth Garouste and Mattia Bonetti consists of branches, felt, raffia, velvet, iron and other materials not normally associated with house furnishings. They are very skilled at presenting their dramatic furniture, intricate accessories and interior decoration that is like a stage setting. The two designers do not have a particular stylistic approach but they simply use anything that comes to hand. These masters of ornamentation have been working together since they designed the club Le Privilège (1979), and with their designs for the Néotu and En Attendant les Barbares galleries, the stage designer and furniture designer together developed two concepts: neo-baroque and neo-barbarism. In doing so they put their stamp on the new French design of the 1980s. "We do not worry about rationality and consistency when dealing with objects that can embellish the house," says Mattia Bonetti reasonably. Among their most magnificent pieces are the *Turtle Woman* ceramic ashtray in the shape of a turtle (Blend Collection), the *Prince Imperial* chair with raffia skirt (Néotu) and the *Kawakubo* chest of drawers (David Gill).

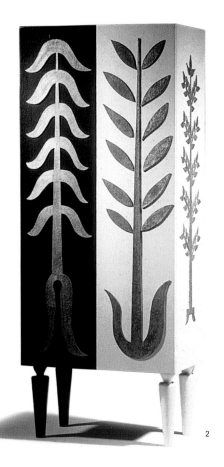

3

1 *Paradis* cabinet, 1998
2 *Armoire Noto* cabinet, 1992
3 *Imperial Prince* chair, 1986

2

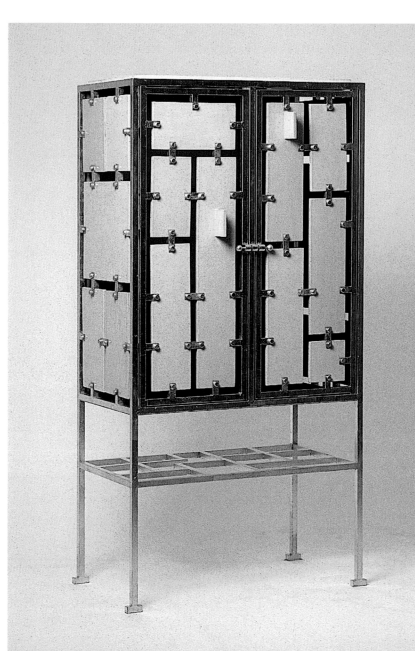

1

Gatti, Paolini, Teodoro Founded 1965 **Italy**

The bag of all bags. Piero Gatti, Cesare Paolini and Franco Teodoro became famous almost overnight with a single piece of furniture, the legendary "bean bag," *Sacco* (1969 for Zanotta). The bean bag adapted itself perfectly to any body shape and weight, and toward the end of the 1960s it represented the progression of anti-authoritarian ideas into furniture. Traditional domestic and seating forms were thrown to the wind and replaced by the leather bean bag, filled with little expanded polystyrene beads. Lounging and relaxing now became the new domestic style. This simple design by the trio of architect, industrial designer and graphic designer (established in Turin in 1965) proved a difficult technical problem to solve. Many attempts were made to mass-produce the bean bag before a solution was found that quickly led to a phenomenal marketing success. Together with the *Blow* chair designed by De Pas, D'Urbino and Lomazzi, the soft bean bag has become one of the icons of pop design.

Sacco chair, 1969

Antoni **Gaudí**

1852–1926 **Spain**

A unique path to modernism.

No one visiting Barcelona could fail to encounter the impressive buildings designed by the Spanish architect Antoni Gaudí, from *Bellesguard*, the symbol of Catalonia, to the *Casa Mila*, whose irregular outside walls look like sand dunes, and the unfinished cathedral of the *Sagrada Familia*. Antonio Gaudí i Cornet developed his own style, which contained Gothic and Moorish elements combined with entirely personal, hardly classifiable forms. Countless avant-garde artists and designers have been inspired by his free variation of forms, styles, materials and decorative details, combined with his willingness to subordinate all rules—even ones relating to construction—to an overall idea. He also created furniture, such as the armchairs with bone-like elements and projecting decoration at the end of the armrests that he designed for *Casa Calvet* in 1898. Such designs marked a clear break with traditional concepts and the transition from Art Nouveau to expressionism. But this brilliant eccentric, who conducted his building workers with a baton, did not become rich through his ideas. When he was run over by a tram in 1926 he was wearing such shabby clothes that he was taken for a vagrant.

Chair for the *Casa Calvet*, c. 1900

Jean-Paul **Gaultier**

b. 1952 **France**

Methodical provocation. Some people find Jean-Paul Gaultier's cone-shaped brassières and mini-skirts for men rather degenerate, but stars like Madonna and David Bowie see this French designer as their guru of taste. Mixing the most varied styles without any scruples, Jean-Paul Gaultier is the great eccentric of the fashion world. The career of this blond tousle-haired artist started in 1970 when he worked as fashion stylist for Pierre Cardin. Six years later he made a bid for independence by launching his own collection, which included fluorescent jewelry, but this was a flop. It was only at the beginning of the 1980s that the world seemed ready to accept the humorous-ironic look of the top designer who could not care less about traditional concepts of beauty or ugliness, or whether Mr. and Mrs. Normal Consumer think that curtains or plastic tablecloths should be used for making clothes. Jean-Paul Gaultier sticks to his motto "fashion is nothing without fun." He has also become involved in the design of perfume bottles and movie sets, thus helping madness to become normal.

Spring collection, 1999

Frank O. Gehry

b. 1930 **USA**

News from the nineties. The young and then unknown Californian architect Frank Gehry launched the *Easy Edge* chair range made from laminated corrugated cardboard in 1972. It caused such a stir that he decided to cease the production of the much-praised but controversial range because he feared unfavorable repercussions on his architect's practice. His fears were groundless and today he is one of the most sought-after international architects and designers. The "deconstructivist" artist sees buildings as sculpture and his eccentric style strongly reflects artistic influences. It has resulted in sensational buildings like the Vitra Museum in Weil, the Toyota complex in Maryland (in collaboration with artists Claes Oldenburg and Richard Serra), and the Guggenheim Museum in Bilbao, an organic spatial landscape whose breathtaking, plastic irregularity is reflected on a smaller scale in his furniture. Like Ron Arad and Tom Dixon, for instance, Frank Gehry also uses everyday materials such as corrugated iron, roughcast plaster, and rectangular wickerwork as well as steel and iron girders. Vitra produces a re-worked version of his corrugated cardboard chairs, while Knoll caused a stir with his *Cross Check* bentwood and wicker chairs and tables (1991). This unusual furniture uses the principles of wickerwork and the manufacturer's technicians had to make no fewer than 120 full-size prototypes of the range before putting it into production. The result is recognized by many as the most radical innovation since the works of Eames and Bertoia.

1

2

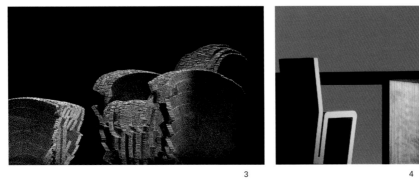

3

4

1 *Wiggle* chair, 1972
2 *Cross Check* chairs and table, 1991
3 *Little Beaver* armchair, 1980
4 *Side Chair*, 1990

Romeo **Gigli**

b. 1950 **Italy**

Simple, romantic and sensual.
Romeo Gigli creates luxurious, sumptuous clothes, and other items such as Venetian glass. His fashion creations revive the beauty of the Italian Renaissance, like the youthful figures in Piero della Francesca. This modest star only rarely appears in public. He first studied architecture but gave it up before completing the course because he preferred fashion. His architectural experience is perhaps reflected in his clear forms of expression, with a tendency towards asymmetry. As well as in art, Gigli finds his inspiration by travelling to distant countries like Asia and South America. While emphasizing the figure, his clothes remain purist and sober in manner, as he feels women should dress. His romantic, poetic style accentuates the flowing, soft materials that seem to caress the body. Gigli has a marked preference for stretch linen, chiffon, cheesecloth, wool and cashmere. He combines natural or rich colors with gold brocade, rich Indian embroideries and lace borders with pearls.

Autumn collection, 1989

1 *Girotondo* trays, 1989
2 *Big switch* light, 1992
3 *Bombo* stool, 1996

Stefano **Giovannoni** b. 1954 **Italy**

Comic messages. Stefano Giovannoni belongs to the class of Italian designers who bring humor and color to modern design. Together with Guido Venturini he designed many playful yet practical household gadgets for Alessi. As the "King Kong" Duo they designed the *F.F.F.* range between 1985 and 1989. Standing for "Form Follows Fiction," an ironic reference to the Bauhaus dogma "Form Follows Function," the *F.F.F.* range included a brightly colored gas lighter in the shape of an erect penis; the *Merdolino*, a toilet brush in a flowerpot; and *Nutty the Cracker*, a nutcracker with squirrel. But this jolly, colorful "comic book" design is not restricted to gadgets; Stefano Giovannoni has also tried his playful, imaginative hand at fashion and furniture. He has created objects such as the *Bombo* stool (1996 for Magis); the *Rocking Chair* (1987), reminiscent of a halved meteorite and made of fiberglass, aluminum, and rubber; science-fiction-like roller skates (1965); and jeans covered with plastic plates (1987 for Levi's).

Giorgetto **Giugiaro** b. 1938 **Italy**

The father of the VW *Golf*. There is hardly a European or an Asian car manufacturer who has not called upon Giorgetto Giugiaro's skills in the past forty years: Alfa Romeo, Audi, BMW, Fiat, Isuzu, Lancia, Renault, Saab, Seat, VW and many others have entrusted their products to this man's feel for form and the spirit of the time. As creator of the VW *Golf*, the Fiat *Panda* and the Fiat *Uno*, he has influenced the image of Europe's streets for decades. Giugiaro's successful career as a car designer and subsequently as a designer of furniture (Tecno), lamps (Bilumen), cameras (Nikon), watches (Seiko, Swatch) and other appliances for Philips, Sony and Johnson & Johnson was quite unexpected, in that he studied art, with industrial design only as a subsidiary subject. His extraordinary talent was spotted by Dante Giacosa, Fiat's technical director, who immediately offered him a job. He learned his craft at Nuccio Bertone's studio where he worked for six years before going on to become an epoch-making car designer in his own right. In 1967 Giugiaro founded his own company, Ital Styling, soon changing its name to ItalDesign, which has so far developed more than 80 cars. Giugiaro founded Giugiaro Design in 1981, to concentrate on the development of functional industrial product design.

2

6

7

1 Nikon *F5* camera, 1996
2 Maserati *3200 GT Coupé*, 1998
3 Bottles for Fonti San Bernardo, 1993
4 *Medusa* light, 1997
5 Copenhagen suburban railway, 1998
6 Alfa Romeo *Alfasud*, 1971
7 Volkswagen *Golf*, 1974

Hubert de **Givenchy**

b. 1927 **France**

4   5

He breathed life into fabric. The secret behind Hubert de Givenchy's successful career is his extraordinary feel for textiles of all kinds: "Fabric is the beginning of everything, a prerequisite for all inspiration," the fashion designer and art collector once said. Givenchy's family had expected him to become a lawyer but instead he went to Paris in 1945 and worked for Jacques Fath as a stylist. Seven years later, still only twenty-three years old, he set up his own fashion house. During those seven years, he had acquired a lot of experience by working for major houses such as Robert Piguet, Lucien Lelong and Elsa Schiaparelli. In 1953 he met the Spanish designer Cristóbal Balenciaga who introduced Givenchy to the world of fabrics. His career suddenly took off in 1954 when Audrey Hepburn asked him to design her wardrobe for the film *Sabrina*. Reflecting the youthful, elegant image of the actress, he created an unmistakable look combining harmonious proportions, a very feminine line and unusual details. His client list has included such famous names as Jackie Kennedy, Marlene Dietrich and Liz Taylor. Givenchy said that It was "the decline of haute couture" that led him to sell his business in 1995. Today it is Alexander McQueen, the "bad boy" of the fashion world, who is ensuring that the venerable house of Givenchy remains in the limelight of fashion. Hubert de Givenchy is now head of the auction house Christie's in Paris.

6

2

3

3

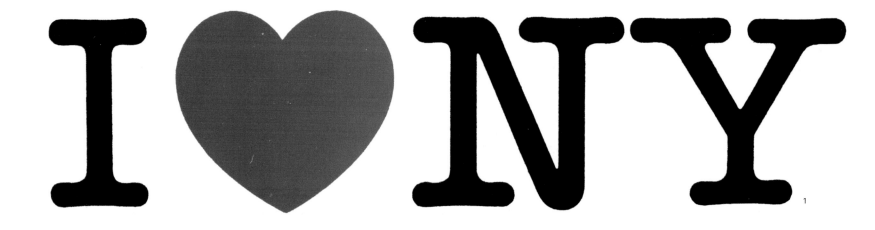

1

Milton **Glaser** b. 1929 **USA**

"I love NY!" The publisher of *Paris Match* gave Milton Glaser hardly a day to redesign the magazine. He reduced the format, increasing the circulation by 20 percent. He designed a new corporate image, range and shop fittings for the Grand Union Central supermarket chain with equal success. He is the guru of American image-making and co-founder of the Push Pin Studio in New York; to him the effectiveness of a statement is much more important than its elegance. After studying art in New York and Bologna, he livened up the then-popular graphic design style—prosaic and Germanic—with elements of humor, expertise and a sense of art. The novelty of his style, strongly influenced by surrealism and hippy culture, lay in the fact that Glaser included romantic elements and complexity in his designs. His posters for Bob Dylan became pop icons, and in the mid-1970s Glaser became closely involved in book and magazine design, working for publications like the *Village Voice*, *Esquire* and *L'Express*. His greatest single success is the device using three letters with a red heart, Milton Glaser's iconographical declaration of love for New York created in 1973. Since then millions of people have worn it on T-shirts, carried it on plastic bags, and displayed it as car stickers.

1 Sticker, 1973

2 Poster (Bob Dylan), 1966

3 *Glaser Stencil* typeface, 1974

4 CD cover (Louis Armstrong), 1990

5 Logo and mascot for the *Twergi* range (Alessi)

6 Cover for the book *Alessi: Die Traumfabrik*, 1998

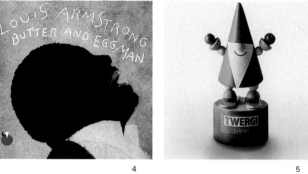

4

5

6

Kenneth **Grange** b. 1929 **Great Britain**

Product design instead of designer product. To Kenneth Grange, co-founder and partner of the Pentagram design agency (until 1998), product design is total. There is no compromise between form and function. As an industrial designer, Grange sees design as an integral part of the production process, with the visual identity of the commissioning client always in the foreground. This idea is explained in his book ambiguously entitled *Live through Design*, and it means that millions of consumers will know the product designed by him (and the manufacturer) but not the designer himself. He has designed all kinds of celebrated products, such as the *Image* sunglasses (for Polaroid), and the *Compact* wet razor (for Wilkinson). This unusual self-abnegation in a creative artist goes hand-in-hand with a marked sense of mission for design, an area increasingly dominated by the cult of personality. Prominent clients such as Kodak, EMI, Parker, Kenwood, Connolly and British Rail all appreciate this designer's self-effacement.

1 London taxi, 1997

2 Kodak *Instamatic* camera, 1966

3 Razor, 1997

4 Pocket cameras (for Kodak), 1975

5 Kenwood *Chef* mixer, 1986

6 Iron, 1993

3

4

5

6

Michael **Graves**

b. 1934 **USA**

When design came into the kitchen.
Like Robert Venturi, Michael Graves is a
leading representative of American
postmodernism, which rehabilitated the
figurative that had been displaced by the
abstract. He believed that the rejection of
all cultural and historical links had led to
alienation and loss of imagination. Unlike
other representatives of the new
eclecticism, he has applied this philosophy
to the creation of very successful everyday
objects. His whistling bird kettle (1985, for
Alessi) was bought by over half-a-million
people, marking the arrival of fun design
in the home. After he studied architecture
in Harvard and Rome, from 1964 Graves
lectured at Princeton, where some of his
best early buildings are to be found. His
more recent projects include hotels for
Walt Disney and the extension of the
Whitney Museum in New York. Michael
Graves has also long been interested in
furniture design, producing sketches since
the 1970s. His first piece of furniture,
Plaza, was a dressing table (1981, for
Memphis), and he also designed
tableware, lamps, rugs and jewelry.

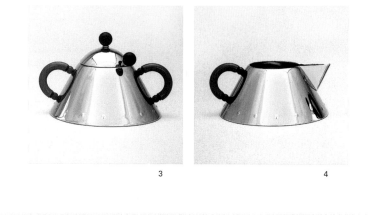

3

4

1

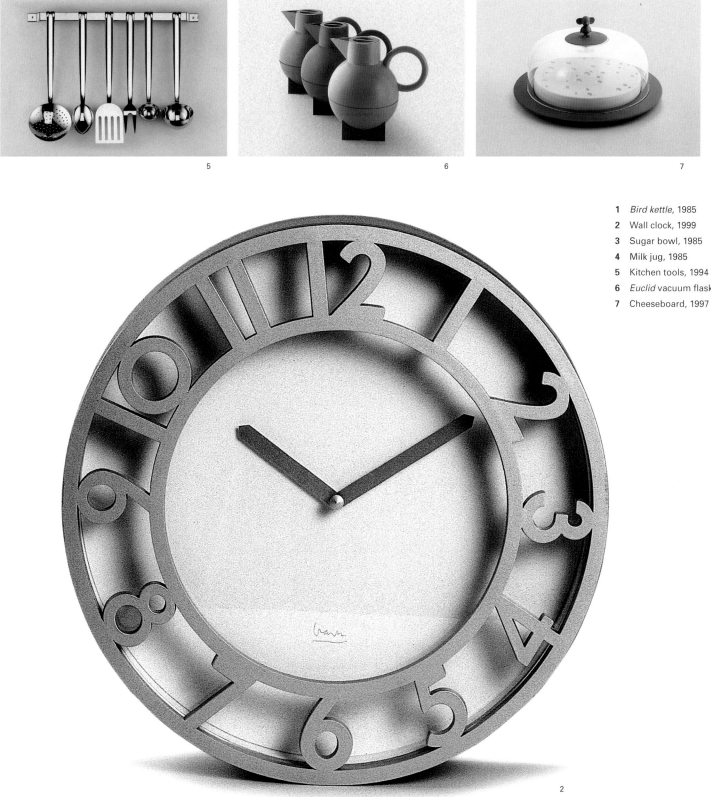

1 *Bird kettle*, 1985
2 Wall clock, 1999
3 Sugar bowl, 1985
4 Milk jug, 1985
5 Kitchen tools, 1994
6 *Euclid* vacuum flask, 1995
7 Cheeseboard, 1997

5

6

7

2

Eileen **Gray** 1878–1976 **Ireland and France**

Pioneer of modernism. Eileen Gray shared the fate of many artists: she was little known during her lifetime but greatly admired after her death. In spite of the small amount of work she produced, this Irish-born designer and architect is recognized today as one of the pioneers of Modernism. She was also one of the first women to be taught at the Slade School of Art in London. In 1902 Eileen Gray moved to Paris where she began her artistic career producing lacquerware. She applied up to twenty coats of lacquer to folding screens, panels, furniture, bowls and plates, and even discovered new colors for her Japanese-style domestic objects. In 1913 Eileen Gray exhibited her lacquerware for the first time at the Salon des Artistes Décorateurs. Jacques Doucet, one of the most famous couturiers of his time, noticed the young woman and became her mentor. The contacts the young craftsman made as a result of this support helped her secure many commissions. Eileen Gray set standards in the use of neon light with her *Prophetic* lights, while her houses *E-1027* (1929) and *Tempe a Pailla* (1934) in the South of France were considered quite futuristic. Gray's initial passion for precious furnishings later gave way to a more sober functionalism. She experimented with tubular steel, and she designed chairs and tables in chrome and glass which still look very modern today.

1

2

4

5

6

1   *Rivoli* desk, 1928
2   *Tube Light* standard lamp, 1927
3   *Monte Carlo* sofa, 1929
4   Round table, 1927
5   Day bed, 1925
6   *Blackboard* carpet, 1910

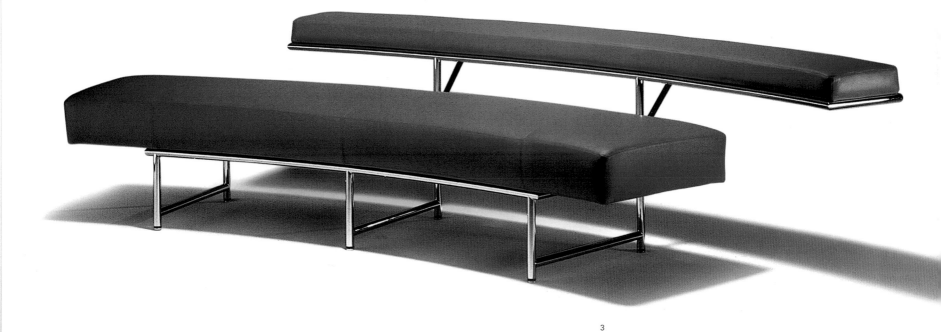

3

1 *SK4 Phonosuper* radio and record player
   (with Dieter Rams), 1956
2 *Sixtant* electric razor, 1962

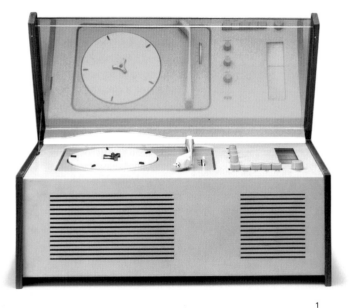

1

2

Hans **Gugelot** 1920–65 Indonesia, Netherlands and Germany

Mass-produced neo-functionalism. In the mid-1950s Hans Gugelot with Dieter Rams designed the remarkable *Phonosuper SK4* combined radio and phonograph (1956, for Braun). It was compact and user-friendly, with no unnecessary decor and no "back." Because of its revolutionary Plexiglas lid, the apparatus was popularly known as "Snow White's coffin." This unusual radio-phonograph was one of the first examples of sober, functional design in mass-produced consumer equipment. The *SK4* also marked the first example of the extremely successful "Braun Design" style that continued to bear Gugelot's imprint long after his death; it is frequently equated with German design. The Indonesian-born Dutchman made his mark in Max Bill's studio as a proponent of neo-functionalism. In the early 1950s he followed Bill to the Ulm Academy for Design, where he ran the product design division from 1954 onwards. Gugelot produced pioneering designs for Braun, such as the celebrated *Sixtant* electric razor (1962), and for other manufacturers. He set up his own studio in 1960, doing work for the sewing-machine makers Pfaff as well as designing ranges of office furniture and the classic *Carousel* slide projectors (1963, for Kodak).

Tricia **Guild**

b. 1951 **Great Britain**

Flowers to the people. As a child of the hippy generation, Tricia Guild transferred her typically English love of flowers and plants to fabrics and other materials with such success that her studio Designers Guild (since 1970) can today offer the consumer a comprehensive lifestyle concept with over 2,500 patterns of fabric and carpets. In 1972 she opened a boutique in the King's Road, then still a slightly shabby part of London. It has now become the flagship shop of the company, offering a "Total Look" from curtains to sofas. The company has about 250 employees, it exports 60 percent of its production, and it produces a range of decorating books. It also creates designs for international manufacturers, such as a tea service for Rosenthal. In 1994 the award of the European Design Prize confirmed the excellence of this "floral" company. It should however be recognized that Tricia Guild succeeded in converting a nation enamoured of botanical motifs to a modern interpretation of this floral theme.

1

1 *Quanjin* fabric, 1994
2 *Kavahana* fabric, 1996
3 *Furn* coverings, 1998

2   3

Alfredo Walter **Häberli,** Christophe **Marchand** b. 1964, b. 1965 **Switzerland**

Unreservedly constructive. Alfredo Walter Häberli and Christophe Marchand both graduated from design school in 1991 and they work together as a successful team in furniture and product design. Their works include the adaptable *Ricreo* secretaire (1997, for Zanotta), which has a steel frame, several compartments, drawers, filing drawers and glazed cupboards, offering endless possibilities with its flexible modules. The *S 1080* table (1999, for Thonet) can be pushed into the corner on two wheels and is very space-saving with its overlapping tabletop. As well as system furniture designed to achieve the most efficient writing position and solutions for changing sitting positions, such as the *Wing* table (1999 for Edra), the pair has also designed a series of smaller accessories like the *Pinocchio* bookends (1997, for Danese) and a flyswatter (1999, for Authentics). Since the 1980s the two have been responsible for arranging many exhibitions at the Design Museum in Zurich.

1 *SEC* furniture system, 1997
2 *Wing* bed, sofa and table, 1999

1

2

156

Edward **Hald** 1883–1980 Sweden

The glass poet. Hald's fascinating glass engravings with delicate, figurative motifs combined classic elements typical of the time with modern art. They appeared on utility goods such as the *Feuerwerk* (fireworks) dish (1921) as well as on decorative objects like the prizewinning bowl *Ball spielende Mädchen* ("Girls Playing with Ball," 1920). His luxurious showpieces revealed his love for lyrical compositions, small, detailed, accurate engraving and the human sexual act. A critic invented the definition "Swedish grace" to describe his poetic style. Edward Hald's work is synonymous with that of Sweden's most famous glass manufacturer, Orrefors. Since 1917 this company had taken on established artists and it had been very successful with this approach (like Hald, Simon Gate made a name for himself there). Hald had studied architecture and painting in Dresden, Copenhagen and Paris, and he had a European reputation before he started working for Orrefors. He became widely famous for his glass engraving after the Paris Art Deco exhibition in 1925, where he won several prizes.

1   *Girls Playing with Ball* vase, 1920
2   *Graal* vase, 1956

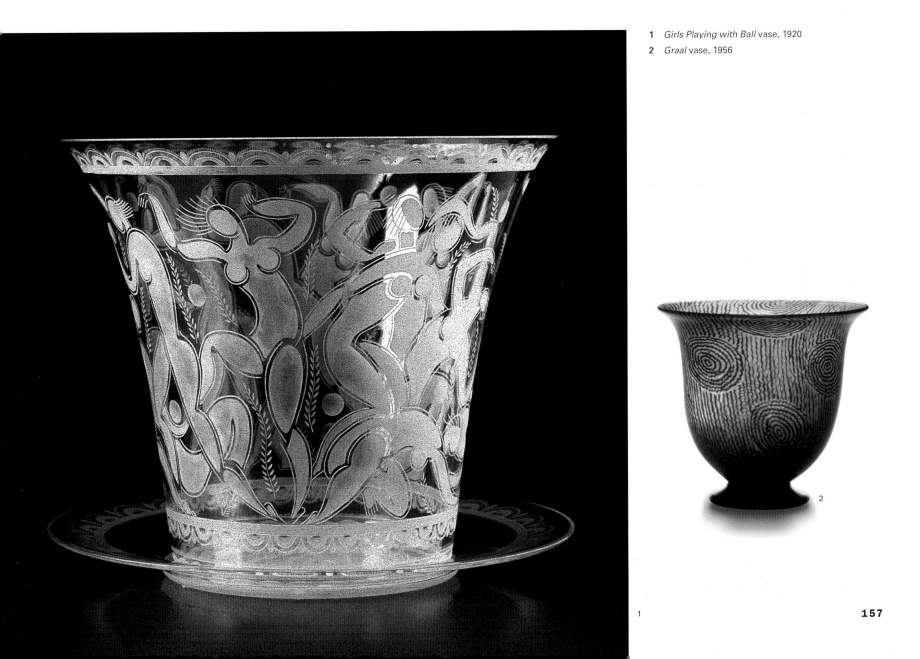

1/2 *Haugesen* table, 1984

3 *X-Line* table, 1977

Niels Jørgen **Haugesen** b. 1936 **Denmark**

The minimal maximum. Niels Jørgen Haugesen has achieved considerable success with only a small number of perfect designs. Often he leaves his projects to mature for several years before returning to them. His preferred material is metal, which he often combines with wood. When an American department store announced a competition for new types of furniture, he won second prize with his design but attracted the most attention. The jury was fascinated by his *Haugesen* folding table that could be unfolded in no time. The leaves simply disappear under the table, using a principle he invented. Trained as a cabinetmaker, Haugesen worked for many years in architects' offices, and also for Arne Jacobsen, whose imaginative approach to design and to the work itself greatly influenced him. Niels Jørgen Haugesen sees furniture as a constructional task whose internal logic must be fully thought out. For instance, his *X-Line* stacking chair visually expresses the underlying principle of the design and the forces that make it work.

158

Rolf **Heide**

b. 1934 **Germany**

A lover of shapes. "Too many unnecessary objects are being designed," says the man with an unmistakable penchant for geometric shapes and ascetic aesthetics. After studying art and cabinetmaking, Rolf Heide worked as an interior architect. In this capacity, for seventeen years he designed ideal rooms for the interior design magazine *Schöner Wohnen* ("Beautiful Lifestyle"), a publication whose influence on German interior design cannot be underestimated. Heide applies his minimalism to a very wide range of furniture: from unit furniture systems (1965) to stackable divans (1966), highly functional kitchen units (1974), or a very practical lamp like *Aruga* (1995). Heide's exhibition stands have always caused a sensation. For instance, he pushed the principle of minimalism to the limit when he designed a stand for the carpet manufacturers Vorwerk: inside a cube with a barely recognizable entrance, the products of the manufacturer were missing.

1   *Futo* standard lamp, 1998
2   *Container* cupboard, 1971

2

1

Poul **Henningsen**

1894 – 1969 **Denmark**

Light shapes. Poul Henningsen was a keenly critical observer of the urban milieu, and he was irritated by the enormous luminous power of lightbulbs that was wasted so thoughtlessly. In his own lights he tackled the problem scientifically and designed them as anti-glare reflecting machines, but with remarkably artistic results. From the mid-1920s he marketed them under his initials PH, and gradually adapted them to the most varied purposes. Their appearance alone was impressive. For instance, the *Kogelen* pendant light (1950s, for Louis Poulsen) consisted of a complex structure three feet high made up of a series of plates; it looked very striking, and it also fulfilled its purpose perfectly. Before World War II PH lights were Denmark's most important industrially designed product and they were popular with architects including Alvar Aalto and Ludwig Mies van der Rohe. But Henningsen was not only a maker of lights. The chain-smoking cultural critic was also an architect, writer, publisher, songwriter, theater producer and furniture designer—all in all, a Danish institution.

1 *Kogelen* ceiling light, 1957
2 *PH* table light, 1933
3 *PH 5 Pendant* ceiling light, 1958
4 Winding chair, 1932

3

4

2

Josef **Hoffmann** 1870–1956 **Austria**

The cubist. Whether buildings, interiors or vases, the work of Josef Hoffmann is always distinguished by its masterful geometry, its rejection of historic decorative elements, and its admirable sense of utility. This aesthetic approach was seen by many as the true expression of the industrial era and as such far ahead of its time. Josef Hoffmann first formulated his progressive ideas in the radical "Secession" group, to which Joseph Maria Olbrich and artists like Gustav Klimt belonged. They created the "Viennese Modern" style in about 1900, and they also played an important part in the development of international architecture and design. For instance, the Art Deco movement of the 1920s and 1930s would have been quite unthinkable without Hoffmann. He developed his famous "cubist" expression of forms for the sanatorium in Purkersdorf (1906), with its then very unusual flat roof. Like his mentor Otto Wagner, he conceived his projects as a synthesis of the arts, seeing the interior decoration as part of the architecture, as for instance in the Stoclet House in Brussels (1905–11). Hoffmann's best-known item of furniture is a dining chair, a "sitting machine," as he called it himself.

1

2

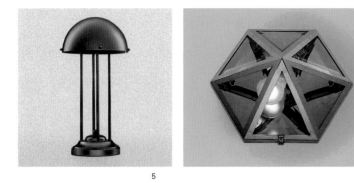

5

6

1 *Kubus* armchair, 1910
2 *Club* armchair, 1910
3 *Sitzmaschine* chair, c. 1908
4 Nesting tables, c. 1900
5 *Hans Henneburg* light, 1904
6 *Villa Spitzer* light, 1903

3

4

Hans **Hollein** b. 1934 **Austria**

Originally a postmodernist. Hans Hollein studied architecture in Vienna, Chicago and Berkeley. Since 1964 he has run his own studio in his hometown of Vienna, where he soon attracted attention with his luxurious extensions and alterations. For the Retti candle factory (1965) he took the theme of the airplane. For the headquarters of the Vienna tourist information center (1978) he arranged golden palms and truncated antique columns in a glass-vaulted pavilion. Ornateness and witty touches are also typical of Hollein's work as furniture designer. For instance, he decorated his Art Deco dresser with real ostrich feathers. No less extravagant were his sofa prototypes *Marilyn* and *Mitzi* (for Poltronova). His *Schwarzenberg* table from brier wood which he showed in the 1981 Memphis collection made a lasting impression, confirming once again his reputation as a pioneer of the post-modern and as a brilliant blender of tradition, kitsch and pop-art.

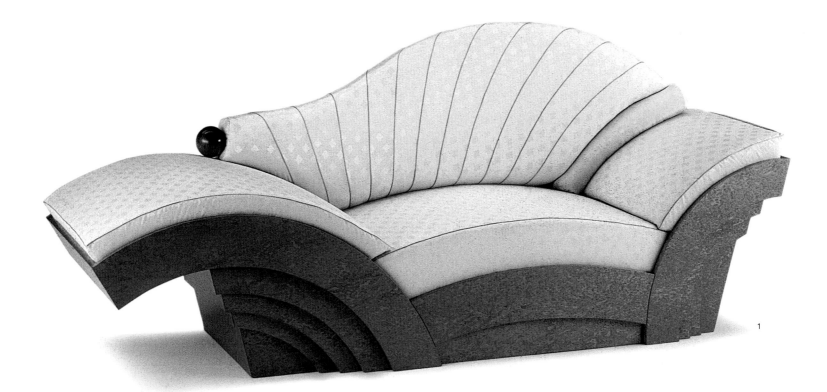

1

1 *Marilyn* sofa, 1980
2 *Schwarzenberg* table, 1980
3 *Piazza* tea set, 1983

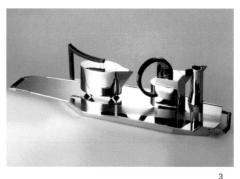

2

3

2

3

1 *d-line* door handle, 1972
2/3 *Quinta* lights, 1992

Knud **Holscher**

b. 1930 **Denmark**

The timeless. Knud Holscher is a celebrated architect and product designer, one of the Danes most in demand on the international market. A pupil of Jacobsen, Holscher maintains a cheerful functionalism which is usually described as timeless, because any decoration would blur the clear lines of the object. His numerous projects include desk lamps (for Erco), bathroom fittings, sound panels, energy-saving devices and guideline assistance for the blind. His work includes many examples which confirm his main premise, that in the end quality is always accepted. A case in point is the *d-line*, a range of impressively simple fittings made from stainless steel (for Petersen) which has been in production for over 25 years and just will not age.

1

Fujiwo Ishimoto

b. 1941 Japan and Finland

A Japanese in Helsinki. Fujiwo Ishimoto is a textile designer whose work combines Far Eastern and northern elements. Whether using sweeping brushstrokes, lithographic colored surfaces, scrawled crayon lines or fantasy landscapes from the photocopier, his designs always reveal a boundless creativity and great force of expression for which the adopted Finn has received many design prizes and international recognition. The applications of his fabrics are as varied as their visual appearance: curtains, duvet covers, tablecloths, scarves, and so on. Ishimoto was a graphic artist in his native country, and he discovered his love for Finland when working for a Scandinavian interior design company. He has by now designed several hundred patterns, almost all of them for Marimekko, Finland's most famous textile manufacturer, which was following the "lifestyle" trend as early as the 1960s.

Maisema fabric, 1982

Alec Issigonis 1906–88 Great Britain

Little car, big success. Alec Issigonis was born in Turkey and emigrated to England in the early 1920s. He started his career as a specialist of automobile wheel mounting, quite a long way from his most important creation, the *Mini* (1959, for Morris). This was a car with a short wheelbase, small outside but surprisingly spacious inside. Compact with a sporty look, it became the mobile symbol of the "Swinging Sixties." Issigonis had already designed the fairly traditional *Morris Minor* (1948), but with the *Mini* he created a completely new type of vehicle, the minicar with the sloping tail, that was to dominate the rest of the century. His anti-limousine was also the first cult car for all, also available in station wagon, van, and pickup versions. Apart from its obvious fun qualities, it had many advantages: it was within everyone's reach, it was economical to run, and it fitted into the smallest parking space. It was a perfect illustration of engineer Alec Issigonis's basic design principle, which was that the best styling was the natural by-product of the best technical solutions.

1   Morris *Mini* car, 1959
2   Morris *Minor* car, 1948

Arne **Jacobsen**

1902–71 **Denmark**

Silhouetting the furniture. The most brilliant designs are often inspired by the works of others. The Danish architect Arne Jacobsen installed the plywood chair designed by the American artist Charles Eames in his own studio, and it became the inspiration for one of the most successful models in the history of design. The shell-like three-legged chair *Myren* (1951) was sold in millions of copies and is still considered a timeless classic today, used in canteens and classrooms all over the world. It consisted of just two elements, the legs and the springy bowl-shaped seat, and it was extremely economical to mass-produce. Later Fritz Hansen brought out a four-legged stacking version, *3107* (1955). In 1960 Jacobsen succeeded in producing a modern *Gesamtkunstwerk* (a synthesis of several arts) with his Hotel Royal in Copenhagen, a multistory building situated in the center of the city. He was responsible for every detail of the interior design—both furniture and furnishings—from the chairs to the pastry forks. In their rooms guests would sit in an *Aeget* armchair or a *Svanen* suite of two armchairs and a settee, both made from pressed Styropor, reminiscent of Henry Moore's abstract sculptures and the subject of many jibes from the press. Arne Jacobsen had been very taken with the Bauhaus in the 1920s and some of his designs included free cubist lines. Overall he was someone who amalgamated the most varied trends to develop a style of his own. His chairs marked a definitive departure from the traditional craftsmanship which characterized Danish furniture. The creation of purely industrial furniture was probably his greatest innovation.

1

1   *Myren* (Ant) chair, 1951
2   *Svanen* (Swan) chair, 1958
3   *Aegget* (Egg) and *Svanen* (Swan) chairs, 1958
4   *Cylinda* range, 1967

Grete **Jalk**

b. 1920 **Denmark**

The sculptress. The furniture designer Grete Jalk won the sought-after prize of the Copenhagen Joiners' Guild for the first time in 1946, and she was a member of that exceptionally creative generation that in the 1940s laid the foundations for the dominant position that the Danish Modern style would achieve. She freed herself from the traditions of the past and, like Aagaard Andersen and Nana Ditzel, she had the courage to experiment. She studied modern materials such as plywood. For the two-part construction of her ingenious laminated wood chair (1963, for Jeppensen), the material is formed in a way that at first seems almost impossible, advancing into the third dimension and giving an overall appearance that is convincingly sculptural. Her tubular steel tube armchair (1964, for Fritz Hansen) also captivates with its compact construction. In 1987 Jalk published the book *Dansk Møbelkunst* ("The Art of Danish Furniture"), a survey of the achievements of the Danish furniture industry.

Plywood chair, 1963

2

3

Georg **Jensen**

1866–1935 **Denmark**

The smart silversmith. "From backyard workshop to silver emporium" could be one way of describing Georg Jensen's story. Trained as a potter, he opened a workshop where he designed silverware shortly after the turn of the century. This was the start of a rapidly rising career. The Art Nouveau style was very popular in metal design and the Danish variations created by the House of Jensen were successful internationally, to such an extent that he opened subsidiary companies in New York, Milan and Munich. One of his most famous designs from the early years is a teapot decorated with a pumpkin flower (1904). These exuberantly decorative forms subsequently gave way to modern functionality with designs developed by house designers such as Johan Rohde and Henning Koppel. The most distinctive characteristics of Jensen's silverware were maintained, including its matt, moon-like surfaces achieved by skilled craftsmanship and the use of a layer of polished platinum.

1 Teapot, 1904
2 Scissors, 1915
3 Spoons, 1912 and 1916

1

1

Jacob **Jensen** b. 1926 **Denmark**

Equipment as a cult object. Jacob Jensen attended the Copenhagen Arts and Crafts School. From 1963 to 1991 he designed radios, phonographs, amplifiers, and loudspeakers for Bang & Olufsen, the top-of-the-line Danish manufacturer, that completely changed the appearance of audio components. These polished objects with their sparse graphics and sober lines were quite unlike the appliances of the past. The *Beolit 600* portable radio (1965) was an elegant, slender parallelepiped. Never again would projecting control buttons bother the eye and irritate the fingertips. One of the many innovations was not surprisingly the flush slide-rule station selector such as that of the *Beomaster 2000* (1974) receiver. Jensen's products have become cult objects. His amplifier could be hung on the wall like a picture and his phonograph placed on an altar to pop music. In 1978 the Museum of Modern Art organized a one-man show of his work. His designs still exercise the same magic, whether it be a vacuum cleaner (1992, for Nilfisk) or a cooker (1993, for Gaggenau).

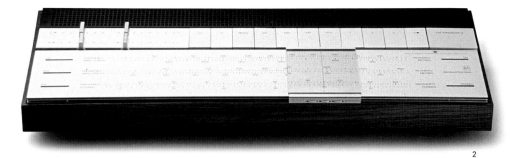

1 *Beogram 4000* record player, 1972
2 *Beomaster 1200* receiver, 1969
3 *Beolit 600* portable radio, 1965

Hella **Jongerius** b. 1963 **Netherlands**

Trial and error. "Rubber is a craft material that is very easy to experiment with," says Hella Jongerius. As well as being an excellent material from which to make bathmats (1993), whose knobbly surface massages the feet while also catching the water, she has also demonstrated that it is ideal for flower vases (1994) and washbasins (1997, both for Droog Design). These objects have a glass-like appearance that does not look cheap. The Dutch designer attended the Academy for Industrial Design in Eindhoven in the early 1990s. She is fascinated by the unexpected, and like an alchemist she creates her designs through trial and error and painstaking experiment. The results are often strikingly archaic in appearance. Hella Jongerius enjoys using materials in unusual and therefore surprising contexts; in addition to rubber, she has worked with Porzella, from which she made a surprisingly strong stool (1997, for Rosenthal), and with bright high-tech fibers from which she made another stool (1997, for Droog Design).

2

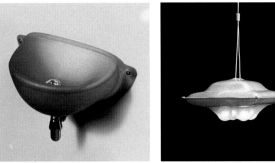

3

4

1 *Soft* vase, 1996
2 *Soft* wash basin, 1997
3 Pendant light, 1997
4 Bathmat, 1994

1

2

Finn **Juhl**

1912–89 Denmark

Modernity in teak. When the Danish version of functionalism in furniture design was about to conquer the world, the architect Finn Juhl called into question this simple style. His "sofa with ears" that he showed at the exhibition of the Copenhagen Cabinet Makers (1939) clearly stated his opposition to the style prevailing at the time and his sweeping disapproval of it. The flowing, sculptural forms of his furniture, reminiscent of modern painting but also of Art Nouveau, soon gained ground and even became synonymous with Scandinavian design. It was Finn Juhl who popularized the use of teak in furniture design. Until then it had been an exclusive material, and it was not possible to use the valuable tropical hardwood industrially. This changed with the introduction of a new sawing technique used in the processing of aluminum. His teak armchair *133* (1953) heralded a new era that made Finn Juhl one of the most important representatives of "Danish Modern."

1/2 *Chief* armchair, 1949

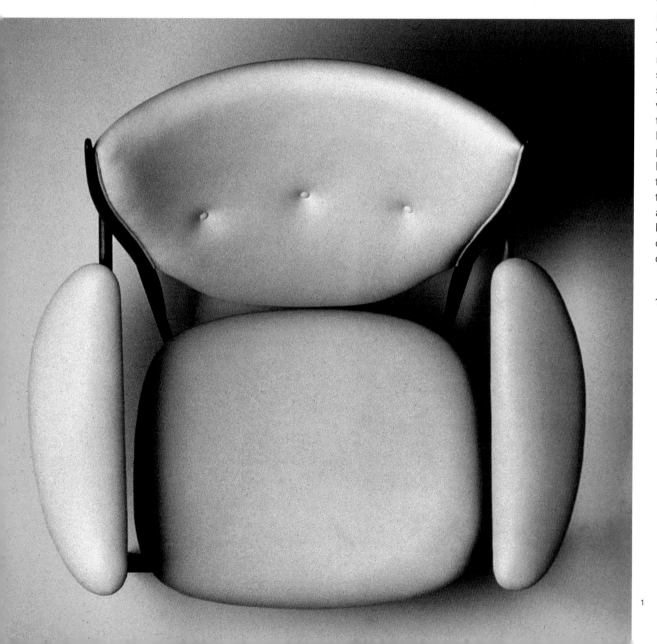

1

175

Yusaku **Kamekura** 1915–97 **Japan**

The triumphant progress of good graphics. In Japan, products judged to be particularly beautiful and practical are allowed to display the *G*-sign, which stands for "The Good Design Selection System." This symbol of design excellence was designed by Yusaku Kamekura in the late 1950s. It was followed by further logos that have become internationally famous, such as that developed for the camera manufacturers Nikon. At the beginning of the 1960s Kamekura worked as a freelance designer for magazines including *Nippon* and *Creation*. He was also a co-founder of the Japan Design Center. However, Kamekura is best known for his posters, particularly those he created for the 1964 Tokyo Olympic Games and the 1972 Sapporo Winter Olympics. In the early 1980s he often chose the circle as the basic motif for his often starkly geometric, strongly typographical posters, but more recently he went back to the more traditional Japanese forms. Kamekura received many international prizes, and in 1994 a doctorate by the Warsaw Art Academy.

1 Poster for the nuclear industry, 1956   **2** Poster for the 1964 Olympic Games

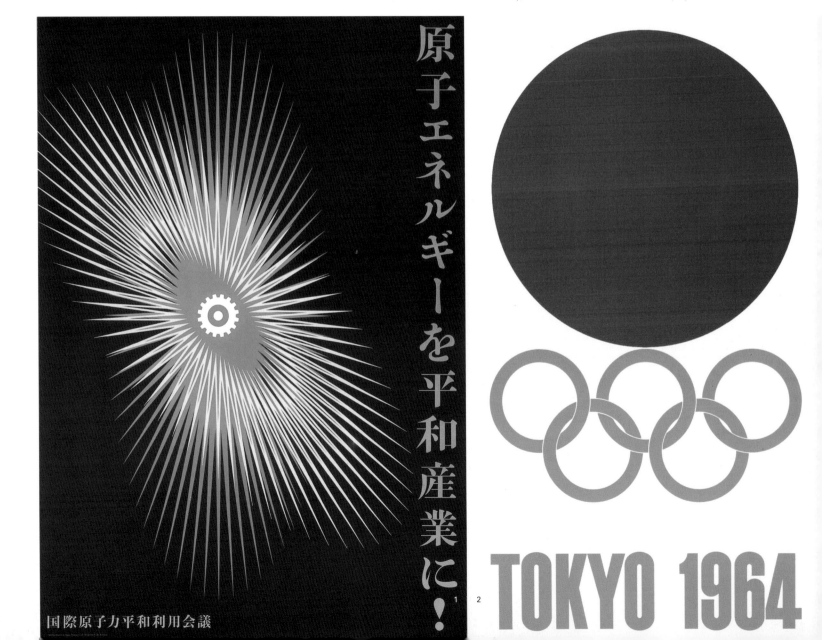

Mitsuo **Katsui** b. 1931 **Japan**

A new size chip. Mitsuo Katsui has been hailed as a pioneer not only in his own country but internationally since the beginning of the 1970s, when he took on the traditional Japanese world of graphic art with his computer-generated brightly luminescent posters. In 1971 he was awarded the prize of the Japanese Typographical Association. Few graphic designers have perceived and exploited the great potential of the computer as early and as convincingly as Mitsuo Katsui. His designs are characterized by combinations of geometric forms, manipulated typographical elements and color gradations. Because he rejects the complete digitalization of his designs and also uses analog manufacturing processes, his creations are less cold and superficial than other digitized products. When Katsui discovered the computer as a creative work tool, he had already been working as a graphic artist for some time, and ten years earlier he had already received an award for advertising posters (1958, for Ajinomoto). He was appointed art director of the 1970 Osaka Expo, a position which he held again at the Tsukuba in 1985.

1 Poster (for Issey Miyake), 1997 **2** Advertising poster for filmsetting, 1985

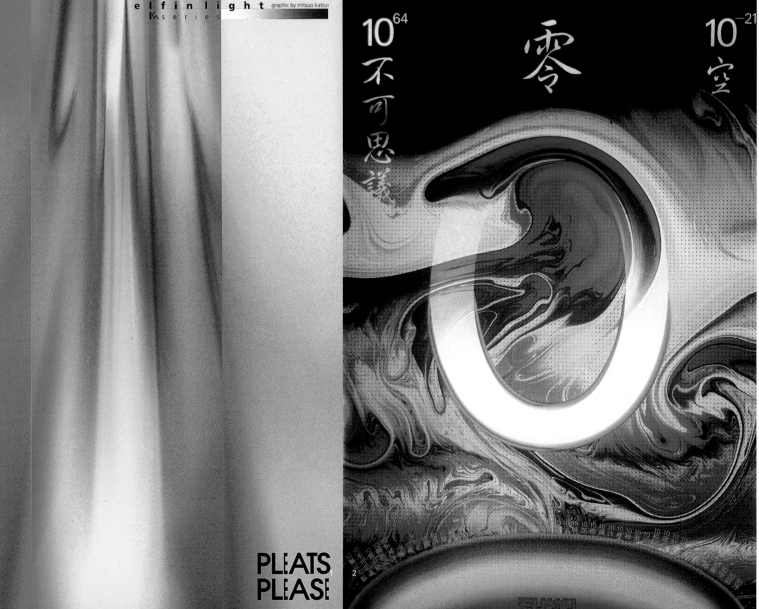

Edward McKnight
Kauffer

1890–1954 **USA and Great Britain**

Posters for the metropolis. The name of the American Edward McKnight Kauffer is inseparable from an institution that is anything but American: the London subway system, the Underground. In the years between the two world wars he designed about a hundred posters for the famous "tube"; they are masterpieces of the genre and are now among the most popular memorabilia of London, whether as posters or postcards. He was the son of a musician from Montana who studied art in Paris (and who went to London at the outbreak of World War I), and he made an enormous contribution to bringing modern graphic art to the people. At the height of his fame, the artist who loved cubism and surrealism worked for many companies including BP, Shell, P&O and the Great Western Railway. He was so much part of the British design scene that he was named Royal Designer for Industry by the Royal Society of Arts. In 1940, having returned to New York, Kauffer was unable to revive his great successes in spite of working for clients such as the Museum of Modern Art and PanAm.

Poster, c. 1945

1

Katsuo **Kawasaki**

b. 1949 **Japan**

Product personalities. Today Japanese kitchen knives are almost as famous in the Western world as Samurai swords. Katsuo Kawasaki has undoubtedly played a major part in this. Traditionally, kitchen knives in Japan have always had wooden handles. Kawasaki's *Artus* knives (1983, for Takefu), on the other hand, consist of a single, individually formed piece of steel. His scissors are even more radical (1985, also for Takefu), hardly resembling scissors any longer, but like the knives they are produced using traditional methods. Kawasaki worked for a few years for the electronics firm Toshiba before setting up his own studio, which has been involved in the design of a whole range of products. He has received many awards for his designs such as his *Clipe us* loudspeaker. Kawasaki is now handicapped as a result of an accident, and today he concentrates on developing products to help the handicapped lead a normal life. In 1989 he designed the *Carna* folding wheelchair made from titanium tubes that weighs little more than 44 pounds (20 kg).

1   *Artus* knives, 1983
2   *Cano* egg timer, 1993
3   *Carna* wheelchair, 1990

Isamu **Kenmochi** 1912–71 **Japan**

An artist of the modern age. In 1958, Isamu Kenmochi designed the prize-winning Japanese pavilion at the World Exhibition in Brussels. Then in 1964 the Museum of Modern Art bought the rattan armchair he had designed in the late 1950s for the bar of the New Japan Hotel in Tokyo (1958, for Yamakawa). This was a dream come true for Kenmochi, the pioneer of Japanese furniture and product design, since it demonstrated that Japanese contemporary design was being recognized abroad at last. Made, like all of Kenmochi's chairs and armchairs, from indigenous wood, the round armchair has a self-contained, timeless appearance. These classics are still produced today with a few modifications. Kenmochi started his career in the 1930s in the cabinetmaking department of the Industrial Arts Institute (IAI) and experimented with plywood used in aircraft construction. After the war, he went on a study tour of the United States where he was the first Japanese to take part in a design conference. Determined to develop a modern Japanese design culture, he adapted new production techniques and combined them with traditional Japanese craftsmanship.

2

1 *38* armchair, 1958
2 *Kashiwado* chair, 1961

1

Kenzo Takada b. 1939 Japan

Kimono and miniskirt. Kenzo Takada became instantly famous in 1970 at the age of 31, when he was the first Japanese to present his collections in Paris. He opened his boutique "Kenzo Jungle" in the Galerie Vivienne, and both press and public reacted with great enthusiasm to his daring creations, which were innovative combinations of designs, colors, fabrics and cuts. His designs appealed to the public particularly because of their original fusion of cultures. Kenzo combined Japanese restraint with the louder elements of Western pop culture to produce cheerful "creations for a more beautiful world." Although the young Japanese has become increasingly celebrated, moving more and more in the select circles of the "beautiful rich," he has never lost his feeling for the wider market. He sells the *haute couture* image at affordable prices, and he has been the initiator of several trends like the "schoolgirl look," the "farmers' look," and the "military look" that have found their way from the catwalk to the high street. Today Kenzo is one of those fashion designers who has acquired the status of international star, with his name on bags, jewelry, perfume, and even a special model of the Renault *Twingo*.

1/2 Autumn collection, 1999
3 Autumn collection, 1996

181

Poul **Kjaerholm**

1929–80 **Denmark**

Cool furniture. Many important architects in the 1960s chose to furnish the houses they designed with Poul Kjaerholm's furniture, the ultimate in uncompromising modern furniture design. His coolly sophisticated designs fascinated the public with their clear, flawless conception, and this is still the case today. Kjaerholm was a skilled cabinetmaker whose opinion of the expressive designs developed by Finn Juhl or Arne Jacobsen was that they were so much rubbish. He was guided by his "awareness of materials" and used wood, tubes and leather which he preferred to combine with steel and glass. He strove to achieve absolute structural openness—as in his *PK 61* sofa table—which he combined with 1920s Bauhaus traditions. Almost all of Kjaerholm's furniture could be mass-produced. His light, airy *PK 22* chair consists of only three easily assembled elements: the steel frame, the brackets and the cane wicker work. How far ahead of his time Poul Kjaerholm was is apparent in his bowl-shaped chair, *PK 0*, consisting of two plywood elements. In the 1950s it was still impossible to manufacture this design cost-effectively, but Kjaerholm was sure that it would be one day. He was right—in 1997 the chair was mass-produced by Fritz Hansen.

1

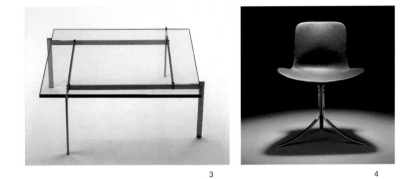

3

4

1 *PK 0* chair, 1956
2 *PK 24* chaise longue, 1965
3 *PK 61* table, 1955
4 *PK 22* chair, 1956

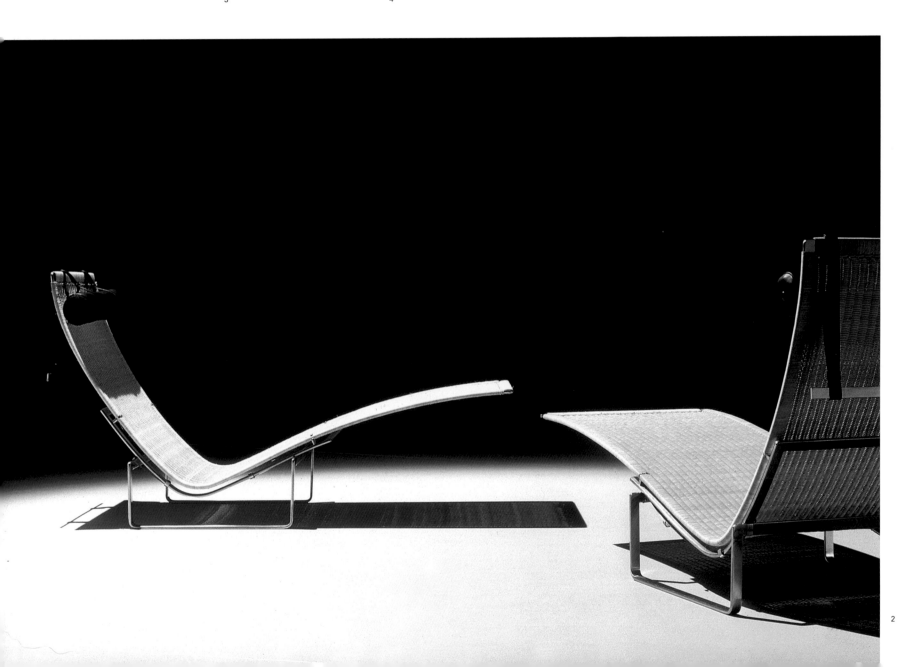

Calvin **Klein** b. 1942 **USA**

Sportswear Inc. Calvin Klein's aggressive advertising campaigns often cause a sensation, notably the provocative androgynous-erotic advertisements to launch his unisex underwear that appeared on billboards all over the world in the 1990s (the children's advertisement had to be withdrawn). Calvin Klein had no formal training and learned everything about the fashion world from scratch. He became famous in the 1970s for the soft lines of his sports clothes that were swiftly recognized as American classics. The "designer jeans" concept was a remarkable coup for Klein, although he actually prefers working with linen, silk and wool. Nonetheless, a growing number of customers are ready to pay more for the benefit of having the right logo displayed on the blue denim. His minimal style without decoration or superfluous detail perfectly reflects the spirit of the times.

1/2 Spring collection, 1999

2

1

Kaare **Klint** 1885–1954 **Denmark**

Conservative renewal. Even as a cabinetmaker's apprentice, Kaare Klint was studying the relative proportions of people and furniture, and collecting accurate data about the size and use of household equipment, thus becoming one of the pioneers of ergonomics. He aimed to develop the fundamental furniture designs that he believed were to be found in history, in eighteenth-century English furniture and also in African and Shaker furniture, which he saw as functional and timeless. In the mid-1920s the innovator and traditionalist founded a cabinetmaking school at the Copenhagen Academy of Arts, becoming master to whole generations of Danish furniture designers. A few of his own designs such as the *Safari* chair (1927) have perfectly survived the passing of time, thus confirming his theories. One of his later designs became a great commercial success: his pleated coated paper lampshades (1944, for Le Klint) have sold in millions.

1/2 Paper lights, c. 1945

3 Church chair, 1936

Florence **Knoll** b. 1917 **USA**

First lady of design. Florence Schust grew up among designers, particularly after being adopted by the family of her childhood friend Eero Saarinen. There were frequent trips to Finland, schooling in Europe, and architectural studies in London before she attended the Illinois Institute of Technology in Chicago where she was taught by Mies van der Rohe. She acquired her first work experience with Walter Gropius in Cambridge, Massachusetts, and Marcel Breuer in New York. She married the German industrialist Hans Knoll whose father had been one of the pioneers of modern furniture manufacturing. As a partner of Knoll Associates Inc., Knoll Textiles Inc. and Knoll International, she continued to run the business after her husband's death. The company still produces design classics by famous artists like Mies van der Rohe, Mart Stam, Marcel Breuer, Eero Saarinen and Harry Bertoia. Florence Knoll's own designs are reserved and cool, severe and angular, reflecting the objective perfectionism of the early 1960s. "I design the gap-fillers that no one else wants to do," she once said modestly about her own role in the company, although the office furniture designed by her and her interior design concepts have definitely set the standards for the company.

2482 table, 1961, and *Credenca* cupboard, 1963

Henning **Koppel** 1918–81 **Denmark**

Silverware as art. Originally a sculptor and glass artist, Henning Koppel transformed Danish silver design. He further developed what had already started with Johan Rohde, using clear, rounded lines reminiscent of Georg Jensen's collection. Without any special coating, his wine carafe (1948) revealed the magical shine of the silver. Koppel's asymmetric fish dish (1954) was a high point in the artist's career. It was admired around the world, a prototype of undecorated silver. Henning Koppel made use of the power of light to contribute to the shape of the object through its reflection. In his old age he became an innovator once more with his famous *321 A* wristwatch without hour markers (1977, for Georg Jensen).

2

3

1 Gravy boat, 1954
2 Silver jug, 1952
3 *321 A* wristwatch, 1977

1

Shiro **Kuramata**

1934–91 **Japan**

Surrealist domestic objects. Shiro Kuramata's furniture, made from industrial materials, is comprised of conceptional innovations that are also extremely poetic. His cupboards stand on tall, slender legs, while a chest of drawers dances the tango (1970, for Cappellini). The *How High the Moon* armchair is an unusual, light construction of great elegance, made from interwoven steel mesh (1986, for Vitra). Shiro Kuramata originally trained as an architect at the Technical High School in Tokyo before studying furniture design at the Kurasawa Design School. He started designing furniture in 1970, pieces whose bold shapes conflicted with traditional visual and seating customs. He was always happy to introduce new combinations of materials into his work—for instance, a glass table resting on spherical rubber legs. The seat and back of the *Miss Blanche* chair (1988, for Kuramata Design) are made of transparent acrylic in which paper roses have been cast. During the 1980s, he designed furniture for famous companies like Memphis, Cappellini, Vitra and XO. Last but not least, Kurumata was also responsible for the interior design of the Issey Mikaye boutiques in Tokyo, Paris and New York.

1

2

4

1 *Pyramide* chest of drawers, 1968
2 *Side 2* chest of drawers, 1970
3 *How High the Moon* armchair, 1986
4 *Sofa with 2 Arms*, 1982
5 *Solaris* table, 1977
6 *Koko* table, 1986

5

6

3

1

2

Masayuki **Kurokawa** b. 1937 **Japan**

The soul of materials. "When I design materials it is like creating life," says Masayuki Kurokawa, who likes to compare the creative process to a cat playing with a mouse. As a result his designs are often very playful. The *Cobra* table lamp (1973, for Yamagiwa) has a bendable stem made of ribbed rubber which makes it flexible and reminiscent of a snake. The architect and designer first became famous for his innovative use of materials, combined with a particular talent for giving even the most ordinary objects a decorative, striking character. Contrary to the traditional views according to which desk accessories, clocks and door handles should be made from metal or hard plastic, he developed the *Gnom* series (1973, for Fuso Gomu). Kurokawa became internationally famous with exhibitions in New York and San Francisco, and he was a member of the group of five designers (including Toshiyuki) that was awarded the much sought-after Mainichi prize for the exhibition "Hi-Pop-Design" in 1985.

Christian **Lacroix**

b. 1951 **France**

Baroque display of magnificence.
Christian Lacroix's career shows courage: at the very moment in the 1980s that haute couture was declared dead, he opened his own fashion house. He caused a stir in the fashion world with his very first collection. This had a French period look that took everyone by surprise, with models parading on the catwalk in crinolines and powdered Louis XIV wigs. Christian Lacroix's professional training perhaps explains the historical aspects of his fashion. He originally studied history of art in Montpellier before enrolling at the École du Louvre to study art restoration. Through his wife Françoise he met Karl Lagerfeld and Yves Saint Laurent's partner, Pierre Bergé, and he showed his designs to them. As a result of these contacts he went to work at Hermès in 1978 and then joined the Patou fashion house in 1981. There he developed his characteristic baroque style, ornamental, very feminine, that caused such a furor at his fashion shows.

Spring collection, 1999

Karl **Lagerfeld**

b. 1938 **Germany and France**

An emperor with a ponytail. The designer Karl Lagerfeld is always full of surprises, but he invariably follows the two important guidelines of luxury and exclusivity. Born the son of a Swedish banker in Hamburg, he moved to Paris at the age of fourteen where he attended a school for diplomats' children. Two years later he entered a fashion drawing in a competition and won a prize. The fast-speaking workaholic jack-of-all-trades was soon offered a job with Pierre Balmain, subsequently moving to Jean Patou where he produced two haute couture collections a year. Karl Lagerfeld set up as an independent fashion designer at the beginning of the 1960s. His amazing versatility and remarkable productivity is reflected in his ability to work for several fashion houses at the same time, such as Krizia, Chloé, Charles Jourdan and Fendi. Lagerfeld confirmed his reputation as one of the most important trendsetters in the fashion world when he was appointed chief designer of the House of Chanel, where he had been working since 1983. He has also launched perfume, watches, house furnishings and other fashion accessories under his own name. As if this was not enough, he has also made a name for himself as an artistic photographer. His ability to surprise is illustrated by his collaboration with the inexpensive mail-order firm Quelle. In explanation, Karl Lagerfeld says: "I believe in two kinds of snobbery: very expensive, and very good value."

Autumn collection, 1997

René **Lalique** 1860–1945 **France**

The beautiful sparkle. The perfume bottles which René Lalique designed at the turn of the century are today among the most sought-after collector's pieces of the Belle Époque. The goldsmith and jeweler was one of the most important representatives of Art Nouveau, but he also used classical and symbolist stylistic elements, frequently with exotic and erotic allusions. He became known to a wide public when his work was shown at the Paris Universal Exhibition in 1900. Lalique subsequently became one of the most successful producers of accessories and precious objects for the new, rich elite, and a symbol of France's love of luxury. In his designs, dragonflies, nymphs and peacocks came to life in enamel or semi-precious stones. Then Lalique specialized in glass, designing over a dozen scent bottles for Coty. Later he also worked for several other companies, creating scent bottles in fanciful shapes such as skyscrapers or acorns. Lalique also experimented with pressed glass for mass-produced objects. Today the House of Lalique is run by the founder's grandchildren.

1 *Serpent* vase, 1924

2 *Le jour et la nuit* table clock, 1926

3 Scent bottles, 1931

1

2

3

Jack Lenor **Larsen**

b. 1927 **USA**

The man with a mission. The man who revived American textile design founded Jack Lenor Larsen Incorporated in New York in the 1950s. This soon grew to be a multinational company producing a wide range of products, running from expensive fabrics to elegant tableware, all reflecting a particular stylish way of life. It was his admiration for designers such as William Morris, Tiffany and Fortuny, his great interest in ancient cultures, and his excellent knowledge of ancient weaving and dyeing techniques that led him to his first innovation: machine-produced fabrics that looked as if they were handwoven. Larsen's design studio was already producing printed velvet and stretch fabrics for upholstering furniture by the late 1950s. This manufacturer and prize-winning designer travels widely for inspiration, finding it in the Shibui screens in Japan, the soft pastel shades of early Chinese porcelain, the earthy nuances of his northwestern American homeland, and the brilliance of the South American sunlight.

Landis polychrome fabric, c. 1970

Ralph **Lauren**

b. 1939 **USA**

The American way of fashion. Ralph Lauren's career looks as if it was taken from a picture book of the American dream. In the late 1950s, Ralph Lipschitz, as he was then still called, worked as a glove salesman for a department store, and every evening he would study economics at night school. In the mid-1960s, he was working at Beau Brummel when he had his decisive idea, inventing the "Polo" brand name with its overwhelming associations of high quality. Within a year, this inspiration had led to the establishment of Lauren's first firm, Polo Fashion, making menswear. Women were catered for in 1971 and a year later he changed the brand name to "Ralph Lauren," launching a comprehensive women's collection characterized by cashmere, cotton and tweed. Ralph Lauren became known all over the world in 1974 as suit designer for the cult movie *The Great Gatsby*. At the end of the decade he launched the Prairie Look (1978), a range that was both lighter and more sophisticated, a prototype for "made in USA" casual fashion.

1 Autumn collection, 1995
2 Autumn collection, 1999
3 Chair, 1999

2

1

199

Le Corbusier

1887–1965 **Switzerland and France**

A pseudonym for modernism.
Charles-Édouard Jeanneret, known as
Le Corbusier, was one of the most
important architects of the twentieth
century. His projects were by no means
all unopposed; for instance, the *Plan
Voisin* (1925) called for the total
demolition and rebuilding of a part of
Paris, and it was never realized.
Nevertheless, the functional sobriety
propounded by Le Corbusier played a
major part in the shaping of modern
architecture and design. He developed
the concepts which enabled prefabricated houses to be built. For the rebel
Le Corbusier, the house was merely a
machine for living in, and its purpose
was to function as smoothly as
possible. In his *Pavillon de l'Esprit
Nouveau* shown at the Paris Art Deco
exhibition of 1925, bare walls and flexible furniture revealed Le Corbusier's
ideal representation of living in the
future. One of his best known furniture
designs is the *Chaise Longue à Réglage
Continu* (1927). Together with Charlotte
Perriand he developed the *LC* range in
the late 1920s, made from tubular steel
with leather upholstery (originally for
Thonet in France). His *Grand Confort*
chair (reproduced by Cassina, I Maestri
collection) is now one of the most
famous classic armchairs. The architect,
town planner, designer, sculptor and
writer subsequently developed a more
organic style, expressed in the chapel of
Ronchamp and *La Maison de l'Homme*
in Zurich.

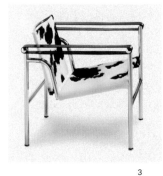

3

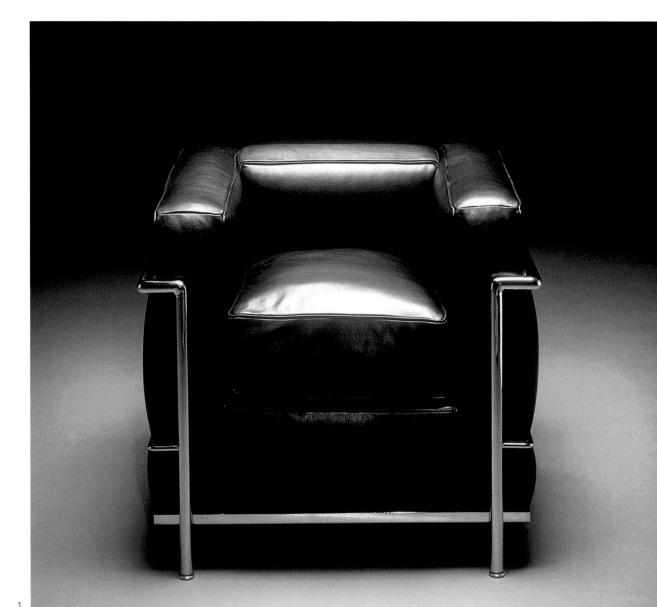

1

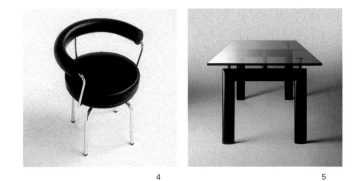

1 *LC3* armchair, 1928
2 *LC Casiers Standard* shelving unit, 1925
3 *LC1* armchair, 1928
4 *LCT* chair, 1928
5 *LC6* table, 1928

4

5

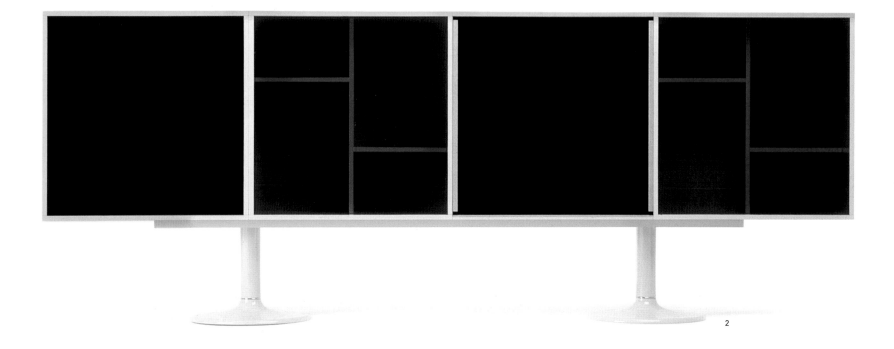

2

Alain **Le Quernec** b. 1944 **France**

Eyecatcher. Alain Le Quernec has developed into one of the most sought-after French graphic designers with his original illustrative style, ingenious collages and unusual typographic elements. He studied at the Lycée Claude Bernard in Paris at the beginning of the 1960s. In 1972 he won a scholarship to the Academy of Fine Arts in Warsaw where he was taught by Henryk Tomaszewski, who was to prove a great influence on Le Quernec's future style. Back in France, he designed very striking, half-dramatic, half-witty posters for social and cultural institutions in Brittany that attracted much attention. In the style of the modern Polish poster tradition, Alain Le Quernec's eye-catching work advertises museums, festivals and opera and theater performances. The celebrated designer and university lecturer is also well known for his logos.

1 Poster, 1991 **2** Poster, 1992

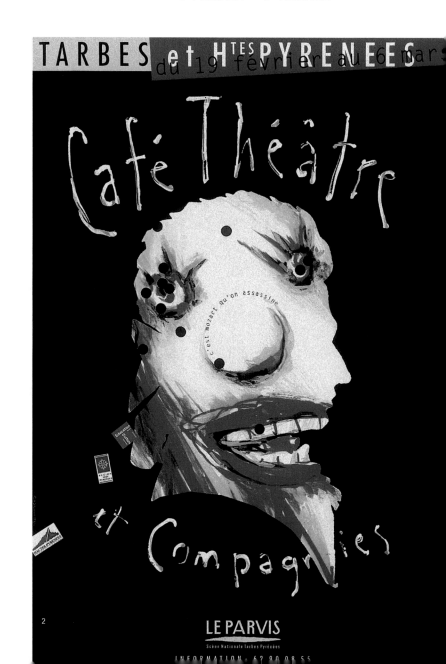

David Lewis b. 1939 Great Britain and Denmark

Equipment for the discerning. David Lewis is of one of those product designers who has changed people's everyday life and way of seeing while remaining unknown himself. Born in London, Lewis studied at the Central School and then in the early 1960s moved to Denmark. His breakthrough was the *Beolap 5000* (1965) for Bang & Olufsen, the first advanced audio system made by the high-end manufacturers, for whom it immediately became a great export success. Among the details invented by Lewis were the slide-rule controls copied by others so often and so badly. His next task was the design of B&O's televisions. With the revival of the company as a top-level manufacturer of sophisticated audio equipment, the Englishman's career received a new impetus; he set up his own studio in Copenhagen and is now responsible for the design of new systems, for example the large-scale *Beosystem AV 9000* (1993). Lewis's work has been recognized at home in Great Britain by the award of the title Royal Designer for Industry.

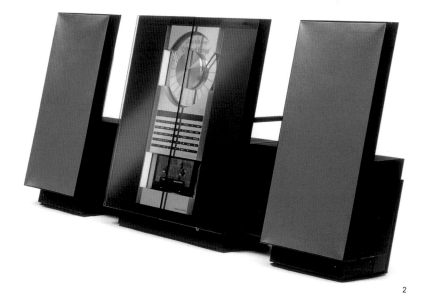

1   *Beovision MX 4000* television, 1994
2   *Beolit 2300* CD-player, 1995

1 *Brousse* chest of drawers, 1990
2 *Nagato* stool, 1986

Christian **Liaigre** b. 1943 **France**

Prophet of the new simplicity. Christian Liaigre is one of France's most successful interior designers. Preferring custom-made objects to mass-produced ones, he is famous for his Zen furniture which was inspired by Japanese art. Here the purist form of the object is underlined by the use of well-chosen, warm and natural materials such as wood, leather, linen, granite and raffia, and the range of colors is exclusively based on natural tones. The much admired pioneer of the new simplicity, Liaigre originally studied painting, but fear of "loneliness at the easel" drove him to interior design. He designed his first chair in the late 1970s and since then he has left his stamp all over the world, driven by a desire to discover new cultures and new impressions. He has designed furniture, hotels and apartments in places as far apart as London, Bora-Bora, Australia and France. Regardless of whether the project is public or private, Liaigre's creations are always fully rounded compositions: "Interior design is a complete work," he explains very much in the spirit of Aalto and Behrens. "That is why I also design all the fabrics, furniture, lamps and even the doorknobs."

Börge **Lindau**

b. 1932 **Sweden**

A surprise from the North. The *S 70* bar stool (1968, for Lammhults) which Börge Lindau designed with his permanent partner Bo Lindekrantz caused an uproar in his native land. The stackable bar stool with its cantilevered steel tubes 1¼ inches (32 mm) in diameter went against the traditional Scandinavian love of wood, but it became a classic far beyond Sweden's borders. After studying at the Gothenburg School of Arts and Crafts, Lindau and Lindekrantz set up their own studio in 1964 and within a decade they had become famous for their unusual furniture, all produced by Lammhults. Whether designing sofas, chairs or conference tables (including one that could be used both as a dining table and as a table-tennis table), Lindau and Lindekrantz rejected all existing rules with great brazenness. In the early 1980s they went their separate ways. Lindau set up his own furniture company, Bla-Station, in the south of Sweden, which is also involved in contract furniture for business, such as the new administrative headquarters of Absolut distillers. He also works for other companies such as the light manufacturers Zero.

1 *S 70-3* stool (with Bo Lindekrantz), 1968
2 *Hannah* chair, 1994

1

Ingeborg **Lundin**

b. 1921 **Sweden**

The beauty of rejection. As designer at Orrefors, Ingeborg Lundin influenced Swedish postwar glass design between the 1940s and the 1970s. Within the internationally extremely successful group of Swedish designers, she belonged to that generation who had to first prove themselves against the great names in the field, such as Edward Hald. Ingeborg Lundin designed both art objects and everyday items, and she made a name for herself by the simplicity of her products and the rejection of all the expensive techniques that had made Orrefors famous. Her best-known creation is the *Apple* vase (1955), a strikingly simple design that is almost a metaphor for clarity. Later she tried her hand at often bold experiments while using traditional methods, such as, for instance, the Graal technique that led to the creation of many beautiful objects.

1   *Mela* (Apple) vase, 1957
2   Vase, 1960

2

1

Claus Luthe b. 1932 Germany

From the bath to the wedge. Claus Luthe caused a great stir at the 1967 Frankfurt Motor Show with the NSU *Ro 80* that he had designed. This was the first sedan with a twin-disc rotary piston engine, and a total of 40,000 examples of this innovative car were produced. Its aesthetically pioneering exterior marked the start of a new era of car design. With its flat hood, rising waistline and short tail the *Ro 80* introduced a new design style: the wedge shape that remained current until well into the 1990s. As head of design development at BMW, Luthe continued to create variations on this theme throughout the 1980s and 1990s. Claus Luthe started his career in the mid-1950s at a German subsidiary of Fiat before moving to NSU, a manufacturer of small compact cars whose "bathtub shape" was striking and compact. Luthe had borrowed it from the Chevrolet *Corvair* and interpreted it once before in the NSU *Prinz 4* (1961). After NSU was taken over by VW (the company later merged with Audi), he worked for a time for Germany's largest car manufacturers, designing models such as the VW *K70* and Audi *50* (1974).

NSU Ro 80, 1967

Charles Rennie **Mackintosh** 1868–1928 **Great Britain**

The genius from Glasgow. Most Britons know two things about Glasgow: it is in Scotland and it is the birth place of Charles Rennie Mackintosh, the most important exponent of early British design. The artist created his own world of forms whose distinctive graphic rigidity set it apart from the predominant Art Nouveau style. The high-backed chair (1897) that he produced in several versions is among the most famous pieces, its unusual proportions never failing to catch the eye. His lamps and windows also reveal his very individual, unmistakable style, as do his illustrations which are characterized by abstraction, stylistic Celtic elements and sparse coloring. To him Glasgow owes its most famous building, the Glasgow School of Art (1897). Like many other Scots, after his apprenticeship (with the architect John Hutchinson) he turned his back on Scotland and looked to the Continent for cultural inspiration. Back in Scotland, he founded a group of four independent architects who published articles in influential magazines such as *The Studio* and *Dekorative Kunst* and began to spread his views of design throughout the world. Mackintosh-designed rooms are integrated works of art in which everything, down to the smallest detail, has been carefully designed. The recently renovated Hill House in Helensburgh, Miss Cranston's tea rooms, and his own house in Glasgow are but a few examples of his genius. In later years, clients seemed to desert this brilliant designer and Mackintosh moved to the south of France when he retired.

1

2

1 *Busnelli* chair, 1918
2 *322 D.S.1* table, 1918
3 *Ingram* chair, 1900
4 *Hill House* chair, 1902
5 White painted cupboard, 1901
6 *Berlino* table, 1905

_{Vico} Magistretti

b. 1920 **Italy**

The communicator. Vico Magistretti is one of the most outstanding Italian designers of the postwar years. After studying at the Milan Polytechnic he worked as architect in his father's company. His career as a designer started with the *Carimate* chair (1959) that he developed for Cesare Cassina, who soon mass-produced it. This chair with its woven rush seat clearly illustrates Magistretti's design philosophy; simplicity and an impression of spontaneity are the main characteristics of his designs. He is also very versatile: for instance, he has a passion for furniture that can be folded or taken apart (like the *Kenia* chair, 1995 or the *Ospite* chaise longue, 1997, both for Campeggi). He firmly believes that ideas arise from dialogue, so his design process has involved the executives in charge of design at the large companies for whom he works such as Artemide, De Padova, Fritz Hansen and Kartell. The results have been very successful: lights such as *Atollo* (1997, for O Luce) or *Eclisse* (1965, for Artemide), the *Maralunga* and *Veranda* sofas (1973 and 1983, both for Cassina) and the plastic chair *Selene* (1969, for Artemide) have all become classics.

1

1 *Atollo* desk light, 1977
2 *Selene* chair, 1969
3 *Golem* chair, 1970
4 *Eclisse* light, 1965

3

4

2

Erik **Magnussen** b. 1940 **Denmark**

A love of steel cylinders. Erik Magnussen was attracted to the arts from an early age and in the 1960s he produced freehand ceramic sculptures with considerable appeal. He had designed his first tableware in 1956 for the well-known china manufacturer Bing & Grondahl, and he was only twenty-five years old when he thoroughly modified the image of domestic tableware. The coffee pots, tea pots, jugs, dishes, and cups and saucers he designed were stackable and versatile. The range's name was provocatively functional, *Form 679*, after the production number. Technical sophistication continues to sum up his design philosophy today, and he often pushes these principles to the limit of design, as in his recent *Click* range of work tables (1994, for Fritz Hansen). These very light tables have tubular steel legs and can be clamped together. Tubular or cylindrical steel is the very symbol of modernism and Magnussen uses it in a wide variety of ways, for instance in his famous cylindrical vacuum flask (1975, for Stelton). He devised an ingenious T-shaped lid for this that opens and closes automatically when tipped. Since the 1960s he has created several variations on the theme of the steel chair, such as the small, minimalist chair (1989, for Paustian) consisting of a curved tube and a sheet of steel, only joined at one point.

2

1

4

5

3

6

221

John **Makepeace** b. 1939 **Great Britain**

Master of wood. The British craftsman John Makepeace saved the Arts and Crafts movement from oblivion, dragging it from the nineteenth century into the present, thereby ensuring the survival of the century-old tradition of high-quality designer cabinetmaking. He considered becoming a priest, but he chose the rival calling of cabinetmaking and has devoted his life to a particular mission: the greater appreciation of wood as a material. In a mere forty years, the name Makepeace has become synonymous with three achievements. He is a designer and maker of barely affordable, unique pieces of furniture, he is the most famous champion and teacher of the noble art of cabinetmaking, and he is a pioneer of ecological design and manufacturing. His own creations are modern antiques. The college he set up as a foundation in an Elizabethan manorhouse in Parnham in southwest England in 1977 is the only private training center in the world offering an integrated course in design, cabinetmaking and business management. In 1983 he founded Hooke Park College, where modern scientific research is carried out in the field of ecological building techniques and their practical application in housebuilding and furniture making. "To industry, wood is just a material," says Makepeace, "but to me, it is the most wonderful substance ever." John Makepeace has been uniquely successful in reviving wood as material and bringing about a renaissance in the world of cabinetmaking.

1   *Whale* table, 1992
2   *Sylvan* chairs, 1975
3   *Swaledale* throne, 1994

Robert **Mallet-Stevens** 1886–1945 **Belgium and France**

In favor of geometry. Robert Mallet-Stevens abhorred superfluous decoration. He preferred simple, geometric forms and rejected everything that was not absolutely necessary to the construction of his buildings and furniture. In doing so he broke with the typically French tradition of lavish interior decorating. He preferred using modern materials such as tubular steel, metal sheeting and concrete, but he softened the austerity of these materials by using bright colors, lacquer, leather and rare woods. Robert Mallet-Stevens studied at the École Spéciale d'Architecture in Paris in the early years of the twentieth century. He was strongly influenced by the Vienna architect Josef Hoffmann who built the Stoclet House in Brussels for one of Mallet-Stevens' uncles. Between the two World Wars he was in contact with Le Corbusier and other representatives of the international style. Besides designing showrooms for companies like Bally and Alfa Romeo, Robert Mallet-Stevens also worked on films by Marcel L'Herbier, he taught at his former art school, and he was the founder and the first director of the Union des Artistes Modernes. The complex white house that he built in 1927 in the rue Mallet-Stevens in Auteuil, Paris, is today one of his most admired creations.

2

1   Chair, 1930
2   Armchair, 1927

1

223

Peter **Maly** b. 1936 **Germany**

Praise for the status quo. Peter Maly believes that "rapid change is the death of any significant development." This explains the restrained style that is typical of his designs, with which he tries to avoid the effect of fast-moving changes. Trained as a cabinetmaker and interior architect, he worked in the 1960s for the magazine *Schöner Wohnen* ("Beautiful Lifestyle"), and set up his own design studio in the 1970s. Initially he was interested in the Danish school of furniture design, which reflected his philosophy of modern living. Later he discovered the Bauhaus, since when his designs have incorporated mathematical forms, as in the *Zyklus* armchair (1984, for Cor) and his rugs for JAB Anstoetz, whose motifs consist exclusively of circles and squares. But even when he is using geometric motifs, this perfectionist still considers the need for comfort and functionality, his initial sketches paying attention to spatial factors and surroundings—and the longevity of the piece. As Maly says, in an era of scarce resources it is important that furniture should be passed on to the next generation.

1   *Zyklus* armchair, 1984
2   *Cena* chair, 1996
3   *737* chair, 1994

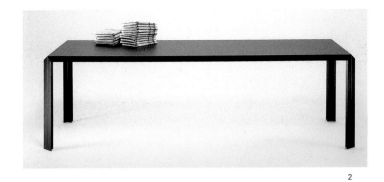

2

1   *Ad Iovis* light, 1998
2   *T* table, 1998

Angelo **Mangiarotti**

b. 1921 **Italy**

The material from which forms develop. Whether it be marble, wood, plastic or fiber glass, it is the material itself that interests Angelo Mangiarotti. The architect, furniture and product designer is always influenced by the various characteristics of the different materials when he designs a product or object. But when he is working on a new project he pays as much attention to the product's user-friendliness as to the possibilities of new technologies. After studying at the Milan Polytechnic he taught as a guest professor at the Institute of Design at the Illinois Institute of Technology in Chicago. Back in Milan, he founded his own studio and worked with Bruno Morassutti between 1955 and 1960. In 1956 he co-founded the Associazione di Disegno Industriale (ADI). He has also carried out important research on the processing of various materials. He has designed a large number of lights and pieces of furniture, famous for their simplicity, for renowned firms such as Artemide, Poltronova, Baleri and Skipper, but in spite of this the emphasis of his creative activity lies in architecture.

1

Enzo **Mari** b. 1932 **Italy**

The design-grouch. Opulence does not interest Enzo Mari. He has always preferred simple, timeless designs, whether designing vases, ashtrays or chairs. The querulous, leftist, rational theoretician and aesthete has written more on the subject of design than any other designer in the past, and by doing so he has made important contributions to debates both in Italy and internationally. Mari studied art and literature at the Brera Academy in Milan. He sees his work as a criticism of the consumer society, in particular the widespread wastage. Even though he himself has added to the glut of designer objects with his products, he responds to mainstream design with formal reduction. To a self-taught person affordability is as important an aspect as utility. That was certainly the case when Enzo Mari started designing for Danese as a twenty-four-year-old, and it is still true today for the man who is now chief designer of the Royal Prussian China manufacturers in Berlin, where he has been since 1993.

1

2

4

5

1 *Pago Pago* vase, 1969
2 *Timor* calendar, 1966
3 *Putrella* dish, 1958
4 *Tonietta* chair, 1985
5 *Ambo* table, 1987

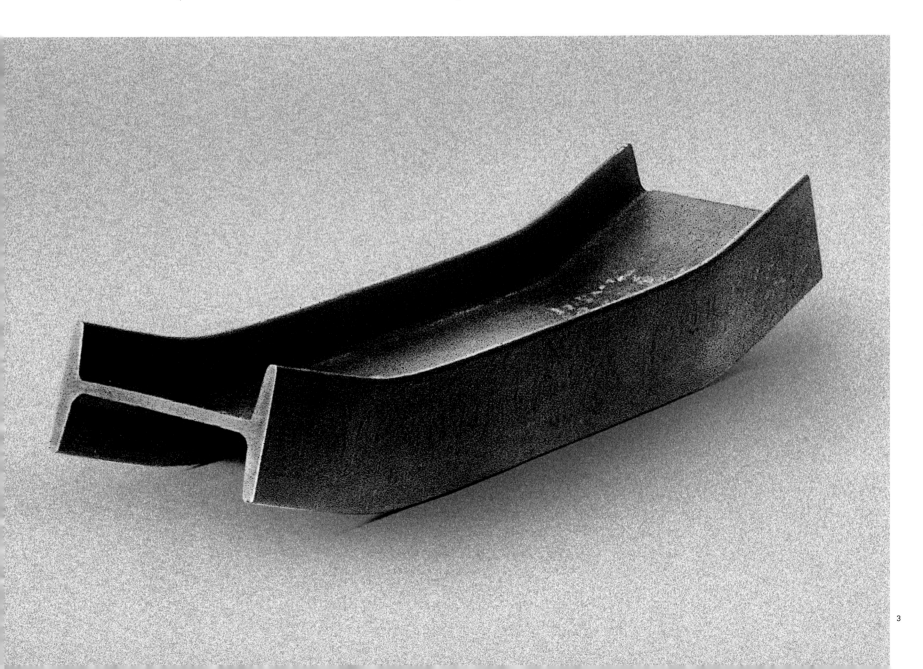

3

Maurice **Marinot** 1882–1960 **France**

The glass experimenter. Maurice Marinot set new French standards in glass design by developing innovative decoration techniques and manufacturing processes for the medium. For instance, it became possible to achieve new effects by special surface treatment. Marinot originally trained as a painter at the École des Beaux-Arts in Paris and was a member of the group of artists known as the Fauves. In 1911 he met Eugène and Gabriel Viard who owned a glass factory in Bar-sur-Seine, and through the two brothers he started working with glass. At first he made pieces with external enamel decoration. In 1913 he learned how to blow glass and from 1921 he started producing thick-walled objects with decorations such as rising bubbles inserted in their sides. Besides using processes like etching and oxidation, he also added strong, bright colors to achieve the effect he wanted. During the 1920s his glass objects became widely popular through many exhibitions, but they were already so expensive that only museums and the richest collectors could afford them. After World War II Maurice Marinot returned to painting.

Flacons, 1930

1 *Alessandra* armchair, 1995
2 *Hilton* serving trolley, 1981
3 *The 21 Hotel* armchair, 1997

2　　　　　　　　3

Javier **Mariscal**

b. 1950 **Spain**

Design in comics. Javier Mariscal is one of the best-known international designers and a leading light of the Spanish design scene. He has succeeded in establishing his own eccentric style in wide-ranging activities that include neo-baroque sculptures, ceramics related to Kandinsky, and kitsch objects like grinning cats. When still studying at the Elisava design school in Barcelona, he made a name for himself as a talented graphic artist for underground comics. Commissions for posters and printed textiles followed from this. But Mariscal also worked as an interior designer, a product designer and a furniture designer with the stylistic approach of the comic strip artist; a characteristic feature of his work is a preference for zigzag lines. Even the first piece of furniture he created, the *Duplex* bar stool he designed in 1980 for a bar in Valencia, looked like a three-dimensional translation of his cartoons with its drunk-making, asymmetrical legs. His *Hilton* serving trolley attracted international attention. It was a bold combination of metal and glass that he conceived with industrial designer Pepe Cortés for the 1981 Memphis exhibition. The *Arana* light, reminiscent of a spider, is another very beautiful example of the collaboration between Mariscal and Cortés.

1

Michael **Marriott** b. 1963 **Great Britain**

A use for everything. Michael Marriott has caused international amazement with his work using recycled materials. In the mid-1990s he baffled the design world with creations like the *Seven Series* shelves made from sardine tins, a clothes stand made from cooking spoons, and the roll container *Citrus Light*, with drawers made from old cardboard boxes. The ideas for recycling used objects arose from a combination of financial necessity and the materials available. Today Michael Marriott prefers using familiar objects rather than items salvaged from garbage: for instance, he uses baseball bats for the legs of the *Skittle* coffee table, and the frame of the *4 x 4* table (both for SCP) is screwed together with a coin instead of an Allen key. The recognition value plays a decisive part in Michael Marriott's designs. He has been fascinated by the Bauhaus since his school days. He took on a variety of jobs between studying at the London College of Furniture and later at the Royal College of Art. He worked in an antique shop, and for the light manufacturer Shiu-Kay Kan, he tried his hand at graphic design and exhibition design, and he was a foreman in a furniture factory. One impression remained with him, the wastage in industry. Michael Marriott responded by developing his Secondhand Design.

1   *Seven Series* storage unit, 1990
2   *Drop* vase, 1997

230

Bruno **Mathsson** 1907–88 Sweden

Eva's ergonomics. It was a chair whose concept departed from everything that had gone before. *Eva* (1934) had a frame of light, bent beech wood with broad webbing woven over it for the seat and back. But the most interesting features lay in the soft, flowing forms that gave it an unusual dynamic appearance, and in the completely new type of concept for a chair. The sitter feels almost pressed into this comfortable desk chair because the body's point of gravity is low. In later years Mathsson successfully developed variations on this principle, such as the elongated chaise longue *Pernilla* (1944). This member of an old dynasty of cabinetmakers developed his skills to those of a master craftsman, but he also developed pioneering ergonomics concerning seating based on anatomical studies. These innovative methods made him one of Sweden's most celebrated furniture makers. Mathsson always broke new ground in his work, as he did for instance with his *Superellipse* (1964), a sophisticated oval table whose outline was based on the calculations of inventor Piet Hein, or with his computer work stations of the 1980s. Even his sales approach was new for Europe, in that he sent his furniture directly to the customer by mail.

2

1 *Eva* chair, 1934
2 *Superellipse* table (with Piet Hein), 1964

1

Ingo **Maurer**

b. 1932 **Germany**

Sheer poetry of light. This master of the poetry of light could easily fill a whole catalogue with his range of designs. *Knitterling, Glatzkopf, Lampampe*—since the mid-1960s over 100 lamps and light systems have been created in the Munich studio of this gifted typographer, all as original and unmistakable as their names. At the start there was the *Bulb*, the giant bulb shape containing a lightbulb, an object that perfectly matched Eero Aarnio's pop furniture: eye-catchingly bold, yet playfully light. From that moment on light learned to fly. Ingo Maurer's often-imitated low-voltage halogen system *YaYaHo* was Germany's lighting design success of the 1980s. The buyer of the system is supplied with assembly instructions and becomes their own lighting director. The paper propellor *Willydilly* is simple, foolproof and good value for money, secured to the cable by the red plastic clothes peg provided with the package. The *Lucellino* winged bulbs are interactive and typically Maurer. They only begin to glow when the earth connection is made by touching them.

234   1

1 *Lucellino* light, 1992
2 *Zettel´z* light, 1997
3 *YaYaHo* lighting system, 1984
4 *Mozzkito* light (detail), 1995
5 *Los Minimalos* light, 1995

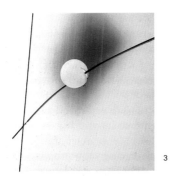

3

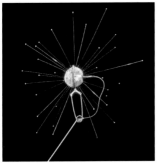

4

5

2

235

Warren **McArthur**

1885–1961 **USA**

A forgotten innovator. Warren McArthur was not only a pioneer of tubular steel and tubular aluminium furniture; he was also one of the great precursors of system furniture and the rationalization of manufacturing processes. Born in Chicago, he grew up in a house designed by Frank Lloyd Wright, who was a friend of his father. After completing his studies, he settled in Phoenix, Arizona. The various projects he became involved in reflected his passion for every kind of technical progress. He was the first car dealer in Arizona, he founded the first radio station in the state, and he developed the *Wonderbus*, a forerunner of the mobile home. After the sensation caused by the furniture he designed for the Arizona Biltmore Hotel, he set up his own furniture company in Los Angeles in 1930. This was the beginning of McArthur's great period of success. In the years that followed, his furniture would be found everywhere: in restaurants, dining cars and airplanes, in offices and hotel lobbies, and also in elegant, private living rooms.

1 *Two-tier* table, c. 1940
2 *Ambassador* armchair, 1932
3 Occasional table, 1934

2

3

1

Alexander McQueen b. 1969 Great Britain

Most non-belonging. In his *Highland Rape* collection (1995), Alexander McQueen had women wearing antlers, wrapped in PVC, and snapped at by bloody hunting dogs. This avant-garde fashion designer began working at the age of sixteen for a tailor in Savile Row, the home of London's finest bespoke tailors. After a flying visit to the Milan fashion designers, he enrolled himself at the St. Martin's School of Art. His first collection in 1993 immediately established him as the new *enfant terrible* of the international fashion scene. His harsh, intentionally obscene style, with shirts and trousers slashed to make overt reference to the erogenous zones, caused a shock that no one would have believed possible after the extremes of Jean-Paul Gaultier and Vivienne Westwood. His most successful innovation was his *Bumsters*, pantaloon-like trousers without a belt, hanging from the hips. In spite of the shocking nature of his creations, which is their most evident feature, it should not be overlooked that Alexander McQueen is one of the most imaginative and technically expert fashion designers. In 1996, when he was just twenty-seven years old, the rebel became chief designer of the House of Givenchy in Paris.

Autumn collection, 1999

239

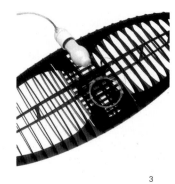

3

1

Alberto **Meda** b. 1945 **Italy**

Research into new forms and materials. Alberto Meda loves the isolation of his Milan studio where he has worked alone since 1979. There he experiments with different materials, their processing and their application to new contexts. The end result tends to be extremely innovative such as the lightweight chair *Light light* (Alias), or the *Titania* and *Lola* lights (Luceplan) that he developed together with Paolo Rizzatto. He was product development manager at Kartell in the 1970s and there he soon discovered his talents as a designer. The knowledge he acquired in his daily dealings with plastics and other materials covered areas as varied as car construction, furniture and lighting. Meda's high-tech products are often surprisingly poetic. For him technology is always only a means to an end, namely to speed up the well-trodden path of product development as much as possible.

4

5

6

1/3 *Titania* lights, 1989

2 *Longframe* chaise longue, 1994

4 *Light Light* chair, 1987

5 *OnOff* table lamp, 1988

6 *Meda* office chair, 1997

2

David **Mellor**

b. 1930 **Great Britain**

Better knives. Where would the British cutlery industry be without David Mellor? Probably still in the Victorian era with its love of decoration. It was by no means inevitable that Mellor would be the cutlery industry's savior, because at first the Sheffield-born silversmith seemed more likely to become a craftsman, producing unique pieces for the prosperous British dining rooms, or to have a career as a designer in the civil service. He carried out commissions for the railways, various government ministries, and the post office, for whom he designed new filing cabinets (in 1968). Fortunately for the modern dining table he kept up his interest in cutlery, a decision justified by his success. When the British government decided to introduce new cutlery in its canteens, they naturally approached David Mellor. The resulting range of cutlery was called *Thrift* (1965), a name that referred as much to the economical production costs of this stainless steel cutlery as to its simple form. So British civil servants came to experience the pleasure of eating with well-designed, mass-produced cutlery. Mellor has designed several other ranges of cutlery, among which *Pride* (1954), *Café* (1985) and *City* (1998) are the best known. These were sold in his own shops that he set up in the 1960s. Not content with just being a designer, in 1975 he started to manufacture his designs in his Sheffield workshop, and subsequently in a factory in nearby Hathersage.

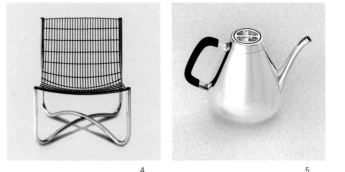

4   5

1

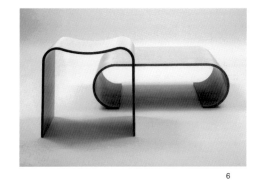

6

2

3

1   *City* cutlery, 1998
2   *Pride* cutlery, 1954
3   Children's cutlery, 1978
4   *Abacus 7000* chair, 1973
5   Teapot, 1963
6   *Canto* table and stool, 1997

Alessandro **Mendini** b. 1931 **Italy**

The gentle rebel. How much decoration can an object carry? In the case of Alessandro Mendini this question need not be asked. He has never been frightened of color and decoration—one need only look at the armchair *Poltrona di Proust* (1978, for Alchymia, reproduced in 1993 by Cappellini) or the *Cosmesis* and *Metroscape* watches (1990, both for Swatch), all of which could be interpreted as declarations of independence from the industrial constraints that surround us. Mendini studied architecture at the Milan Polytechnic until 1959 and then worked for ten years at Nizzoli Associati (1960–70). The 1970s heralded his radical awakening. He cofounded the Global Tools Design School (1973) and Alchymia (1976), and finally he was also one of the members of Memphis. At the same time he worked for a series of magazines such as *Casabella* (1970–76). He founded *Modo* and was its editor-in-chief between 1977 and 1979. Between 1979 and 1985 he was editor-in-chief of *Domus*. In 1988 he founded the magazine *Ollo*, a loose-leaf collection published together with Alchymia as a "medium without a message." Alessandro Mendini is not just a designer, theoretician and journalist; he also teaches at various colleges, and he is design consultant to Alberto Alessi, whose private house he designed. He has been increasingly involved in architecture since the early 1990s.

3

2

1

1 *Proust* armchair, 1978
2 *Kandissi* sofa, 1979
3 *Anna G.* corkscrew, 1994

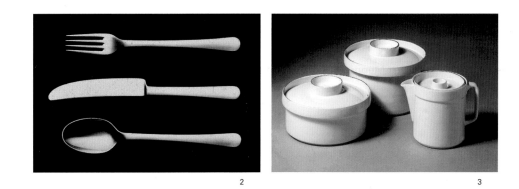

Grethe Meyer

b. 1918 **Denmark**

Ideals of a designer. Grethe Meyer's *Boligens Byggeskabe* storage units (1952, with Børge Mogensen) have become a Danish furniture icon for which design enthusiast pay enormous sums. But it would be unfair to reduce the merits and qualities of this architect, designer, ceramicist and product designer to this one classic piece. In the 1950s Grethe Meyer contributed to the *Bau-Buch*, a significant book on architecture and design in which she wrote the chapter on furniture and interior design. She also played an important role at the Royal Copenhagen porcelain company in the 1960s, developing a new, robust style and simple forms with echoes of the rural world. Many of her designs including the *Blakant* faïence tableware and the *Ozean* vase are still produced today, not least because they are still selling well. Over the years Grethe Meyer's work has always been distinguished by its combination of high quality and a desire to meet the needs of the consumer, guided in this by her own standards.

1 Clay bowls, 1967
2 *Copenhagen* cutlery, c. 1960
3 *Blåkant* crockery, 1965

1

2

Ludwig **Mies van der Rohe** 1886–1969 **Germany and USA**

A monument. Mies van der Rohe wrote that "Architecture is a language, and when you are very good you can be a poet." On these terms, there is no doubt that this architect and furniture designer wrote some beautiful verses in his career. His steel-framed buildings with large-scale glazing like the Seagram Building in New York (1958) and the Nationalgalerie in Berlin (1968) are landmarks of modern architecture. He approached furniture design with the same philosophy of "no trivial decoration." His most famous pieces include his tubular steel cantilever chairs *MR20* and *MR10* (1927, for the Weissenhof development in Stuttgart, produced today by Tecta), the famous *Barcelona* chair (1929, reedition by Knoll International), and the *Tugendhat* table of strip steel and glass. Mies van der Rohe learned the craft of masonry from his father at the Aachen Cathedral building school. He was a furniture designer and plasterer before moving to Berlin in 1905. There he worked first with Bruno Paul and later Peter Behrens, also meeting Walter Gropius and Le Corbusier. He began to design glass houses in the early 1920s. He became a lecturer at the Bauhaus, and he was its last director until 1933. In 1937 he emigrated to the United States where he was appointed head of the architecture department at the Illinois Institute of Technology. When he died he was the most sought-after international architect in the world.

1 *MR10* chair, 1927
2 *MR20* chair, 1927
3 *Barcelona* furniture, 1929
4 *Brno 255A* chair, 1930
5 *248L* chaise longue, 1929

Issey **Miyake** b. 1938 **Japan**

The limit of the wearable. More than any other fashion designer Issey Miyake has pushed the boundaries of fashion into the unknown. He has redefined the concept of clothes and discovered new, unexpected connections between garment and body, experimenting with new materials like rattan, bamboo, iron, synthetics and paper. Miyake moved from graphic art to fashion design, studied in Paris and worked in New York for a year. In the 1970s he designed clothes which gave the impression that they were made from a single piece of fabric. He occasionally worked with the graphic artist Tadanori Yakoo who designed the motifs on his silk garments. In the early 1980s he caused quite a stir with garments incorporating daring plastic cups, developed from original casts of the female body. Faithful to his philosophy that there are no boundaries in fashion design so long as one's imagination can run free, in 1982 he designed a cage-shaped, rattan breast harness, reminiscent of the Samurai armor of the Sengoku period. He is a creator of light-hearted fashion for a mobile society that combines functionality with simple design and innovative manufacturing processes, appropriate to the mood of the end of the century.

Spring collection, 1994

248

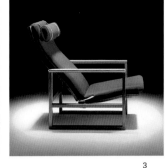

2   3

1 *Spanish Chair*, 1958
2 Armchair, 1964
3 *2254* armchair, 1969

Børge **Mogensen**

1914–72 **Denmark**

Furniture for everyone. No other pupil of Kaare Klint has followed the master's ideals as uncompromisingly or as independently as the versatile cabinet-maker Børge Mogensen. As head of the design development department of the Danish cooperative stores in the 1940s, the furniture that he designed had to be simpler and better. Since the 1940s his practical furniture, suitable for everyday use, has been found in large numbers in typical Danish houses. With his light beech wood chair and cupboards he created designs to counterbalance the then popular, much imitated mahogany, and he was responsible for many innovations such as interiors for children like *Peter's Room* (1940), and the legendary *Boligens Byggeskabe* system of storage unit whose versatility enabled it to be used in living rooms, bedrooms and dining rooms (1952, with Grethe Meyer). His sturdy furniture soon became fashionable among the wealthy, leading furniture makers to take note of him. When a small furniture manufacturer in Frederica wanted a new collection in the mid-1950s, he turned to Mogensen, whose designs for the company included the *Spanish Chair* (1958), a classic in wood and leather. Børge Mogensen remained faithful to natural materials because, according to the eco-pioneer, they are problem-free.

1

Bill **Moggeridge** b. 1943 **Great Britain**

Man and mouse. If there is one designer who has struck gold with a single product, it must be Bill Moggeridge, who designed the computer mouse. At least seven million examples of this indispensable object are sold each year. The graduate from the Central School of Art is an emigrant from England who moved in 1970 to Palo Alto, already the center of the computer and electronics industry. There he set up ID Two (a second leg of Studio Design Developments that he had started the previous year in London), with clients such as Conversion Technologies, Decision Data and Grid Systems. In 1981 he founded Ideo Product Developments with David Kelley and Mike Nuttall in San Francisco, and by the end of the 1980s this was one of the most successful design studios in the United States, winning award after award. As well as the daily clicking of the mouse, the consumer can benefit in everyday life from other creations by Ideo, such as the *Neat Squeeze* toothpaste tube they developed for Proctor and Gamble. Ideo's new development of Ford's audio system catapulted the market share of this product from 13% to 97% in six months, and is probably the best example of Bill Moggeridge's design concept. He combines British inventiveness with American business skills. In other words, an excellent design has to pay off.

1   Mouse, 1988
2   Radio (model), 1998
3   Electronic book, 1998

1 Book, 1925
2 Book jacket, 1930

László **Moholy-Nagy**

1895–1946 **Hungary, Germany and USA**

From artist to constructivist. Moholy-Nagy originally wanted to become a lawyer, but in the military hospital he discovered painting. After a short expressionist phase he concentrated on photographic experiments, strongly influenced by the Russian constructivists and Berlin Dadaists. When Walter Gropius saw his work in an exhibition he was so impressed that he brought the young Hungarian to the Bauhaus in Weimar. Here he was able to reveal the versatility of his talents; he was a successful photographer, he created scenery for ballet and theater, and he developed new typography for the Bauhaus books. As head of the metal workshop, he became the model and mentor for such great designers as Marianne Brandt and Wilhelm Wagenfeld. In 1923 he left the Bauhaus and went to Berlin where he worked as a commercial artist, attracting a lot of attention. László Moholy-Nagy's importance lay not only in his unusual creations but also in his scientific approach his work, such as the application of newly developed photographic techniques. Like so many other Bauhaus teachers Moholy-Nagy also fled from Nazi Germany, travelling first to Amsterdam and then to London. Here he produced advertisements for London Transport and designed shop window displays for the Simpson's department store. He subsequently left for the United States where he founded the New Bauhaus, which later developed into the Chicago Institute of Design. Here he was able to integrate his ideas on art and technology into an ambitious teaching program. His books *The New Vision* and *Vision and Motion* still play a useful part in the training of designers and artists.

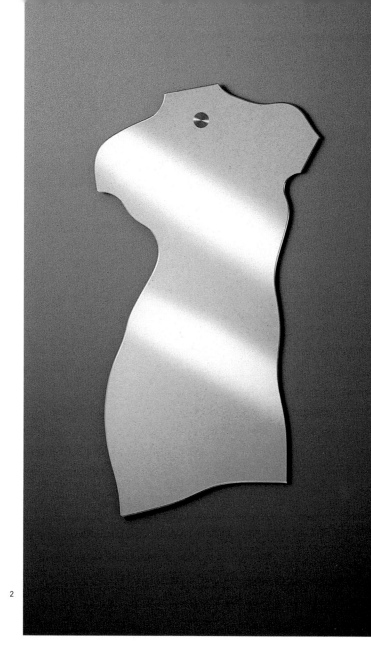

Carlo **Mollino** 1905–73 **Italy**

A lover of curves. Carlo Mollino was a man who could be called a universal genius. The architect not only carved hardwood into curves, thus playing an important part in the predominance of organic forms in furniture design of the 1950s; he also organized exhibitions, designed houses, and photographed works of art and events, as well as designing stage scenery, movie sets, ladies' fashion and shoes. In addition to this Mollino was also a gifted and successful sportsman, as horseman, skier, stunt pilot and racing driver on the international circuit. Relating to his sporting activities, he built the Ippica riding school in Turin in 1937 (demolished in 1960), in 1951 he published a book on skiing, and he also designed and built cars and airplanes. Described at the end of the 1940s as "Turin Baroque," his curvaceous furniture could be bizarrely representational, with forms often reflecting those of the female body.

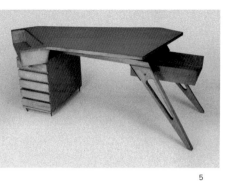

1 *Ardea* armchair, 1944

2 *Milo* mirror, 1937

3 *Arabesco* table, 1949

4 *Gilda* armchair, 1954

5 Writing desk, c. 1950

4

5

3

Claude **Montana**

b. 1949 **France**

A liking for zips. Zippers in places where they are definitely not needed and excessively broad shoulders are the trademarks of Claude Montana's creations and the unmistakable style which made him famous in the 1980s. He is also famous for his love of very soft leather. He combined this soft material with a new, angular, hard line that corresponded with women's new image and conception of themselves. Born in Paris, Montana first went to live in London where he started his career as a designer creating papier mâché jewelry (for Vogue). He launched his first collection when still in his twenties. Three years later he set up his own couture house in an old banana warehouse in Paris. He finds his inspiration in works by young sculptors and painters. Simplicity, clarity of line and the play of colors sum up Montana's approach to style. This trendsetter exclusively uses expensive, single-colored materials like cashmere, leather, wool and silk. Montana declares, "I am not interested in being good. What matters is to be the best."

1/2 Autumn collection, 1993
3/4 Spring collection, 1997

2

3

4

1

Hiroshi **Morishima**

b. 1944 **Japan**

Sheet by sheet. Hiroshi Morishima's cone-shaped vase, reminiscent of a lampshade, has a special charm, but its unique quality only becomes apparent when it is looked at more closely. In designing his delicate lamp in 1986, he used a sheet of handmade paper (*wagami*), made from three layers of mulberry tree bark. The air pockets formed between the layers during the manufacturing process produce an irregular grain on the surface of the shade, giving the light a warm tone and soft glow. After studying in Tokyo and Pasadena, Morishima worked in New York as a graphic artist. He then returned to Tokyo in 1973, working for the Nippon Design Center. Here he demonstrated a strong preference for paper as material, processing it in ways that created interesting structures, breaking up the light in a complex manner. He founded his Time-Space-Art studio in 1980, while continuing his fruitful collaboration with the paper manufacturers from northern Japan who are masters in the traditional craft of handmade paper.

Table lights, 1980

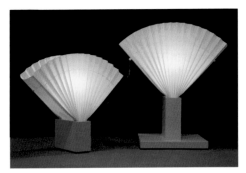

255

Bruno **Munari** 1907–98 **Italy**

The playful element. Bruno Munari was one of those fascinating men who cannot be categorized: fantasist, graphic artist, painter, musician, teacher, artist, and designer, he was well aware of his capabilities when he said, "Everyone knows another Munari." He started in the 1920s as a Futurist painter. His real passion (and this is not unfair to the multitalented artist who retained his childlike curiosity throughout his life) was the playful object, unpredictable and amazing. For adults he built mobiles that he called *Useless Machines* (1993), and he designed corresponding *Unreadable Books*. For children he developed educational or other toys, made from new materials like the monkey *Zizi* (1953, for Pigomma), made from a kind of expanded foam developed by Pirelli. Among his classics are the *Falkland* hanging lamps (1964) made from metal rings and jersey fabric, and the *Cubo* aluminum ashtray (1957, both for Danese). He always remained the magician who said of himself, "Give me four stones and a sheet of tissue paper and I shall create a wonderland."

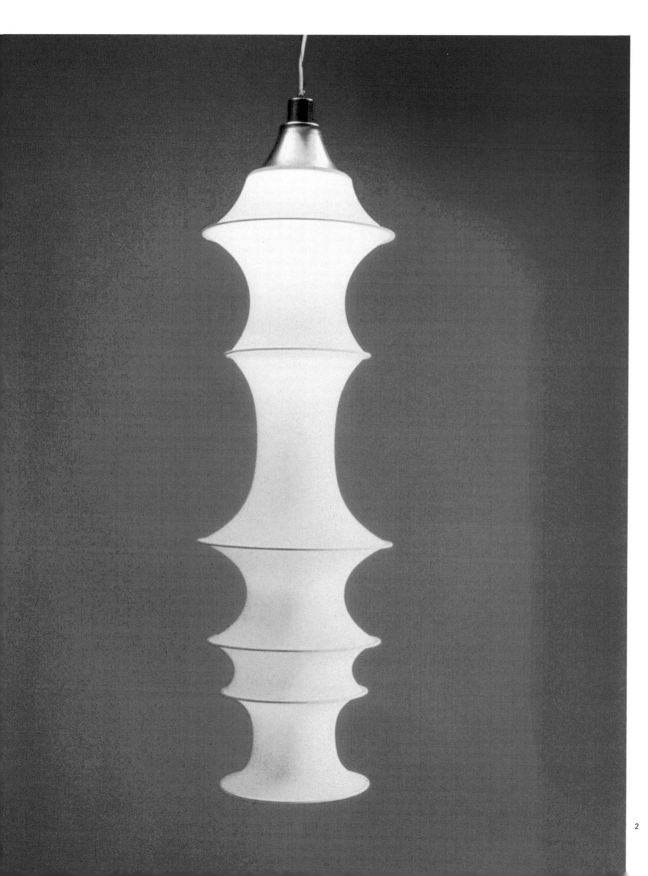

1 *TMT* ice bucket, 1954
2 *Falkland* light, 1964
3 *Cubo* ashtray, 1957
4 *Spiffero* screen, 1989

3

4

2

George **Nelson**

1907–86 **USA**

The intellectual prodigy. George Nelson began studying architecture at Yale University at the tender age of sixteen, after which he studied art. Shortly after completing his studies he was awarded the Architecture Prize of the City of Rome. He was a genius in every discipline, including design, and he would start every design project with the questions "Why?" and "Why not?" Ambitiously, he defined good design as "a manifestation of the ability of the human mind to go beyond its own boundaries," by discovering new ones. His *Storagewall* shelving units could also be used as a room divider, thus revolutionizing the concept of the office. This dramatic solution to a problem encouraged the furniture manufacturer Hermann Miller to persuade this brilliant designer to come and work for it, and there he led a formidable, unbeatable team including Charles Eames, Alexander Girard and Buckminster Fuller. With his multidisciplinary approach he developed his wall shelving unit to produce the very successful *Action Office* system, designed with Robert Probst, which was soon found in many offices in America. Among Nelson's countless design classics are the *Marshmallow* sofa, made from bar-stool seats (1956, for Miller), *Florence Ware* melamine tableware (for Prolon), and the *Editor 2* typewriter (1968, for Olivetti).

1

3

1 *Marshmallow* sofa, 1956
2 *Coconut* chair, 1955
3 *Sling* sofa, 1964
4 Chest of drawers, 1949
5 Table, 1954
6 Tables, 1954

2

4

5

6

Alexander **Neumeister** b. 1941 **Germany**

Design on wheels. "I strongly distrust the popular version of the general designer who today designs a vase and tomorrow an airplane," declares Alexander Neumeister, who is himself the opposite of a "general designer." A graduate of the Ulm Design School, he became famous as a specialist designer of vehicles running on rails. His most famous creations are the *Transrapid* magnetically supported train (1982) and the *Ice* high-speed train for German railways (1985) with its cool, smooth, rounded profile. Neumeister studied for a time in Tokyo and he sees himself as a team worker. In the mid-1970s he coordinated a working group "Design in Developing Countries," and he later set up a studio in Rio de Janeiro. Besides trains of all kinds he has designed appliances for data communication and medicine. His client list includes such well-known names as BMW, Bosch, Deutsche Telekom and Siemens.

JR-West 500 train, 1997

Mark **Newson** b. 1962 **Australia and Great Britain**

The jack-of-all-trades. Mark Newson currently shares his time between Milan, London, Los Angeles, Tokyo and La Chaux-de-Fonds. He has created designs for famous lighting and furniture manufacturers including Alessi, Cappellini and Flos Magis. For Moroso, for instance, he has designed a television-seating combination with chair and sofa made from steel and foam rubber. He has designed the interior of many offices and restaurants, such as the Pod Bar in Tokyo, the Crocodile Boutique in Hong Kong and the Coast restaurant in London. He was also responsible for designing the Belgian Walter van Bierendonck's chain store W&LT, and for the renovation of all the Apple businesses in the United States. Newson obtained his diploma in sculpture and jewelry design in Sydney in 1984 and he is widely regarded as among the most talented and succesful all-around designers. One of his most recent projects is a range of mechanical watches. To achieve this his Pod interior design studio merged with the Swiss manufacturer Ike to form the Ikepod brand. The aim is "to develop design consciousness in the fast-moving world of watches."

1 *Orgone* table, 1991
2 *Felt* chair, 1997
3 *Lookheed* chaise longue, 1986

Bruno **Ninaber van Eyben** b. 1950 **Netherlands**

Time for ideas. Dutch people handle Bruno Ninaber van Eyben's designs every day. As co-founder and co-director of the successful Dutch design bureau Ninaber/Peters/Krouwels, or NPK, he designed the Dutch coinage in 1982. With the introduction of the Euro, van Eyben's designs will again fill the purses of his country, because in 1998 he was commissioned to design the Dutch version of the Euro. After completing his studies in Maastricht, he set up his own studio in the early 1970s in order to escape the constraints of industry. During that period he also launched his own make of watch. Among his best-known designs is the *Pendant Watch* (1976), an aluminum watch with a rubber neckband whose black dial is interrupted only by a narrow white line running from 12 to 6 o'clock, and by two equally white hands. Between 1985 and 1997 van Eyben deviated from his course and developed designs and products for NPK to order. At the end of the 1990s he is working independently again and is once more involved in product design and graphic design.

2

1 Netherlands coinage, 1982
2 *Pendant Watch*, 1976

1

Marcello Nizzoli 1887–1969 Italy

The master of curved lines. Paolo Lomazzi of Studio DDL once described Marcello Nizzoli as "the first real Italian designer." Soft curved lines distinguish the machines whose functionality is in no way hindered by the beauty of their organic forms. Designs such as the *Lexikon 80* (1948), *Lettera 22* (1950) and *Studio 44* (1952) typewriters, the *Tectactrys* calculator (1956, all for Olivetti) and the *Mirella* sewing machine (1957, for Necchi) made their designer world famous and typified the lively Italian style of the 1950s. Nizzoli had studied architecture and art in Parma. Before contributing to the postwar boom of Italian design, he had worked as a commercial artist, for Olivetti and Campari among others, and as a painter. Between 1931 and 1936 he worked with the architects and designers Giuseppe Terragni and Edoardo Persico, and he too worked as an architect as well as a designer.

1 Poster, 1959
2 *Mirella* sewing machine, 1957
3 *Elettrosumma 14* adding machine, 1946

2

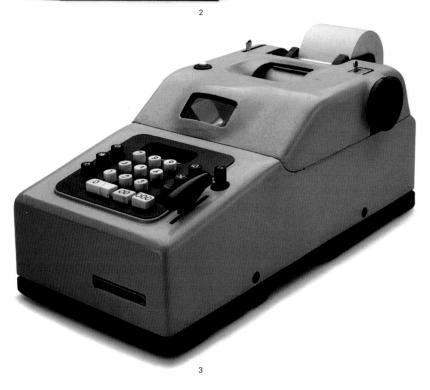

82 DIASPRON

olivetti

1

3

Isamu **Noguchi** 1904–88 **USA**

A much-copied designer. Isamu Noguchi was born in Los Angeles, the son of an American writer and a Japanese poet. He spent his childhood in Japan and his school years in America. After switching from medicine to sculpture and working for a while in France and Japan, he moved to New York in the early 1930s and worked there as an artist/designer. He created play areas and scenery for the dancer Martha Graham as well as some spectacular furniture and other products. Among his best-known creations are the *Nurse* Bakelite radio (1938). For Norman Miller he designed a genuinely sculptural glass dining table and the elegant coffee table (still available) whose glass top rests on a structure whose shape is reminiscent of a Japanese Kanji character (1947). For Knoll he designed the celebrated *Akari* range of lamps, constructed from paper and wire, which made him famous internationally. Noguchi has always been much copied, but his objection is less to the plagiarism of his work than to the that fact the quality of the objects is diminished in the process.

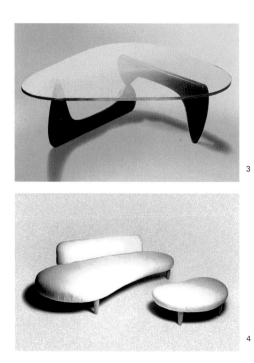

3

4

1

272

5

1 *Nurse* radio, 1938
2 *Akari XP1* table light, 1952
3 Table, 1950
4 *70* and *71* sofa, 1946
5 *Rocking stool*, 1954
6 Hanging light, c. 1950

2

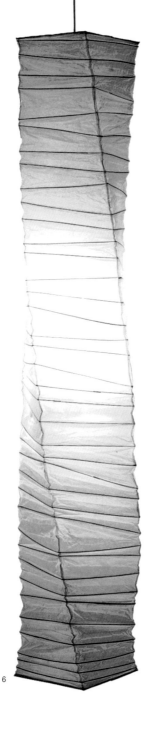

6

Jean Henri **Nouvel**

b. 1945 **France**

The styleless architect star. "I do not draw at all," says Jean Nouvel, the innovative architect who designed such famous and unusual buildings as the Institut du Monde Arabe (1987), the Fondation d'Art Contemporain (1991, both in Paris) and the Cultural and Congress Center on the shores of Lake Lucerne (1998, in Lucerne). While still studying at the École Nationale Supérieure des Beaux-Arts he worked part-time in Claude Parent's studio. In 1970 he set up his own first studio and in 1988 he merged with Emmanual Cattani. Nouvel's favorite materials are glass and concrete. His motto when designing buildings is: "I shall go not beyond the limits of imagination but beyond the limits of the possible." He does not have a particular style and none of his buildings is like another. However, all his buildings surprise the viewer with their unusual, sophisticated solutions and their ever-present functional elegance. This is also true of his furniture such as the *Élémentaire* armchair (1990, for Ligne Roset), or the *Milana* wickerwork armchair (1994, for Sawaya & Moroni).

1 *Elémentaire* armchair, 1990
2 *Milana-FTL* chair, 1994
3 *Saint James* chair, 1991

2

3

1

Eliot **Noyes** 1910–77 **USA**

Identity proposals. The American architect and industrial designer Eliot Noyes is known as the man who designed the corporate image for IBM: not so much the graphics, which he entrusted to Paul Rand, but the definition of the complete image of the company from its architecture to its staff policy. Noyes had learned the importance of the holistic approach from Marcel Breuer, Walter Gropius, and Norman Bel Geddes, whose studio he ran after World War II. Eliot Noyes was the first director for industrial design at the Museum of Modern Art, and among many exhibitions he organized the legendary furniture show Organic Design. His involvement with IBM began while he was working with Norman Bel Geddes, and it continued after he set up his own studio where he created several products like the *A* and *B* typewriters and the IBM *Selectric* (1961), all of which set new standards for electric typewriters. Known in professional circles as "The industrial designer with the most remarkable knowledge," he expects all his clients to accept his philosophy in full, which is that the problem to be solved must be clearly defined, as well the solution. This applies even to big clients such as Xerox, or Mobil, for whom he designed the first generation of modular gas stations (1965) and launched a campaign against accidental road deaths.

1   IBM typewriter, c. 1975
2   IBM *Selectric* typewriter, 1961

Antti Nurmesniemi

b. 1927 **Finland**

The internationalist. Antti Nurmesniemi started small. His breakthrough as a product designer followed the design of a range of rather unassuming enamel jugs (1957), but they were soon found on nearly every Finnish coffee table. Meeting the requirements of utility, they were also very popular in the kitchen and today they are recognized as classics. The latest design by Finland's most prominent industrial designer is at the other extreme: he designed monumental high-voltage transmission towers for a power station, aesthetically ambitious "landscape towers" of pylon construction. Nurmesniemi belongs to the emerging generation of the 1950s and 1960s who had left the war behind and were interested in creating a modern Finland, inspired by the international rationalism that was already emerging in the cheerful sauna of the Palace Hotel in Helsinki, an early project by Nurmesniemi for which he designed the functional *Horseshoe* stool (1951). He remained faithful to his philosophy of clear lines, whether in the *Triennale 001* desk chair (1960), the development of the Helsinki railway system (1968), or in the *Antti* ultra-flat table telephone (1984 for Fujitsu) that was far ahead of its time and—unusually in the field of product design—seems hardly to have aged at all.

1

2

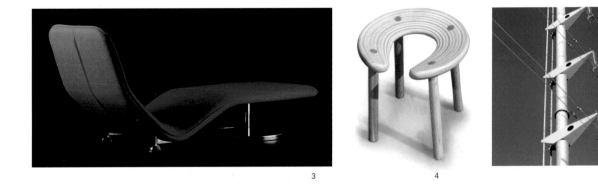

3   4   5

Vuokko **Nurmesniemi** b. 1930 **Finland**

Pop model and protest fashion. She is considered by many to be the inventor of pop fashion, because in the early 1960s she was already incorporating current trends in modern art into her creations and turning fashion shows into "Happenings." In 1953 at the age of twenty-three Vuokko Eskolin (as she was then called before her marriage to the designer Antti Nurmesniemi) was put in charge of the collections produced by textile manufacturers Marimekko, and as such she was also the first Finnish female fashion designer. Her simply cut clothes made from cotton marked a complete break with traditional fashions in clothes and her bold but plain designs later came to typify the image of Finnish clothes fashion. For instance, the *Everyboy* striped shirt is still a best-seller today. In the protest atmosphere of the 1960s when pop music was still considered subversive and young people were for the time developing a lifestyle of their own, the simple unisex clothing from Finland was perfect. It became an unexpected export success, not least in the United States where the First Lady Jacqueline Kennedy swore by Marimekko. Later with her own, hardly less successful brand Vuokko, Nurmesniemi has continued to influence fashion with her innovative ideas.

1 *Perhonen* dress, 1975
2 *Hood* dress, 1966
3 *Puff* dress, 1985

1 *Celebration* shelving unit, 1989
2 *Full Moon* chair, 1989
3 *Child of the Wind* stool, 1984

3

Sinya **Okayama**

b. 1941 **Japan**

Codes and metaphors. The architect and product designer Sinya Okayama always gives his lamps and furniture evocative names. For instance, he called a shelving unit that looked like a snow-covered mountain ridge *Rooftop of the World*, while *Condor* is the name of a cupboard reminiscent of a bird in flight. His pioneering, postmodern designs force a dialog between the object and the consumer. His specialty is the use of forms and lines based on familiar symbols, which are immediately interpreted as graphic codes by the viewer. The *Kazenko* ("Child of the Wind") stool, designed in 1984, is part of a series of creations whose design is inspired by the Japanese Kanji characters. The soft rounded seat corresponds to the Japanese character for "wind." The masterpiece of the series is the *Kotobuki* shelving unit, which follows the same principle with a shape resembling the character for "fire." Okayama set up his own studio in Osaka in 1970 and since the 1980s he has been working for international companies like Memphis, XO, Vitra, Cappellini and Alessi. He is also known for his collaboration with the Italian architect Alessandro Mendini, which was carried out entirely by post.

1

2

Vaughan **Oliver** b. 1957 **Great Britain**

Pop plus culture equals cult. At the beginning of the 1980s when Punk was still making a noise and New Wave had just arrived, the graphic designer and typographer Vaughan Oliver was working for 4AD, an independent record label in London. In collaboration with 4AD's head Ivo Watts-Russell and the photographer Nigel Grierson, Vaughan Oliver produced some of the most innovative designs on the contemporary music scene. The team called itself 23 Envelope. Oliver frequently created his sophisticated, art-oriented designs by working with already existing, superimposed motifs, and the results appeared on the record sleeves of groups such as the Cocteau Twins, the Pixies and Lush. He subsequently worked as an independent graphic artist for record producers, and also for book publishers, theaters, museums, chain stores and television. His exhibition catalogue for Ron Arad and an image brochure for John Galliano brought him cult status and new customers.

1 *Pixies: Doolittle* album cover, 1989
2 *Lush* album cover, 1994
3 *Xymox* album cover, 1987

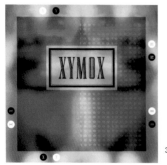

2

1

3

1 *Variable* chair, 1980
2 *Gravity* chair, 1985

2

Peter **Opsvik**

b. 1939 **Norway**

A social seat. At the beginning there was *Triptrapp* (1972), the famous, much-copied children's chair that marked the start of the collaboration between committed designer Peter Opsvik and furniture manufacturer Stokke. It was also the start of the amazing success story of the adjustable chair seat, an example of typically Scandinavian social design whose roots lay in the Balans Group of which Opsvik was a founding member. One has to learn to sit on an Opsvik chair as one has to learn to ride a bicycle. *Duo* (1984), 39 inches long by 48 inches high (1 m by 1.23 m), is the largest desk chair in the program. It clearly shows how such "sitting machines" are constructed. With its curved rockers, the chair reacts to tiny movements in the weight of the body, so that everyone can find their own point of balance, both in a forward working position or when sitting back to relax. The space between the seat and the chair back supports the sitter's back in its natural position. The headrest is compatible with using a mobile telephone. The plywood construction of the chair was influenced by Alvar Aalto's ideas, this material being stable yet light. *Flysit* (1990) is another Opsvik armchair whose legs are on coil springs so that the sitter can jump the chair from one position to another—a great help when a meeting becomes stuck. In case anyone does not know or has forgotten: chairs are also a means of communication.

1

Verner **Panton**

1926–98 **Denmark and Switzerland**

Visionary and never boring. Verner Panton was never interested in the quality label "Danish Design" that had made his designer colleagues famous throughout the world since the 1950s. He roamed through Europe in a VW *Microbus* before finally leaving his homeland for good. He was a rebel who could be described as the exponent of the cosmopolitan opposite of the native teak style. He became famous for his exuberant pop-baroque and his psychedelic creative happenings such the *Visiona Environments* (1968 and 1970) for which he fitted out the hull of a Rhine steamer with the synthetic materials of his client Bayer AG. His portfolio also includes the *Panton* chair (1967, for Herman Miller) that became a design icon of the 1960s, symbolizing a striking formal concept: the first one-piece plastic cantilever chair, a perfect design that exploited the qualities of the new material to the fullest. Verner Panton's motto was that "a failed experiment can be more important than a triviality." This jack-of-all-trades who developed a special seating system for his landscaped interiors was also a color theoretician and a skillful user of light in creating an atmosphere. His *Panthelle* mushroom lights (1970, for Louis Poulsen) are still produced today.

1

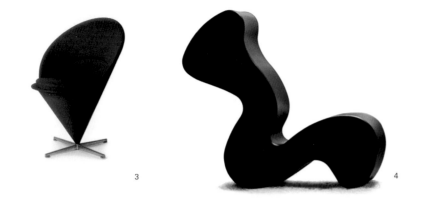

1 *Panton* chair, 1967
2 *Geometrie I* chair, 1961
3 *Cone* chair, 1958
4 *Lupoflex* chair, 1996
5 Seating, 1963
6 *Visiona 2* synthetic environment, 1970

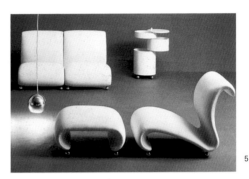

5

6

Charlotte **Perriand** b. 1903 **France**

The colleague of Le Corbusier. Charlotte Perriand was one of the pioneers of modernism and the most important French designer of her generation. In 1920 she was awarded a scholarship at the École de l'Union Centrale des Arts Décoratifs in Paris. The furniture she presented after her examination in 1925 led to her joining Le Corbusier's studio in 1927. For ten years she worked with him and Pierre Jeanneret, creating some of the most famous tubular steel furniture with the two cousins. Since the late 1970s, Cassina has gradually relaunched her famous *LC1* to *LC7* designs. As the only surviving member of the trio, Perriand is an invaluable adviser in this project. Her early tubular steel furniture elevated Perriand to the status of avant-garde designer. Her stays in Japan and Indochina in the early 1940s had a lasting influence on her, but at the moment little is known of her creations after 1950. The autobiography that the ninety-six-year-old is writing may perhaps shed some light on this. One of her recent projects is a Japanese teahouse in the south of France that she was commissioned to design in the mid-1990s by UNESCO.

LC4 reclining chair, 1928

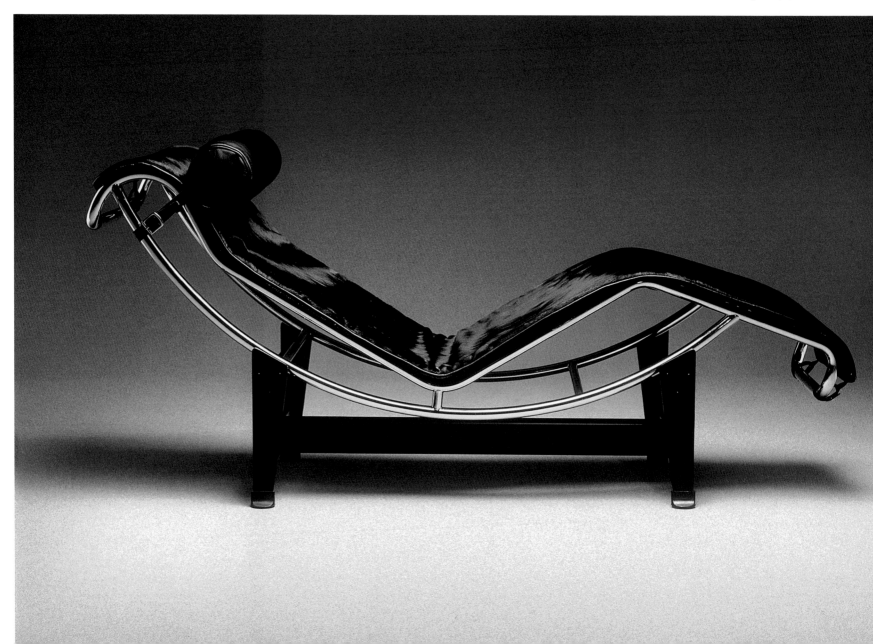

Gaetano **Pesce** b. 1939 **Italy**

In the face of good taste. Elegance and beautiful shapes are concepts that experiment-loving Gaetano Pesce most opposes. The artist, architect, designer and film maker became world-famous suddenly at the end of the 1960s with his *Up* range of armchairs. In 1969 he developed flexible fabric-covered seats made from polyurethane foam for C&B. The armchairs could be compressed to a tenth of their volume and stored in flat, airtight boxes. It was only when they were unpacked that these classics like *Up 5 Donna* assumed their real shape and size. In creating these Pesce was inspired by vacuum-packed coffee. The armchair of the *I Feltri* range (1987, for Cassina) is a cross between a felt cover and throne. After completing his studies in Venice, Gaetano Pesce was fortunate in finding a backer happy to take risks in the person of Cesare Cassina. This entrepreneur did not shrink from experimenting with new materials. Pesce as a result was able to develop his *Dalila* range of synthetic chairs, in which every piece is different from the other, the limited edition of the *Sansone* polyester-resin table (1980) and the *Sansonedue* sofa (1987, all for Cassina) made from metal lattice and epoxy resin.

2   3

1 *Up 5 Donna* armchair, 1969
2 *Dalila* armchair, 1980
3 *I Feltri* armchair, 1987

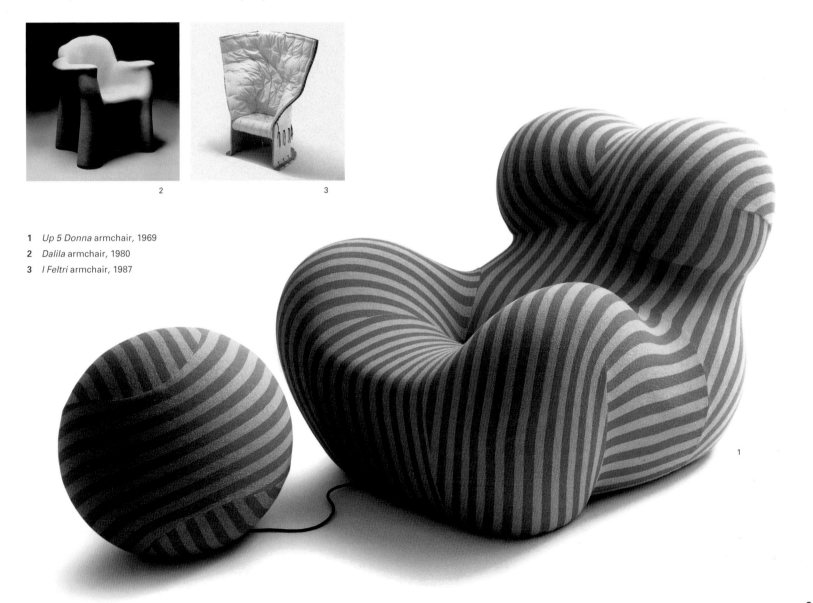

1

Roberto **Pezzetta**

b. 1946 **Italy**

Friendly house appliances.

Roberto Pezzetta reminds us that housework can be fun with his *Oz* refrigerator and *Zoe* washing machine (for Zanussi); both seem to have originated in another world, a fantasy world full of wonderful things. The round, slightly asymmetric lines, the friendly appearance and the pastel shades are reminiscent of the blissful 1950s with their optimism bordering on naiveté. "We want the rediscovered natural shapes of our products to be at the opposite pole to the high-tech kitchen environment, creating emotions and identifications," Zanussi's chief designer for household appliances has declared. This could be the first important change in the kitchen since America's product designers turned the sterile white refrigerator into an icon of the Western lifestyle. The Treviso-born artist who helped develop this new refrigerator originally worked as product designer for Zoppas, a well-known Italian household brand. After a brief stint designing sports articles for Nordica, manufacturers of wintersports equipment, Pezzetta returned to the world of "white goods," which certainly belie their name at Zanussi.

1   *Zoe* washing machine, 1992
2   *Oz* refrigerator, 1994

1

2

288

Christophe **Pillet**

b. 1959 **France**

Freedom and essence. Christophe Pillet is one of the most successful designers of the younger generation. He is a great traveler in the design field, commuting regularly between France, Italy and Japan. After studying at the École des Arts Décoratifs in Nice, he attended the Domus Academy in Milan. Immediately after completing his course he began working with one of the younger members of Memphis, Martine Bedin. Back in Paris, Pillet joined Philippe Starck's studio before setting up his own company in 1993. The great variety of clients of the "Designer of the Year 1994" include Artelano, Cappellini, Ceccotti, Écart International and XO, clearly reflecting the French designer's remarkable versatility. His furniture and Murano glass accessories are characterized by predominantly soft, flowing lines. Visually simple, Pillet's designs are reduced to the essential, with emphasis added by the use of color and contrasting surfaces, for instance by combining wood and fiberglass. The purist postmodernist Pillet is a great admirer of Andrea Branzi and he uses every kind of substance, from metal, wood, plastic and glass to other completely new types of material.

1   *Y´s* chair, 1995
2   *Sunset* chair, 1997
3   *Agatha Dreams* chaise longue, 1995

1

Warren **Platner**

b. 1919 **USA**

Elegance and steel wire. The architect Warren Platner studied in New York and then worked for the legendary designers Raymond Loewy and Eero Saarinen before leaving to concentrate on steel wire furniture in the 1950s. This only went into production after lengthy experiments (1966, for Knoll). The furniture consisted of hundreds of round steel wires, constructed in such a way that they produced a moiré effect. A single armchair had 1,400 welded joints. At the end of the 1960s Platner set up his own studio in North Haven, Connecticut, which concentrates mainly on interior architecture for large companies. His most spectacular project is probably the glamorous *Window to the World* restaurant in the World Trade Center in New York on which he worked with Milton Glaser.

1 Table, 1966
2 Tables and chairs, 1966

2

1

Paul **Poiret**

1879–1944 **France**

The liberator. Paul Poiret proved that it was possible for women to do without corsets, thereby propelling fashion to the twentieth century. The son of a Paris cloth merchant, Paul Poiret designed simple, loose flowing, Empire-style clothes in 1906 that freed women from the pinching constraints of several layers of female underwear. Poiret trained originally with an umbrella maker. He succeeded in selling some of his drawings and in 1899 he joined the fashion house of Doucer. He moved to Worth in 1901 and set up his own workshop two years later. He soon attracted attention with his exotic gowns with soft silhouettes, reminiscent of tunics or kimonos, made from unusual fabrics. The wearer's chest and waist were no longer constricted, and in this way Poiret completely changed the image of women, anticipating fashion by at least twenty years. Ironically in 1911 the liberator of the woman's body introduced a garment that to some extent restricted it again, the narrow, ankle-length "pencil-skirt." Paul Poiret was also known for his fabrics, furniture and hair creations, and he founded the École Martine, a girls' school teaching fabric and furniture design. Paul Poiret closed his workshop during World War I and when it reopened he was unable to repeat his previous success.

Dresses, c. 1900

Ferdinand A. **Porsche**

1875–1951 **Austria and Germany**

Sacred metal. The automobile engineer Ferdinand Porsche registered more than a thousand patents and he was involved in several areas of mechanical engineering, from the development of airplane engines and racing cars to the design of armored vehicles for the German army. The Bohemia-born designer was appointed chief designer at Daimler-Benz in Stuttgart in the 1920s, and in 1930 he set up his own studio. Here the legendary "Volkswagen" was designed, known in Germany as the "Kraft-durch-Freude-Wagen" ("strength-through-joy car"). As works manager of the Wolfsburg Works where the Volkswagen was made, Porsche was interned by the Allies. After his release, he and his son developed the first car to carry his name, the Porsche *356* (1950), a legendary sports car derived from the VW *Beetle*. The sports car tradition was continued by his son Ferdinand "Ferry" Porsche and grandson Ferdinand "Butzi" Porsche with the cult model *911* (1963) and other models. In the early 1970s grandson Butzi set up a successful studio for product design that he later moved to Zell am See.

1   Porsche *356A 1600S Speedster*, 1958
2   Porsche *356 Coupé*, 1950
3   VW *Käfer (Beetle)*, 1936

2

3

1

Carl **Pott** 1906–85 **Germany**

A man of principle. The Pott family cutlery company was founded in Solingen, the German Sheffield, at the turn of the century. When Hugo Pott Jr. came to run the company in the early 1930s, he developed a completely new design approach which clashed strongly with the current style and decor inspired by the past. Carl Pott became internationally famous with the first range of cutlery he designed, which was simply called *No. 2716*. It was of Spartan simplicity and ergonomically well thought out. Although the range was awarded a prize at the Paris exhibition in 1937, specialist dealers ignored Pott's creations for a long time. Nevertheless, true to his principles, Pott remained faithful to his philosophy, which was strongly influenced by the Deutsche Werkbund. His economic breakthrough came in the 1950s when he developed light, space-saving cutlery for Lufthansa. Carl Pott designed most of the company's products himself, often spending several years developing new knives, forks and spoons. He was awarded numerous international design prizes. His creations are considered the Mercedes-Benz of cutlery.

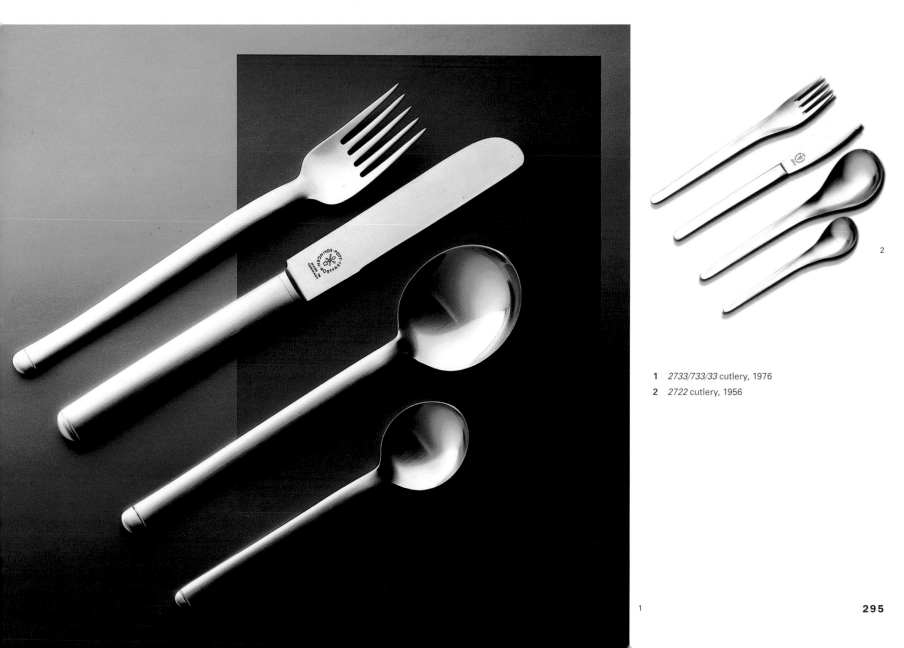

1   *2733/733/33* cutlery, 1976
2   *2722* cutlery, 1956

1

2

Jean **Prouvé** 1901–84 **France**

A fan of sheet metal. The innovative engineer, architect and builder Jean Prouvé came into contact with new artistic movements early on in life: with Émile Gallé, his father Victor founded the Nancy school that became a focal point of Art Nouveau. At the age of fifteen, Prouvé junior became an apprentice of the art metal worker Émile Robert, and three years later he continued his apprenticeship with Szabo in Paris. In 1923 he set up his own studio where he produced artistic doors, banisters and railings in the Art Nouveau and Art Deco styles. But he soon turned to industrial production and the virtues of economy of materials. At the end of the 1920s he discovered his favorite material: thin sheets of steel section. Using this newly discovered material he produced (sometimes in collaboration with Charlotte Perriand) chairs, school furniture, desks and beds, many of which are now being manufactured again by Tecta. His philosophy consisted of always using the newest materials and latest techniques, whether he was designing an armchair or a gas station. This attitude turned the art metal worker into a controversial progressive. Jean Prouvé was a co-founder of the Union des Artistes Modernes with Le Corbusier, and in 1971 he was chairman of the jury appointed to select the design for the Centre Georges Pompidou, which chose the spectacular proposal of Renzo Piano and Richard Rogers.

3

4

5

1 *Fauteuil Métallique* armchair, 1927
2 *Fauteuil de Grand* armchair, 1930
3 *Grande* table, 1950
4 *Standarde Démontable* chair, 1930
5 *Inclinable en Acier* chair, 1924

Andrée **Putman** b. 1925 **France**

Grande décoration. Andrée Putman, the *grande dame* of French design, only became a successful entrepreneur and interior designer after several career changes. She originally trained as a pianist at the conservatoire, and later worked as a journalist. She was attracted by anything that emanated intensity and creativity, and from 1960 she concentrated on industrial design. Her first projects were for the Prisunic chain store. She designed interiors for her friends as well as her own house before finally setting up her own company Écart International in 1978; this specialized in reproducing the work of famous designers of the 1920s and 1930s such as Eileen Gray, Pierre Chareau, Antonio Gaudi and René Herbst. Andrée Putman designed discotheques, hotels, museums and offices, as well as furniture, fabrics, china and glasses, including those for the supersonic aircraft Concorde. She also worked with the English director Peter Greenaway for whom she designed film sets. In designing interiors, perfection is Andrée Putman's motto, and in her opinion "the spaciousness of a room" is its most important quality. But the right combination of materials and surfaces is almost equally important in her designs, which artistically combine luxury and utility. Putman is fascinated by the contrast between hard and soft, using for example wood with glass, or mosaic with concrete.

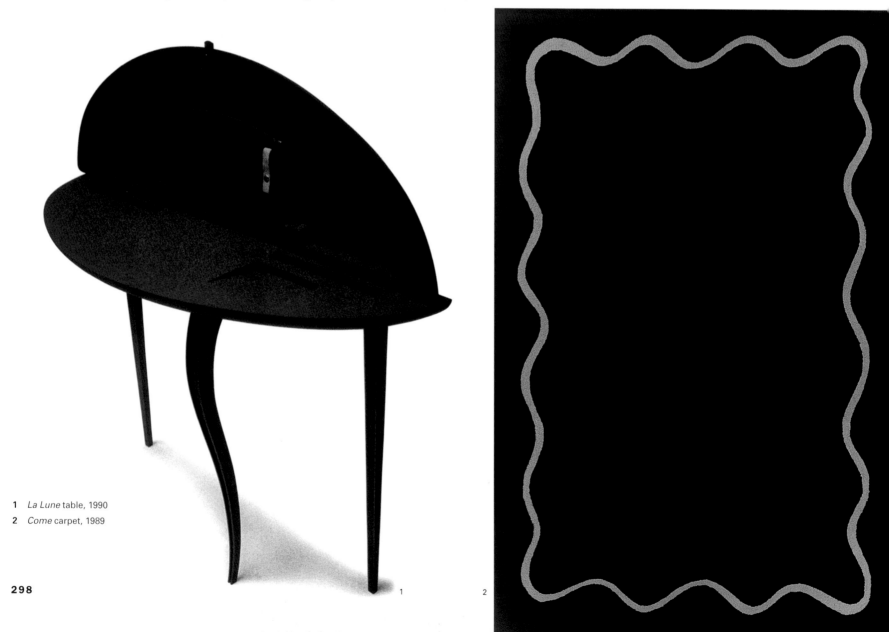

1 *La Lune* table, 1990
2 *Come* carpet, 1989

1

2

Mary **Quant**

b. 1934 **Great Britain**

Mini and more. There is no other field where trends change as fast as they do in fashion. There are far fewer classics in fashion than in the rest of the world of design. It is therefore all the more astonishing when a garment survives time and is even given its own individual name: the miniskirt and Mary Quant are synonymous. A similar phenomenon (though less extreme) had actually occurred in the 1920s, and the shortened garment becoming a symbol for several revolutions, not least the sexual one. The shortening was an act of liberation. Mary Quant turned every street into a fashion parade, introducing other innovations as well as the mini, such as colored tights and a clothes collection made of PVC. It is true that the former art teacher had the good fortune to be around at the right time, the swinging sixties, in the right place, London (which was fast becoming the pop capital of the world), and with the right customers in the form of a fiery mixture of decadent upper-class youngsters and the proletarian youth responsible for street style. Quant revealed an incredible flair for marketing in the growth of her operation. She started as a small boutique owner with a few garments that she made herself for chance customers in her tiny shop; she quickly became proprietor of her first brand Ginger Group (1963), receiving orders from American chain stores; and ultimately she was transformed into the owner of a multinational fashion empire. Whether the competition will admit it or not, there is only one company this century that has succeeded in creating an international brand from just a few inches of fabric.

Collection, 1967

Paco **Rabanne**

b.1934 **Spain and France**

An architect of clothing. Very much in
the footsteps of Dada, Paco Rabanne has
misappropriated plastic, metal chains,
fluorescent leather, ostrich feathers,
aluminum, laser discs, paper, plastic
bottles, and even door handles in the
creation of his radical fashion designs that
trample over every tradition. It was
inevitable that his mad creations should
have made him a famous name in the
world of fashion. He was born Francisco
Rabaneda y Cuervo in Spain, but the
troubles of the Spanish Civil War forced
his family to flee from the Basque region
and settle in France when he was five
years old. At the age of eighteen he went
to the École Nationale des Beaux-Arts
in Paris where he studied architecture.
To earn money to survive, Rabanne
produced fashion accessories, jewelry,
belts and buttons for well-known fashion
houses including Givenchy, Nina Ricci
and Balenciaga. In the mid-1960s he
launched his first collection *Twelve
Unwearable Clothes*. The title was only
partly true, since in spite of the fanciful
materials, the designs were
fundamentally simple.

1/2 Autumn collection, 1995

3 Detail of fabric, 1990

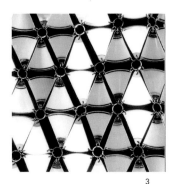

3

1

2

Ernest Race 1913–64 Great Britain

Forerunner of recycling. The architect Ernest Race is internationally recognized as among the most successful English postwar designers. He was one of the first to develop the use of alternative materials because of the shortage of materials caused by the war. The best-known product involving imaginative recycling is the *BA* chair (1945), made from remelted aircraft scrap. With the engineer Noel Jordan he set up Race Furniture Ltd, which used 850 tons of aluminum alloy scrap to produce 250,000 examples of this lightweight forerunner of the new-from-old philosophy. When this trailblazing chair was shown at the Britain Can Make It exhibition at the Victoria and Albert Museum in 1946, the public was fascinated. The great demand for this classic led to a resumption of production. Innovative design combined with an awareness of materials also characterize his other designs, such as the Race *Antelope* and *Springbok* chairs (1951). The filigree lightness and organic silhouette of the bent steel rod frame and the plywood seat reveal the influence of Marcel Breuer and Charles Eames. These chairs were designed for the Festival of Britain in 1951; they too became immediate classics and are still available commercially.

1 Folding chair, 1961
2 *Antelope* table and chair, 1951
3 *Antelope* bench, 1951

Ingegerd **Råman**

b. 1943 **Sweden**

A small distinction. In the 1980s when glass objects were becoming increasingly large, Ingegerd Råman made small ones. At the time, traditional glass shapes like simple schnapps glasses were fast disappearing. The *Bellman* range (1992, for Skruf) reversed this situation. Ingegerd Råman says that it would be "quite easy to make grotesque objects." Her simplicity is unusual among Scandinavia's many glass artists. The most striking feature of her work is the total rejection of the spectacular and the matter-of-factness with which she combines form, function, proportion and decoration into a convincing homogenous whole. Because her objects are so fundamental, she pays particular attention to perfect craftsmanship. Even the smallest imperfection would detract from a perfect overall impression. However, when everything is right, the clarity of the glass is emphasized by the unpretentious shape, bringing out the properties of the material, its lightness and its fragility to full advantage. While always carefully varying her designs, she creates families of objects with their own vases, bottles and carafes. Her objects are always refreshingly simple, and the details often quite surprising. For instance, the ball-shaped stopper of the *Oil Bottle* (1990) is flat in one place so that it does not roll off the table. "I cannot see a difference," it was recently said, "but I know there is a difference." That is indeed the most appropriate comment on her work.

1

1 *Mamsell* carafe, 1990
2 Brandy glass, 1997
3 *Samuraj* carafe, 1989
4 *Gras* vase, *1995*

3

4

2

303

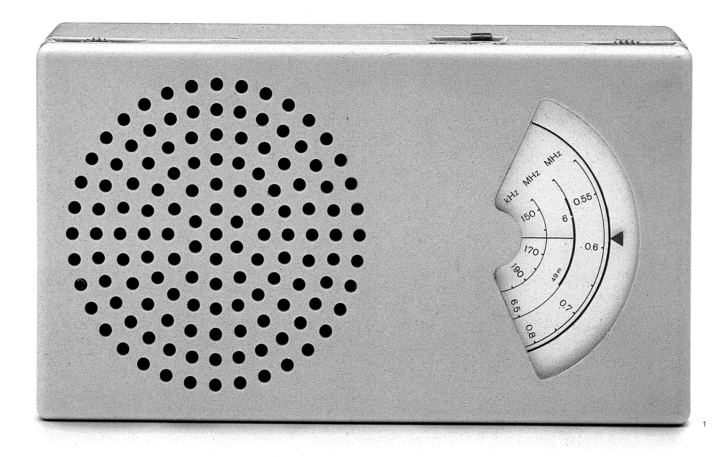

Dieter **Rams** b. 1932 **Germany**

Purely on principle. Dieter Rams wants to improve the world. When he designs a product he always tries to ensure that it fulfills its role better than its predecessors. He studied at the Arts and Crafts School in Wiesbaden, with a temporary interruption to study cabinetmaking, and in the late 1950s he worked in an architect's office. At the age of twenty-three he was appointed architect at Braun, the company that was to become almost synonymous with postwar German design. Its image has been shaped by Dieter Ram since 1960 when he became Braun's head of product development. He applied the ideas of the Bauhaus and the Ulm Design School to the development of functional products that shaped the face of whole groups of appliances through their pure, well-thought form. A classic example was the *Phonosuper SK4* combined radio/phonograph (1956 with Hans Gugelot). This came to be known as "Snow White's coffin" because of its innovative Plexiglas lid, and it heralded the end of the old-fashioned radio cabinet. Equally, the *Audio 1* radio receiver (1961) was an entirely new, fully transistorized appliance with audio quality that set the aesthetic and technical standards for the new era of stereo equipment. Other famous designs by Rams include the *KM2* mixer (1965) and the *ET44* pocket calculator (1977); both have become classics that are still copied over and over again.

1 Portable radio, 1959
2 *ET44* pocket calculator, 1977
3 Radio *RT20 Tischsuper*, 1961
4 Table lighter *TRG2*, 1968

Paul **Rand** 1914–96 **USA**

Mr IBM. Paul Rand influenced graphic art in America more than any other artist and he played an important role in establishing the discipline on a professional basis. His work as an illustrator, advertisement designer and image-maker is always fascinating with its subtle humor and the directness of its message. He had the amazing ability to reduce the most complex facts to their strongest common denominator. As art director of the magazines *Esquire* and *Apparel Arts*, as creator of the excellent cultural magazine *Direction*, and during his many years of collaboration with the Weintraub advertising agency, Rand was one of the first to practice the dynamic integration of text and images. He borrowed several elements from modern European art movements, such as the use of color, the technique of collage and visual contrasts. In his work for IBM Rand applied the newly designed logo to every aspect of the company, and his work there was very influential in the field of corporate identity. It became an example of the genre and led to commissions from major clients including Westinghouse, American Broadcasting, UPS and Revlon. Paul Rand disliked everything that was fashionable and superfluous, but most of all the creator of IBM's graphic identity deplored Computer-Aided Design.

3

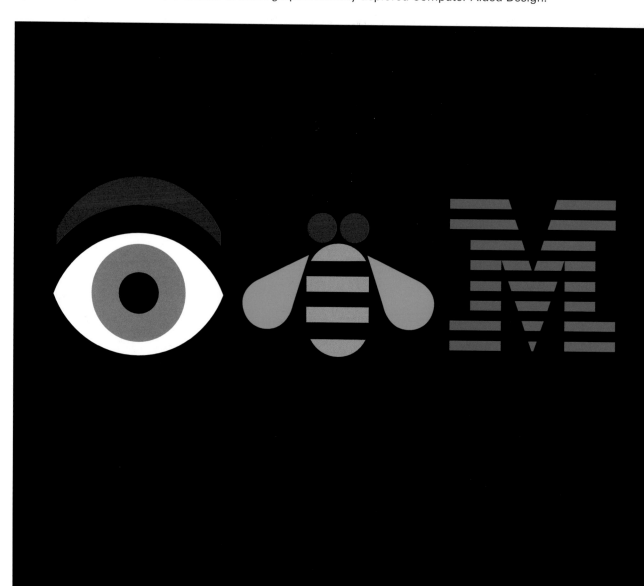

1

Page ⁴

5

2

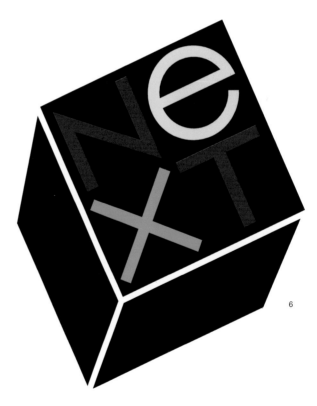

6

Paul **Renner** 1878–1956 **Germany**

Purified writings. Paul Renner never taught at the Bauhaus, but he absorbed the principles of the New Typography that had its origins there. The great achievement of this schoolteacher and typographical experimenter was the development of the clear, functional typeface *Futura* (1928). He derived this from a preliminary version that was more severe and geometrical, a reflection of the spirit of the time. *Futura* was quickly accepted as a classic typeface. From 1927 onwards, Renner worked for several modern book publishers, notably the Munich publishers Georg Müller. He was director of the College for German book printers, but after his dismissal from the teaching profession by the National Socialists in 1933, he became a painter and an author of books on typography and color theory.

ABC**DE**

functionalism

Futura typeface, 1928

Richard **Riemerschmid** 1868–1957 **Germany**

The birth of modern furniture. When at the turn of the century Richard Riemerschmid rejected ornament, his critics condemned him as "unnatural." He was a champion of "natural" furniture and always stressed his respect for the material in his designs. Riemerschmid's typical style of simple, clear construction with exposed joints was found both in his one-off pieces and later in his inexpensive, industrially produced furniture, which he called "machined furniture." After completing his studies at the Munich Academy of Art, Riemerschmid designed furniture, rugs and glasses that were strongly inspired by the Arts and Crafts Movement. He subsequently worked as an architect. He designed products for companies including the Meissen porcelain factory and the Deutsche Linoleum Werke (German Linoleum Factory). He went to work at the Dresdener Werkstätten in 1903 and there designed the garden city of Hellerau, one of his key works. In 1907 he founded the Werkbund, the association which was to change the relationship between art and industry forever. In 1900 Riemerschmid had fallen for the charm of the Jugendstil and designed the Munich theater, a masterpiece of the period, but he soon returned to a more sober, ascetic style.

1 Teaset, 1912
2 *Herrenzimmer* desk, 1905

2

1

311

Gerrit **Rietveld**

1888–1964 **Netherlands**

The early inventor of formal structure. Rietveld worked with his father as a carpenter from the age of eleven, and in between he worked for a jeweler. He founded his own furniture workshop in 1911. The great wish of this socially committed man—who during the World economic crisis designed the primitive *Recession* chair made from planks from packing cases—was above all to make reasonably priced furniture for all. His *Red-Blue* chair was created in the Utrechter Meubelmakerij (1918, re-produced by Cassina), the first constructivist, truly modern piece of furniture, which interestingly enough was originally unpainted. The later painted version reflected Rietveld's interest in Mondrian's paintings, which Rietveld knew well through his connection with the De Stijl movement. Mondrian's abstracts epitomized the artistic ideas of this progressive group of artists: the translation of reality into abstract lines and formal structure. Rietveld therefore added color in order to give his furniture and architecture a spatial structure, because only color defines the position of a line or surface in space. In the mid-1920s Rietveld was able to develop an architectural project for the first time, with the Rietveld-Schroeder House in Utrecht, in which he applied his spatial approach (a central element of his theories) to a building. Rietveld's most important pieces of furniture from this period are his *Stirrup* chairs (1927) and the *Zigzag* chair (1932). After World War II Rietveld concentrated mainly on architecture, building not only private houses but also public projects such as the Dutch pavilion at the Venice Biennale (1954) or the Rijksmuseum Vincent van Gogh in Amsterdam (1973).

3

4

1

1 *Zigzag* chair, 1932
2 *Red-Blue* chair, 1918
3 *Schroeder* table, 1923
4 *L40* ceiling light, 1920

2

Jens **Risom** b. 1916 **Denmark and USA**

Danish elements. When the Danish furniture designer Jens Risom arrived in the United States in 1939 after studying at the Arts and Crafts Academy in Copenhagen, the concept of "Scandinavian design" was still practically unknown there. He contributed substantially to changing this situation. A model house that he furnished in the Rockefeller Center in 1940 attracted much attention and commissions, including ones from Hans Knoll, another immigrant, who was busy building up his own design-orientated furniture business. Risom designed Knoll's first collection including a range of simple birchwood chairs (1941). The woven straps of the seat were ex-army stock. After the war, Risom set up his own company and was one of the first to manufacture unit furniture consisting of interchangeable standard components. This system of modular elements was then new in the United States, and it proved to be ideally suited to the new open plan office, making maximum use of the available surface area. After his company was taken over by Dictaphone in 1973, Risom set up the design consultancy studio Design Control.

1 Birchwood chair, 1941
2 Table, c. 1950

2

1

1 *Berenice* desk light, 1985
2 *Costanza* desk light, 1986
3 *Lola* standard light, 1989

Paolo **Rizzatto**

b. 1941 **Italy**

The creator of high-tech lamps. The lamps designed by Paolo Rizzatto—often in collaboration with Alberto Meda—for his own company Luceplan are among the most innovative designs in the field of light fittings; *Berenice*, *Titania* and *Costanza* have become classics. But being accepted by the market was not without problems; it took a good five years for consumers to accept the unusual forms and materials and for one of his Luceplan lights to become a best-seller. This did not worry the founder of the Milan-based company. "Like the planning of a building, the design of an object is above all a compositional achievement," says Paolo Rizzatto. "It is a question of placing the various parts in relation to each other and assembling them together." When the architect feels that the composition is right, then the product is put on the market, however ahead of its time it may be. But Rizzatto's high-tech projects are not limited to lighting or the lighting of large architectural projects. He also designs furniture for Alias, Cassina and Moltoni while still working as an architect.

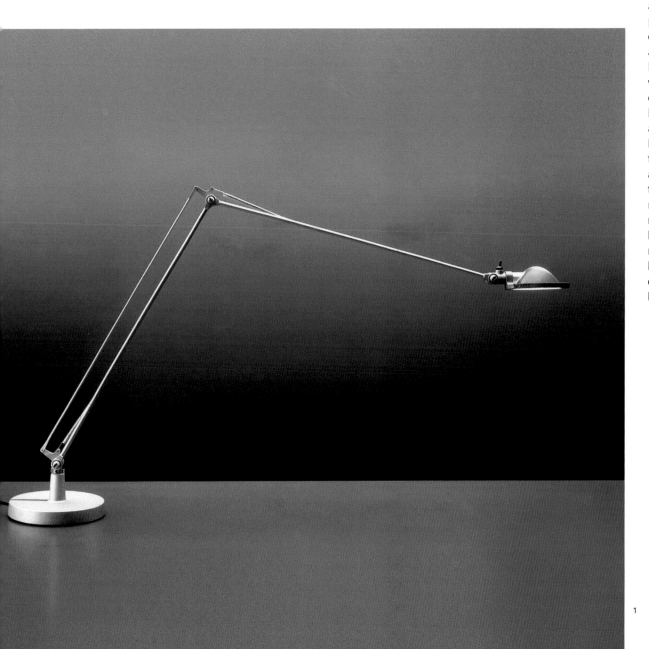

1

Alexander
Rodtschenko

1891–1956 **Russia**

Picturesque and proletarian. In 1914 Alexander Rodtschenko went to Moscow where he designed the Café Pittoresque in order to pay for the completion of his art studies. He later became one of the leading figures of Russian constructivism, the style of the Revolution. He was a lecturer at the *Proletkult* school, the commissar responsible for "industrial art" and in 1930 a professor at the *Wchutemas* workshops, the Russian equivalent of the Bauhaus. From the early 1920s he propagated effective visual communication to serve the Bolshevik cause. He developed his pioneering typography with its clear structure and geometric austerity with the object of encouraging the spread of political messages. Rodtschenko also made use of the new technique of photocollage. He worked on films and became art director of the avant-garde magazine *Lev*. Together with Wladimir Majakowski he produced advertisements (under the name of "Majakowski-Rodtschenko advertisement designers"), banners and kiosks for various Soviet companies and the prototype for a working-men's club. In the 1930s, he and his wife published the magazine *SSR na Stroike* (USSR in Construction), produced for readers in countries outside the USSR, with special issues such as "The Red Army" or "The March of Youth."

Movie poster, 1924

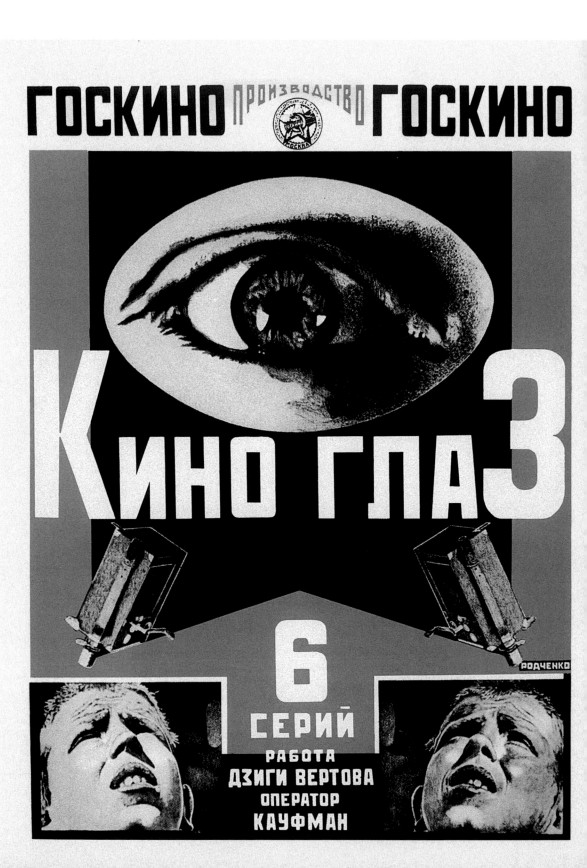

Johan **Rohde**

1856–1935 **Denmark**

A master of clear lines. Johan Rohde's
Coronation Pattern created in 1915
includes over 200 pieces and is still today
the largest-ever range of table silver.
Asked by Georg Jensen to join his
company, Rohde—who was originally a
doctor—became one of the most
influential designers there. Until 1935 he
was responsible for the main trend of the
company as well as the interior furnishing
of the Georg Jensen shops. As a master
of neoclassicism and opponent of
excessively radical modernism, Rohde
developed a style thast was almost free of
decoration. In doing so he became one of
the main representatives of that typically
Danish blend of functionality and
traditionalism, as Kaare Klint was in the
field of furniture design. Rohde's silver
jugs with ivory handles (1925) and his
Arcorn cutlery (1935) are classics of pure
form. Johan Rohde finished the surfaces
of his silverware with countless hammer
blows in order to create the sparkling
aura that has made the Georg Jensen
name famous throughout the world.

Jug, 1920

Aldo **Rossi** 1931–97 **Italy**

Large and small architecture. Aldo Rossi was one of the great architects of the twentieth century, a fact recognized by his being awarded the Pritzker Prize, the highest prize in architecture, for his monumental *Il Palazzo* (1989) hotel in Fukuoka, Japan. The Milan architect also made important theoretical contributions to architecture, particularly with his highly respected book *L'Architettura della Città* ("The Architecture of the City") that debated the role of postmodernist architecture. Rossi systematically reduced the basic forms he used. This is clearly seen in his architectural work such as the town hall square and commemorative fountain in Segrate, near Milan, where he arranged a concrete cube, cylinder and prism. He applied the same sculptural abstraction when designing industrial products. His coffee makers in particular are miniature works of architecture: the models *9094* (1986), *La Cupola* (1988) and *La Conica* (1994, all for Alessi) are like miniature soaring towers, consisting of basic geometric shapes: the cone, the sphere and the cylinder.

1 *Cartesio* storage unit, 1996

2 *La Cupola* coffee jug, 1988

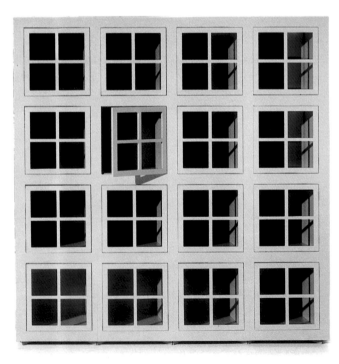

1

2

Jacques-Émile **Ruhlmann** 1879–1933 **France**

A luxury stylist. Only the most precious materials such as the darkest, most exotic woods were good enough for Jacques-Émile Ruhlmann's furniture, whose style was usually Empire, the most French of all styles. The creations of the much sought-after artist and interior architect remained the exclusive prerogative of a select circle of Ruhlmann admirers because of their extravagant luxury and lavishness. His elitist creed was "If only the very rich can afford to pay the price of such decoration, then they are also the only ones who can enjoy it." The son of a painter and decorator, he took over the family business of carpets, mirrors and other household accessories shortly after the turn of the century. In the 1920s he began to market furniture under his own name. The great breakthrough came in 1925 at the famous Art and Industry exhibition in Paris where Art Deco was hailed as the new style and Ruhlmann as the new Art Deco par excellence. However, this success did not last long: by the end of the 1920s Ruhlmann's style was already becoming simpler. He began to use new materials such as metal, glass and laminated wood in his designs. A year before his death Ruhlmann gave up his business. Taste and fashion had changed.

1 Vase, 1928   **2** Table, 1925

1

2

Gordon **Russell** 1892–1980 **Great Britain**

Linking tradition and industry. Gordon Russell's success was based on three fundamentals: solid craftsmanship, a skill he had acquired in his father's antique shop, a feeling for "good form" and his desire to make good design affordable. His aim was to combine the heritage of arts and crafts with the great opportunities offered by industry. In 1929 Gordon Russell Ltd launched Britain's first mass-produced dining-room furniture. In the same year he opened a shop in London whose managing partner was none other than the art historian Nikolaus Pevsner. In the 1930s Russell's company developed an increasingly modern style, stripped of all decoration, and it also manufactured radio sets and early television sets (1937), mostly designed by his brother R. D. Russell (1903–81). The shortage of materials caused by the war and the rising demand created by bomb damage forced the government to set up the Utility Scheme (1942) which included inexpensive, good-quality household furniture, an inititative with which Russell was closely involved. He was chairman of the Utility Design Panel and later became first director of the newly founded Design Council. This *Utility* furniture was the beginning of a comprehensive reform in furniture design.

1 *Cabinet* radio, 1934
2 *Tallboy* cabinet, 1926

1

1 *Womb* chair, 1948
2 *Tulip* seating, 1956

2

Eero **Saarinen**

1910–61 **USA**

The movement of the golden fifties.
Eero Saarinen's TWA airline terminal at
Kennedy Airport, New York (1961) is a
showpiece of postwar architecture, a
glorification of the constructive boldness
that characterized that progress-mad
period. It is an example of the "organic"
style of those years, brilliantly executed
by the former sculptor who was the son
of Eliel Saarinen. The seemingly
unlimited technical possibilities of the
new materials—steel and concrete in
architecture, plywood and synthetics in
furniture design—are strongly expressed
in the sculptural qualities of the building.
Earlier, Saarinen and his friend Charles
Eames had together won the "Organic
Design in Home Furnishings" competition
organized by the Museum of Modern Art.
Their design, the *Organic Armchair* (for
Haskelite), was made from plywood and
foam rubber, and it was the first three-
dimensionally shaped bucket armchair, a
theme that Saarinen continued to develop
in the years that followed. Armchairs like
the *Womb* (1948) and *Tulip* (1956, both for
Knoll) were real trendsetters. In *Tulip*, a
single-legged armchair made from glass
fiber-reinforced polyester resin (accompa-
nied by similar stools and a table), Eero
Saarinen realized his ideal of formal unity,
"because every significant piece of
furniture from the past has a holistic
structure."

1

Eliel Saarinen 1873–1950 Finland and USA

The intermediary. When the Finnish architect Eliel Saarinen decided to settle in America in 1923, mainly for financial reasons, he already had a career behind him. He is rightly seen as the father of Finnish modernism. In the early 1900s he was one of the major representatives of National Romanticism, the first Finnish style. This consisted of elements of national folklore and Jugendstil on which the idea of *Gesamtkunstwerk* (the "total work of art") was based, and it was demonstrated in Helsinki's main railroad station designed by Saarinen in 1914. In America, Saarinen was invited to take part in the design of the Cranbrook Academy of Art, whose director he became in 1932. Famous for his building projects and his involvement in furniture, textile and product design, Saarinen is also recognized as a father figure of American design; Harry Bertoia, Charles Eames and his own son, Eero Saarinen, were among the great names who studied at the Cranbrook Academy, where the ideas of the Old World merged with those of the New. The revival of organic forms in the 1940s that reflected the renaissance of Romanticism would have been unthinkable without Eliel Saarinen.

2

1   *Blue Suite* armchair, 1929
2   Chairs, 1929

1

Lino **Sabattini** b. 1925 **Italy**

Signore Silver. Lino Sabattini's principle is for his designs to develop from the material and not to impose just any particular form on it. He has a reputation as a trendsetting silversmith and he is one of the most important modern metal designers. His approach to his work is possibly due to his complete ingenousness as a self-taught designer. In 1955 he went to Milan where he met Gio Ponti and Bruno Munari. Ponti was much taken by Sabattini's work which he illustrated in his magazine *Domus*. Sabattini became increasingly well-known as a result and he took part in numerous design and art exhibitions, such as the Milan Triennale and the Venice Biennale. Between 1956 and 1963 he managed the Milan branch of Christofle. In 1964 he left Milan for Bregnano and founded the Argenteria Sabattini company. For his work, the very symbol of "Bel Design" with its elegance and modernity, he was in 1979 awarded the Compasso d'Oro, Italy's highest design prize. More recently he turned his attention to a different field: since 1985, he has been developing the range of Rosenthal products, notably with *porcelaine noire*.

Como tea set, 1956

Bruno **Sacco** b. 1933 Italy and Germany

An Italian in Germany. "A maximum of innovation within the bounds of the brand's tradition." This is Bruno Sacco's philosophy as head of the design department of Mercedes automobiles. Sacco himself is not a designer. He studied mechanical engineering at the Polytechnic College in Turin, the car capital of Italy. After spending some time working for the coach builders Ghia and Pininfarina, Sacco joined Daimler-Benz in 1985. There he developed new prototype design concepts and his career developed quickly. After working on several projects under Friedrich Geiger and Béla Barényi he was appointed chief of the body-building and concept design section. As designer-in-chief he was responsible for the development of the 1972 *S-Class* and the *190* series. Sacco has been awarded many design prizes in countries including Mexico, Germany, Italy and the United States. He also played a considerable part in the development of the new *SLK* and *CLK* models, and the spectacular *A-Class*.

1 Mercedes *Vision SLR*, 1999

2 Mercedes *S-Class*, 1972

3 Mercedes *SLK-Class Cabriolet*, 1998

4 Mercedes *S-Class* (detail), 1998

5 Mercedes *CLK Coupé*, 1998

6 Mercedes *C111*, 1970

5

6

4

325

Marc **Sadler**

b. 1946 **France**

Everything in plastic. Marc Sadler's particular fields of interest are synthetics and techniques for processing these very versatile moldable materials. The ski boots that he designed in 1971 for the Italian company Caberare are among the Frenchman's most successful creations—the company became the second most important manufacturer in the world in only three seasons. It is therefore not surprising that Marc Sadler has been concentrating especially on the development of sports articles where plastics have a practical as well as a synthetic use. For instance, he developed the *Motorcyclist's Back Protector* that acted like a beetle's carapace to protect the back of the motorcyclist in case of an accident. It became such a classic that it is now in the collection of the Museum of Modern Art in New York. A resident of Italy for 30 years, Marc Sadler also designs very unusual furniture such as *Hal* (1997, for Cassina), a monstrous, adjustable sitting-machine with a complicated technical "inner life" which seems to have come directly from the cockpit of a spaceship.

1 *Hal* armchair, 1997
2 *Alukit* kitchen, 1997

2

Yves **Saint Laurent** b. 1936 **Algeria and France**

The couturier of the century. Yves Saint Laurent made fashion history by dressing women as no one had ever dared to do before. He dressed them in dinner jackets and he invented thigh-high boots. Even in the liberal sixties, his light gowns and transparent fabrics that revealed the models' stomachs and breasts caused quite a stir, and he dedicated one of his collections to the students protesting on the streets of Paris in 1968. But at the same time, this distinguished Algerian-born couturier with intellectual glasses knew how to dress women in elegant, feminine clouds of the finest fabrics in the world. As a result of this and his love of black velvet he became the darling of the new jet set and the favored couturier of film stars like Catherine Deneuve. He became chief designer at Christian Dior at the age of twenty and later set up his own couture house. Since then he has originated and contributed many different fashions. But one thing is primary: the anatomy of the female body. He says of himself that he was born "with a nervous breakdown," yet with his energy he has also introduced several commercial innovations. He was the first couturier to present a ready-to-wear collection, to perceive the potential of Asian markets, and to add perfume as a lucrative boost to his fashion collections.

1 Spring collection, 1999
2 Spring collection, 1988
3 Autumn collection, 1966

Roberto **Sambonet** 1924–95 **Italy**

The system man. Roberto Sambonet's main field of activity has been with beautiful, practical household objects, the classic craft of "artistic industry" including bowls, plates, vases, glasses, tableware and cutlery. He was notable for the wide variety of materials he used in his designs— high-quality steel and crystal as well as glass and porcelain—and the continuous graphic outline of his designs. Many of his pieces were based on the idea of combination, so that they could be stacked or telescoped like the steel *Center Line* plates (1965) and *Empilage* glasses (1971). Roberto Sambonet was strongly influenced by his collaboration with his friend Alvar Aalto. Before turning to industrial design, he was already famous as a painter and graphic artist. At the beginning of the 1950s he set up his own studio in Milan and in 1956 he founded a company under his own name, specializing in the production of high-quality goods from fine steel. As well as designing his own products, he also designed his company's graphic image with such success that other companies including La Rinascente, Pirelli and Alfa Romeo called upon his services for corporate identity.

1

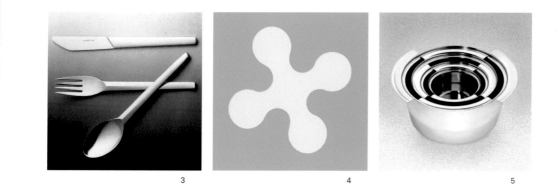

3

4

5

2

1   *Pesciera* fish dish, 1957
2   *Posate Metron* fork, 1960
3   *Posate Metron* cutlery, 1960
4   Logo for the Lombardy region, 1974
5   *Center Line* bowls, 1965
6   Packaging for *Pesciera*, 1976

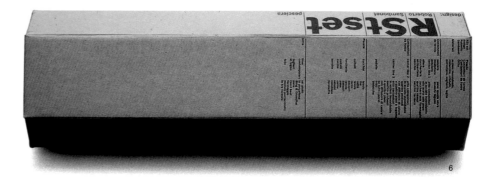

6

Richard **Sapper** b. 1932 Germany and Italy

Design with technical handwriting. Richard Sapper once said, "You cannot learn anywhere how to have an idea." He himself taught industrial design in Stuttgart until 1998. Sapper has never been short of ideas and he finds technically sophisticated solutions for all kinds of objects: espresso coffee machines, kettles, audio equipment, furniture, lights and bicycles. The designer studied philosophy, graphic arts, engineering and economics, and he went to Italy in 1958. There he worked first for Gio Ponti before joining La Rinascente chain stores. Between 1958 and 1977 he designed several brilliant design classics with Marco Zanuso, including the *Doney 14* and *Black 12* television sets (both 1962 for Brionvega). Sapper's best known design is the *Tizio* low-voltage halogen light (1970, for Artemide). Since the 1980s obsession with high-tech, it has been an essential part of every designer's office, just as every designer kitchen includes the famous *Bollitore* kettle (1983, for Alessi), which signals that the water is boiling by producing a harmonious triad instead of a shrill whistle.

1

2

4

5

1 *Tizio* desk light, 1970

2 *V-39* espresso machine, 1978

3 *TS 502* radio (with Marco Zanuso), 1964

4 *9091* kettle, 1983

5 *Ritz-Italora* digital clock, 1971

6 *K 4999* Child's chair (with Marco Zanuso), 1964

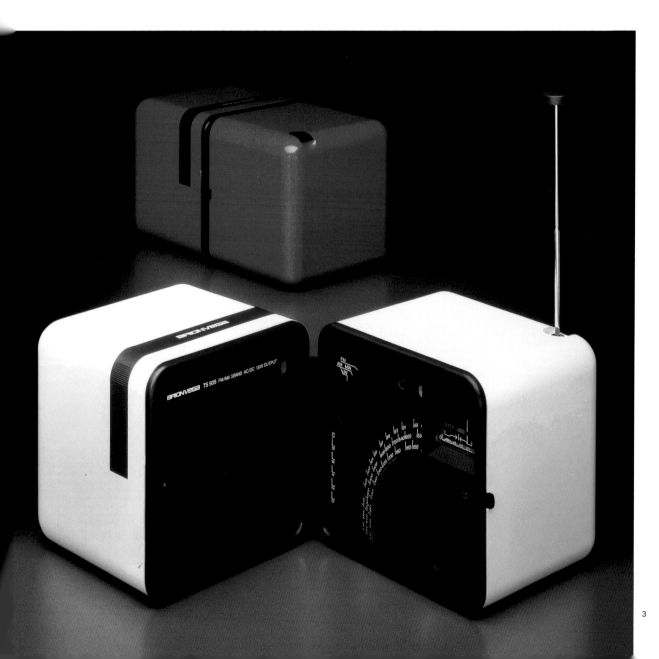

3

6

Gino **Sarfatti**

1912–85 **Italy**

Illuminations for every occasion.
The circumstances that led to Gino
Sarfatti becoming the inventor of modern
lighting were somewhat unfortunate.
While he was studying aircraft
construction and shipbuilding in Genoa,
his father had to give up his business as a
food importer because of the economic
blockade. Consequently, Sarfatti junior
had to abandon his studies in order to
earn a living. He began as a commercial
representative in Milan for Lumen, the
Murano glass manufacturer, but in 1939
Sarfatti went independent and set up his
own company, Arteluce (part of the Flos
group since 1974). He was still only
twenty-seven years old. By the 1950s the
company had become one of the major
designers and manufacturers of lights and
lighting. He held that "decoration and
lighting are two completely different
things," and by reducing his concept to
the smallest denominator he set the
standard for modern lighting design.
Ships, theaters, cinemas, restaurants,
museums, hotels, offices, private houses:
there are few projects Sarfatti has not
tackled. His showroom in the Corso
Matteotti (later in the Via della Spiga)
became a cult address for architects from
all over the world who wanted to see
their projects in the right light.

1

4   5

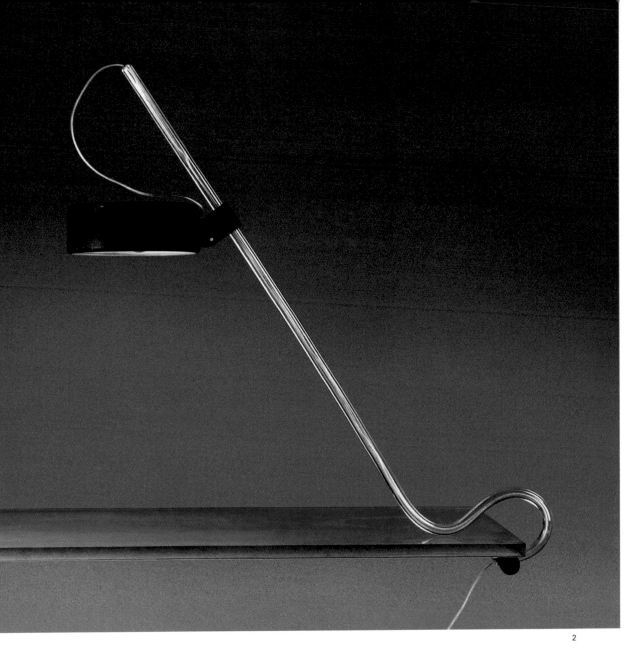

2

3

1 *2097/30* chandelier, 1952
2 Office light, c. 1970
3 *607* office light, 1971
4 *2133* ceiling light, 1976
5 *Metropoli* light, 1992
6 *600* office light, 1966

6

Timo **Sarpaneva**

b. 1926 **Finland**

The designer as star. Timo Sarpaneva's success has been based on innovations of technical production as well as on exciting aesthetic solutions. At the beginning of the 1950s Sarpaneva created a series of glass *objets d'art* using a steam-blowing process, a method then used for the first time. One of the best-known pieces was a vase that the glassblower called *Maailmankaunein* ("The most beautiful in the world," today called *Orkidea*, for littala). Sarpaneva is a living monument to Finnish glass design, a famous eccentric and experimenter, and like a Renaissance man he has made important contributions to other artistic disciplines such as sculpture, painting and graphics. In the 1950s he was, like his countryman Tapio Wirkkala, one of the first international star designers and one of the most honored artists at the Milan Triennale; he was also among the first to design objects with no purpose. He changed direction when he designed the *i-Line* range (1956, for littala), a set of decanters, glasses and plates with which Sarpaneva removed the barrier between luxury artistic glassware and mass-produced goods. The artist himself considers the plates in this range to be one of his best designs. They are glass "watercolours" whose colors run into each other like a rainbow. The *Finlandia* range was produced using a new wood-fired process and is famous for its ice-like surfaces. He followed it in the 1980s with the *Claritas* range of massive, jagged glass sculptures: *Creatura* is nearly three feet (85 cm) high and weighs 1,500 pounds (700 kg). Here the master has brought the cooled-down mass back to life with his chisel.

1

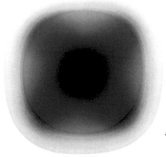

1 *Anubis* vase, 1984
2 *Suomi* service, 1974
3 *i-Line* glass, 1956
4 *Sun in the Forest* glass panel, 1957
5 Casserole, 1973
6 *Kajakki* glass sculpture, 1954

Peter Saville b. 1955 Great Britain

The image expert. The celebrated graphic artist Peter Saville specializes in image creation and has developed campaigns for Christian Dior, Yohji Yamamoto, Jil Sander, John Galliano, Hugo Boss, Vivienne Westwood, the London Whitechapel Gallery and the Centre Pompidou in Paris. But his most successful campaign was not commissioned by anyone. Peter Saville invented the idea of corporate identity in British pop music. The co-founder of Factory Records in Manchester with cult bands Joy Division and New Order, he developed the complete graphic concept, from record sleeves to T-shirts. He subsequently became art director of Virgin's subsidiary Dindisc Records before setting up as Peter Saville Associates in 1983 with typographer Brett Wickens. In 1990 the image maker of pop culture moved to the Pentagram agency and worked on rejuvenating the image of institutions such as the Natural History Museum (with architect David Chipperfield) and the revamping of the image of TV Channel One in Los Angeles. Since the early 1990s Peter Saville has been offering his graphic services as a freelance consultant.

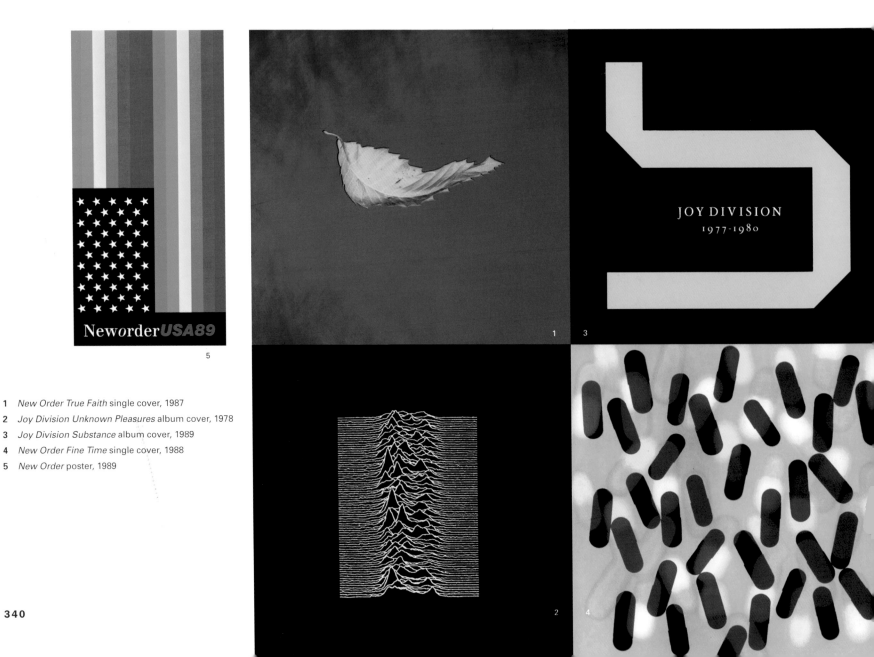

1 *New Order True Faith* single cover, 1987
2 *Joy Division Unknown Pleasures* album cover, 1978
3 *Joy Division Substance* album cover, 1989
4 *New Order Fine Time* single cover, 1988
5 *New Order* poster, 1989

340

1 *Le Diable en Tête* jug, 1995
2 *Ex Libris* shelving unit, 1997
3 *Patty Diffusa* chair, 1993

2

William **Sawaya**

b. 1949 **Italy and Lebanon**

A promoter of plurality. The designer William Sawaya is internationally famous both for his own designs and as half of the Sawaya & Moroni partnership. He graduated from the Beirut National Academy of Arts and then moved to Italy. In the late 1970s he set up the company with Moroni that soon made a name for itself with its unconventional furniture and accessories. The concept of Sawaya & Moroni is simple: they look for out-standing international designers and architects. Famous practitioners like Zaha Hadid, Michael Graves and Jean Nouvel are joined by less well-known but no less inspired designers such as Marco Mencacci and Michael Young. Without having to follow any particular style, the artists can give free rein to their creativity in designing furniture, silverware and glass. The only requirements are that the form should be innovative and that the design should be perfectly crafted, like the pieces created by William Sawaya himself whose unusual glass objects add to the variety of the company's program.

3

1

341

Carlo **Scarpa**

1906–78 **Italy**

The material aesthete. Soon after completing his studies at the Academy of Fine Arts in Venice in the late 1920s, Carlo Scarpa found a soul mate in the person of Paolo Venini. Together they reformed, or even revolutionized, the processes of glass design and manufacture. Scarpa transformed the traditional thin glass into a thick, almost ceramic-like substance made from milky opal glass. Typical of Scarpa's work are geometric forms, luminous colors and unusual glazing techniques. With Venini he enjoyed complete design freedom while achieving true mastery in the mechanical techniques of glassblowing. For his furniture he used durable, precious materials such as marble, wood or crystal, giving the impression that it was created for eternity. Scarpa was especially celebrated for his brilliant exhibition and showroom designs, such as those for the Paul Klee exhibition (1948), several projects for the Venice Biennale, and an Olivetti showroom (1956).

2

1

342

4

3

1 *Decoro a Fili* vase, 1942

2 *Battuto Bicolore* vase, 1940

3 *Murrine Opache* glass dishes, 1940

4 Table from the *34* range, 1934

Peter Schreyer b. 1953 Germany

The new language of car design. "Designers should rebel now and again," says Peter Schreyer. This is something that he has done himself. Since the mid-1990s Schreyer has been head of Audi Design, the automobile company that achieved a feat that no one believed was any longer possible. In the 1970s and 1980s the public was becoming bored because the models produced by the various manufacturers increasingly resembled each other. Audi succeeded in changing this perception radically by making design a priority. Models such as the new *A6* (1998)—whose estate car version was awarded the much coveted Bundespreis (Federal Prize) for product design—and the *TT* coupé (1998) caused quite a sensation with their bold, sensual lines. Schreyer went to work for Audi straight after studying design in Munich and London and he has developed the interior of several models and the concept for the *Quattro Spyder*. In 1991 Schreyer went to work for a year with the VW-design team in California where the idea for the *New Beetle* (at the time still known as *Concept I*) was being developed.

1 Audi *A6*, 1998
2 Audi *TT Coupé*, 1998
3 Audi *A3*, 1997
4 Audi *A4 Avant*, 1996

3

4

2

Peter **Schmidt**

b. 1937 **Germany**

Visualized fragrances. Although his designs have a place of honor in many German households, the name of graphic artist Peter Schmidt is almost unknown. He is the creator of the lilac-colored Milka wrapper, of logos and of packaging for multinationals such as Schwarzkopf, Jil Sander, Joop, Strenesse, West and Boss. His work ranges from the development of new packaging and brand image to corporate identity. But his undisputed specialty is the design of perfume bottles and their packaging. Schmidt's talent lies in his ability to create the right packaging for each fragrance and to develop a range of bottles that reflects the company's image. For example, for Davidoff he created dark-colored bottles, while for Jil Sander he designed austere square glass containers.

1   Scent bottle for Jil Sander, 1979
2   Toiletry bottle and packaging for Hugo Boss, 1996
3   Toiletry bottle and packaging for Hugo Boss, 1997

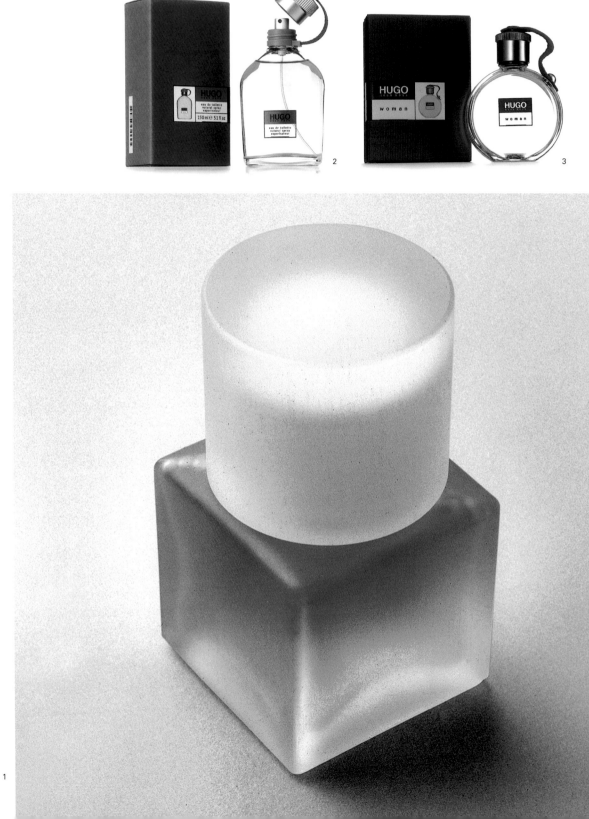

Ben **Shahn** 1898–1969 **Lithuania and USA**

Posters of protest. "You have not converted a man because you have silenced him," declared Ben Shahn's poster promoting *Great Ideas of Western Man* (1960). This is typical of this artist and illustrator whose realistic murals and posters of information and social criticism are always on behalf of the rights of workers, the civil rights movement or the fight against the nuclear weapons. During the Second World War he created propaganda posters for the US Army. The son of Jewish parents who had emigrated to America from Tsarist Russia, he completed his training as a lithographer and then traveled extensively through Europe and Africa. When he returned at the end of the 1920s he shared a studio in New York with the photographer Walker Evans. Many leading American magazines used Shanh's illustrations, which were often distinguished by his ingenious and frequently irregular typography.

1 Poster, 1959
2 Poster, 1960

EXHIBIT- JEROME ROBBINS "BALLETS U.S.A."-U.S.I.S. GALLERY 41 GROSVENOR SQ. LONDON W.1. SEPT. 15- OCT. 23. 1959

1

2

347

Shounsai **Shono** 1904–74 Japan

New dimensions in bamboo. Shounsai Shono became a national hero in his own lifetime, through his use of bamboo. He came from the Oita region that was famous for its artistic bamboo baskets, revolutionizing the tradition of Japanese basket making. But it was not just his innovative designs, regularly exhibited at craft fairs and in museums, that made him such an expert in his field. It was his meticulous study of materials and his knowledge of the quality, the structure, the advantages and the disadvantages of the various ways of using the material that raised his creations above those of the other basket makers. His knowledge of the strength and elasticity of bamboo enabled him to produce objects that would have been thought impossible before him. Shounsai Shono designed baskets for the most varied purposes, creating lively forms that often looked like abstract paintings or imaginative sculptures.

1 *Wellen* basket, 1956
2 *Kuina-bue* vase, 1967

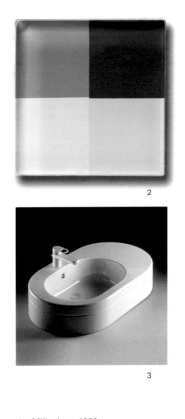

Dieter **Sieger**

b. 1938 **Germany**

From bath to living room. Wash basins, single-mixer faucets, baths, continuous-flow water heaters: Dieter Sieger is renowned as a specialist in elegantly designed bathroom fittings. Several other careers came first. After leaving school, Sieger did a three-year apprenticeship as a bricklayer before going on to study architecture. After two semesters he moved to the Arts and Crafts School in Dortmund. After obtaining his diploma in 1964, he set up his own architect's studio and built some 200 houses. He has also designed the interiors of a couple of yachts, an appropriate task for the keen sailor that he is. Sieger's next career began in the 1980s, and with his sons Christian and Michael he now designs modern bathroom accessories that are restrained yet luxurious. He has diversified further with designs for lights, glassware, and porcelain such as the *Cult* service (1994, for Arzberg) and the *Vinum* range of wine glasses (1999, for Ritzenhoff) created by several designers.

1 Milk glass, 1992
2 *Aquarius* tile, 1998
3 *LavarLo* wash basin, 1986

Ettore **Sottsass**

b. 1917 **Austria and Italy**

The legend. Italian designers welcomed Ettore Sottsass with open arms when he came to Italy, aware that their reputation could only benefit from his innovative designs. He is one of the most creative and influential designers of this century, born in Innsbruck but an Italian national since the 1960s. The adopted Italian studied architecture in Turin in the 1930s. His father was an architect, an important representative of functionalism, and the young man assisted in his father's studios. During World War II he was in the army, but by 1947 he had already set up his own design and architecture studio in Milan. He spent periods abroad to find inspiration for his work—in 1956 for instance, when he went to work for George Nelson in New York, or in 1961 when he traveled to India. His breakthrough as an industrial designer came with the *Elea 9003* computer (1959, for Olivetti), the first Italian mainframe. Other office machines followed: the *Tekne 3*, the *Praxis 48* (both 1964) and the *Valentine* (1970, all for Olivetti). Sottsass still designs lamps, ceramics, household objects, furniture and electronic apparatus for companies like Alessi, Artemide, Poltronova, Vitra, Zanotta and Zumtobel. However, Sottsass does not limit himself to industrial design. He has been a leading figure in influential movements like Radical Design, the Global Tools design research group, and the Alchymia group. With his *Carlton* (1981) shelf unit he created the icon of the Memphis style. It was at that time that he set up his studio Sottsass Associati. He has become a living legend as the influential leader of the Italian design scene that has long been setting the aesthetic and intellectual design pace with international influence.

1

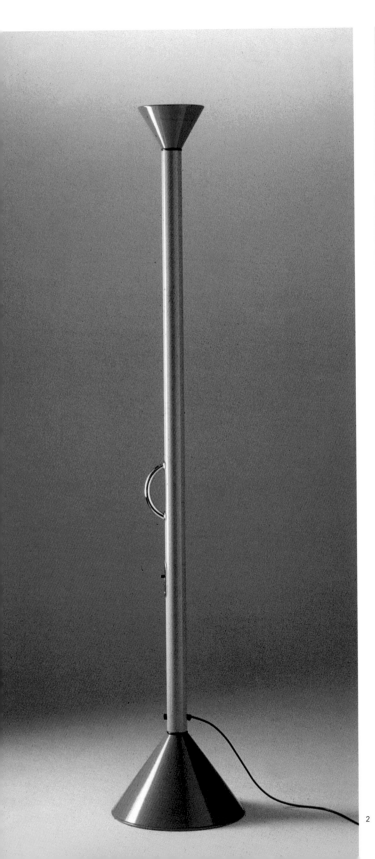

4

5

6

1 *Casablanca* shelving unit, 1981
2 *Callimaco* standard lamp, 1982
3 *Lipari* table, 1992
4 *Carlton* shelving unit, 1981
5 *Valentine* typewriter, 1970
6 *Murmansk* dish, 1982

2

3

Mart **Stam** 1899–1986 **Netherlands, Germany and Russia**

Constructing with utopian vision. Experts still disagree whether it was Mart Stam or Marcel Breuer who had the idea for the first cantilever chair, but in any event Stam's *S32* model (1926, for Thonet) is still considered a classic today. After training as a draftsman in Amsterdam, Stam began his career as an international architect. He worked in Berlin, Switzerland, Paris and Rotterdam, becoming acquainted with modernists like Max Taut and El Lissitzky. At the end of the 1920s he experienced his greatest success with low-cost high-quality housing projects, working on the famous Weissenhof development of terraced houses in Stuttgart in 1927. He was also experimenting with tubular steel to make chairs, a completely new idea at the time. Some of his designs are still produced today and they have been much copied. In the early 1930s, he and his wife Lotte became members of the "May Brigade," communists who designed the plans for the new Soviet towns of Magnitogorsk, Makejewka and Orsk. Back in the Netherlands Stam became director of the Institute of Arts and Crafts in Amsterdam. His political convictions prompted him to go to East Germany after World War II, leaving again after the repression of the uprising of 1953.

2

1

4

1 *S32* chair, 1926
2 *S34* chair, 1926
3 *MSW 27* wall light, 1927
4 S33 chair, 1926

Philippe **Starck**

b. 1949 **France**

Victory of the horns. Philippe Starck is better known to the public than any other designer. His reputation is very much based on his ability to present himself as an *enfant terrible*, an entertainer, a media star, or a politically motivated rebel, depending on the occasion. The entertaining design guru (who has a distinct weakness for motorbikes and scooters) says that he has no taste, that he is not inquisitive, and that he does not like to talk, particularly about design. He has succeeded in blurring the boundaries between high culture and everyday objects. He is skilled in all crafts and works all over the world. His subjects include the interiors of trendy places like *La Main Bleue* and *Les Bains-Douche*, hotels, lights, noodles, sofas, toilets, lemon squeezers, and recently biodynamic food. The shapes and forms vary widely, although early on their common characteristic was that they always included horns. His critics have sometimes said that he was frittering away his talent. But although the Frenchman agrees with them, he is frightened "not to exist any longer" unless he gives free rein to his creativity. The self-taught artist has an interesting artistic approach to his designs: "I do not care what objects look like, I only care about the feelings they arouse in people."

4

5

1

6

7

8

9

1 *w.w. stool*, 1990
2 *Ära* table lamp, 1988
3 *Bubu* stool, 1991
4 *Lord Yo* chair, 1994
5 *Juicy Salif* lemon juicer, 1990
6 *Hot Bertaa* kettle, 1991
7 Toothbrush and container, 1989
8 *Louis XX* chair, 1992
9 Door handle, 1991

2

3

Stiletto b. 1959 Germany

That design denied. Stiletto was a mechanic in the West German army, after which he studied mechanical engineering, then visual communication, and finally sculpture. During this time he saw the squatter scene in Berlin. Stiletto is above all the "clarifier of the existing," and he joined the revolt of young German designers of the 1980s with a true classic: *Consumer's Rest* (1982), a seat made from a shopping cart (there is also a lesser-known child version as well as a sofa and a table). The changed form and the play on words are in the tradition of Marcel Duchamps, who would change a mundane item of practical use into a ready-made piece of furniture with cult potential. The native of Berlin, who ironically describes himself as a "design doctor," has recently made a series of lights that remain true to the lightbulb. The lights are inexpensive because they are assembled from existing elements, and they are called *Revolver*, *Glühwürmchen* ("glowworm") and *Pflanzlicht* ("plant light").

2

3

1 *Consumer's Rest* chair, 1982
2 *Satellight* bedside table, 1986
3 *Honda* light, 1985

1

Giotto **Stoppino** b. 1926 **Italy**

The driving force. Giotto Stoppino has an open mind to new tendencies, materials and technologies, but sometimes he has consciously designed his work to contrast with current trends. For instance, his wicker chair (1961, for Vittorio Bonacina) designed with his partners Vittorio Gregotti and Ludovico Meneghetti was inspired by Art Nouveau, thus contributing to the Neo-Liberty movement that flourished for a short time in Italy in the 1960s. During the 1960s and 1970s he experimented with synthetic materials, resulting among other things in the development of the *Tic-Tac* table lamp (1970, for Kartell). This light's most unusual feature was that it was switched on and off by turning the shade. Stoppino also experimented with aluminum, as in the *Isos* combined table lamp and filing tray (1972, for Tronconi). Together with Ludovico Acerbis he designed a table for the *I Menhir* range, consisting of a harmonious combination of marble, metal and crystal. Giotto Stoppino belongs to the generation of designers whose bold projects contributed to the exciting development of Italian design since World War II.

2

1 *Sheraton* sideboard, 1977
2 *Soffio di vento* cabinet, 1986

1

Studio 65

founded 1965 **Italy**

Flippant Classics. Gianni Arnaudo, Franco Audrito, Adriana Gavizio, Roberto Gibello, Giancarlo Paci, Luciano Paglieri, Paolo Perotti, Anna Pozzo, Annamaria Racchetta, Angelica Sampanioti, Athena Sampaniotou, Maria Schiappa, Janis Skoulas, Ferruccio Tartaglia: hardly anyone remembers any of these names. They were all young Turin-based architects and designers who would have been completely forgotten if they had not formed Studio 65, in which guise they made a brief but important appearance on the international design scene. In the 1970s they were approached by Gufram, who produced limited editions of objects such as the *Cactus* by Guido Drocco and Franco Mello and the *Pratone* rubber seating lawn by Ceretti, Derossi and Rosso. Many people were surprised to be invited to sit down in distinguished furniture shops on *Bocca*, a giant sulking mouth of foam rubber, or on *Capitello*, the dangerously sloping top of an Ionic column. These objects were visual stumbling blocks, so in the latter, for instance, what looked like white marble was actually cold-foamed plastic. *Bocca* and *Capitello* were flippant responses to the conservative concept of seating.

1 *Capitello* chair, 1971
2 *Bocca* sofa, 1971

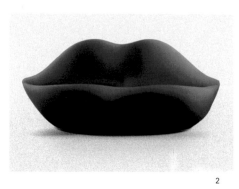

2

1

Gerald **Summers** 1899–1967 **Great Britain**

Simple Furniture. Gerald Summers was one of the few British designers who devoted himself completely to modernism between the wars, and as a result his furniture now fetches amazingly high prices. He used a modern material, laminated wood, and experimented with this to express his love of geometric simplicity and his progressive approach to design. He founded his own company, Makers of Simple Furniture, but he was unable to organize advertising and sales effectively, and few of his designs went into production. Besides beds, tables, chairs and children's furniture, he is particularly admired for his remarkable armchair made from a single piece of plywood (1934), which is considered a classic of British design and often compared with the creations of Marcel Breuer and Alvar Aalto.

Armchair, 1934

Superstudio

1966–78 **Italy**

Continuous protest. Florence was the main center of the design revolution in the second half of the 1960s. Like Archizoom, Superstudio was set up there in 1966. Its founders were Adolfo Natalini and Cristiano Toraldo, and shortly afterwards they were joined by Piero Frassinelli, Alessandro Poli and Roberto and Giancarlo Magris. Together they fought the blandness of functionalism and the omnipotence of industry. In doing this they provided other movements such as Radical Design with the necessary theoretical ammunition. Besides their fantastical, amusing lights made from synthetic materials, including *Passiflora* (1966) and *Gherpe* (1967, both for Poltronova), Superstudio also designed the "checkered" tables and stools of the *Quaderna* range (1971) that are still very popular today. The pattern of black squares on white laminate was inspired by Superstudio's most important project developed in 1969: *Il Monumento Continuo* ("The Permanent Monument"), which rests like a grid structure over the whole world, a symbol of the replaceable nature of existing systems. Superstudio was dissolved in 1978 as the design protest movement died down.

1/2 *Quaderna* table, 1971

3 *Gherpe* table lights, 1967

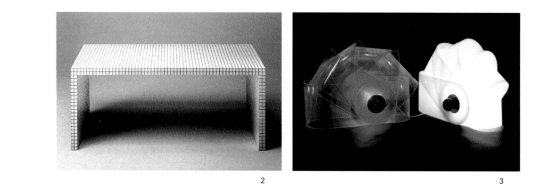

2

3

1

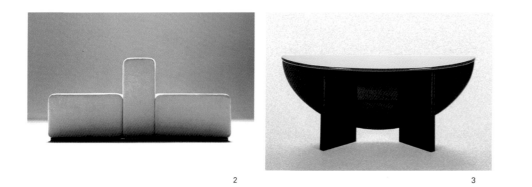

2

3

Kazuhide **Takahama**

b. 1930 **Japan**

East meets South. The meeting between the Japanese designer Kazuhide Takahama and the entrepreneur Dino Gavina at the eleventh Milan Triennale in 1957 was a fateful one. Although they did not speak each other's language there was an immediate "design rapport" between them. This resulted in Takahama designing the *Naeko* angular sofa for Gavina that formed a focal point in the collection. When Takahama's tourist visa expired it seemed likely that the relationship of the two men would end. But Takahama returned to Italy and continued to work for the well-known furniture manufacturer, art lover and "rebel/anarchist/revolutionary," as Gavina describes himself. Among Takahama's numerous designs are simple pieces of furniture such as the *Maja* stacking chairs (with interchangeable upholstery), the *Marcel* table system (tubular legs and a crystal glass top), and the *Godet* seating units made from foam rubber. He has also designed some more complex items, such as the *Redon* bed and the *Rennie* armchair, which is a tribute to the great Charles Rennie Mackintosh. Takahama's lights such as the *Sirio* standard lamp and the slit wall light *Kaori* (both for Sirrah) are considered classics.

1 *Suzanne* chair, 1965
2 *Marcel* sofa, 1965
3 *Anatella* table, 1975

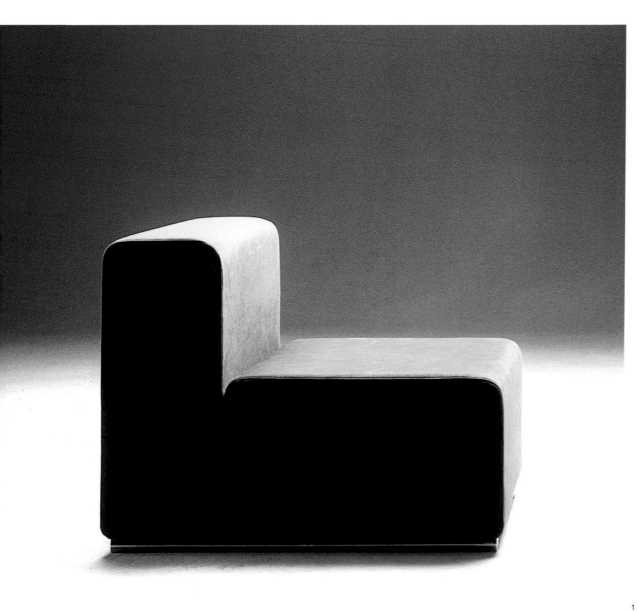

1

Roger **Tallon** b. 1929 **France**

Hard industrial design with soft edges. There is no doubt that Roger Tallon has written a chapter in design history with the television sets that he has been designing for Télévia since the late 1950s, and for the TGV, France's legendary high-speed train. Yet at first nothing appeared to point to a career in design. After graduating from a four-year engineering course in 1950, he joined Caterpillar-France, where he worked on the graphic image of the company. He subsequently moved to Tecnès which had been founded by Jacques Viénot in 1949. In 1963, Tallon was appointed professor at the École Nationale Supérieure des Arts Décoratifs where together with Jacques Dumond he founded and expanded the design department. Roger Tallon's reputation as an extremely competent systematician is based on an approach to work which consists in first analyzing a problem thoroughly before asking the collaboration of the various departments of a company to solve it. As a result he has worked for the greatest names in French industry. But Roger Tallon is also much in demand abroad: he has designed a range of lamps for Erco, the Mexico City metro and buses for Moscow whose interiors he designed in addition to the accessory parts.

2

3

1 *TGV Atlantique* high-speed train, 1989
2/3 Lights, 1973

1

Ikko **Tanaka** b. 1930 Japan

Creative tradition. In 1981 Ikko Tanaka used three black squares and two dark green triangles to create the impression of the traditional hairstyle of a Japanese woman. He used this on his own favorite composition, a poster for the University of California. The other two colored triangles and red squares are somewhat reminiscent of a kimono. "The young generation in Japan probably think of me as a conservative designer," says Tanaka. Many of his creations have been inspired by traditional Japanese sources. But he firmly believes that "it is still possible to be creative when working with traditional ideas." Tanaka has worked as a graphic artist in varied fields since the 1950s, from posters to logos, book design and exhibition concepts, and he has won countless prizes. Tanaka studied at the Kyoto Academy of Art and was involved in the building of the Nippon Design Center. He was already celebrated in the early 1960s for his posters displaying geometric symbols that were abstractions of typically Japanese motifs such as masks, characters and calligraphy. He himself often describes his work as "Japanese perceptions."

1   Theater poster, 1981
2   Poster, 1981

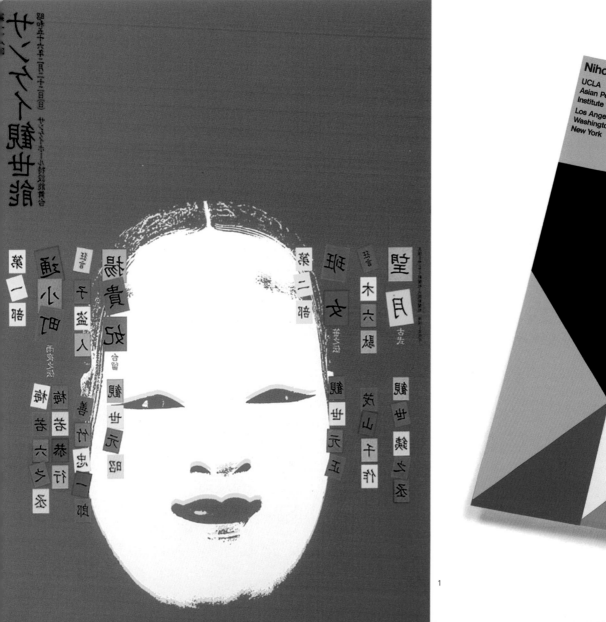

1

2   **365**

Walter Dorwin **Teague** 1883–1960 **USA**

Product design as management. Walter Dorwin Teague studied art and worked in advertising, but the turning point in his career came with a visit to Europe when he became a fervent admirer of Le Corbusier and his functional, unadorned lines. In the late 1920s Teague tried his hand at product design. One of his first major clients was Kodak, for whom he produced a comprehensive consultancy package that started with market analysis and finished with product development. He created the famous *Vanity* camera, the first camera to be marketed as a fashion accessory, with a brightly colored body and a bag with matching silk lining. The *Baby Brownie* (1933) had a plastic case and the *Bantam Special* (1936) was a forerunner of the pocket camera. He also designed pavilions at the 1939 New York World's Fair as well as Pullman carriages. Among his most successful creations were the tiled "icebox" gas stations for Texaco (1937) and the interior design of the Boeing *707* and *727* aircraft (1956) that set the standard for the period. Together with Henry Dreyfuss and Raymond F. Loewy he founded the Society of Industrial Designers of America, becoming its first president in 1944.

3

1

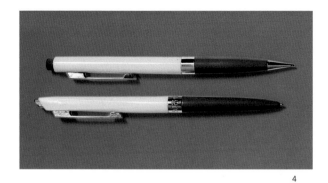

4

1 *Spartan* radio, 1939
2 *Bantam* roll film camera, 1936
3 *No 114* desk light, 1939
4 Ballpoint pen, c. 1940

2

1

1 *Lariana* chair, 1936
2 *Sant'Elia* chair, 1936

2

Giuseppe **Terragni** 1904–43 **Italy**

Sobriety and steel. Giuseppe Terragni's chairs *Lariana* (1936), *Follia* (1934) and *Sant'Elia* (1934–36, all reproduced by Zanotta since 1971, 1972 and 1983) are examples of tubular steel furniture that can justifiably be compared with the designs of Le Corbusier, Mies van der Rohe and Marcel Breuer. Terragni first studied at the Technical Institute in Como before joining the Milan Polytechnic in the mid-1920s. He was a representative of functionalism, or "rationalist architecture" as it was known in Italy. His building projects as well as his chairs reflect the sober lines advocated by the Bauhaus and De Stijl. In 1927 Terragni founded Gruppo 7 with which he took part in the Weissenhof exhibition in Stuttgart. As an architect he worked mainly in Como where he built the Casa del Fascio, the headquarters of the Italian fascists who, unlike the Nazis, flirted for a time with modernism. Originally the *Lariana* chair was designed as conference seating in this monumental building.

1 Chaise longue, 1992
2 *National Geographic* cupboard, 1990
3 *Rex* armchair, 1995
4 *200* sheet steel chair, 1994

Mats **Theselius** b. 1956 **Sweden**

Furniture with meaning. What to do with seventy-five years' worth of inherited *National Geographic* magazines? Mats Theselius has provided the solution: a specially designed, made-to-measure cabinet (which could also take 50 or 100 years' worth of the magazine) is both an homage to the American magazine that is an institution and a parody of standardized bourgeois comfort. It is also an extreme example of functionality. Accomplished stylistic eclecticism is routine for Theselius, compared with other young designers who may create it from time to time. Armchairs like the *200* (1994) or *Rex* (1995), hybrids in leather and metal produced by the avant-garde specialist manufacturer Källemo, are anachronistic and topical at the same time. Mats Theselius plays on alienated meanings and his designs swing between product and environment. He is an artist, designer and ironic interpreter of reality.

Michael **Thonet** 1796–1871 **Germany**

The people's chair. When the cabinetmaker Michael Thonet from Boppard am Rhein presented his first experiments with laminated wood, Germany was still gripped by the charm of Biedermeier, and the idea of mass-production had not yet taken hold. So when Thonet went bankrupt at the beginning of the 1840s and moved to Vienna, his prospects appeared to be bleak. But there seemed to be a greater need for chairs in the prosperous Austrian capital. Using his previous experience with bentwood and laminated wood, Thonet produced the classic coffee-house chair (today Thonet's *No. 14*), the prototype of the modern, industrially produced furniture. The *No. 14* chair is one of the most successful mass-produced items of furniture, over 50 million chairs being sold before World War II. The Thonet family business now owns seven factories abroad and has to defend itself against imitations. The advantages of such furniture lie not only in the endless possibilities of form and the ease of transportation (as unassembled components), but also in the elegance of their construction. Le Corbusier was so impressed by this that he used Thonet's chairs in his pavilion at the 1925 Paris design exhibition. Later Thonet became famous again for another innovative development in furniture design: the tubular steel chair.

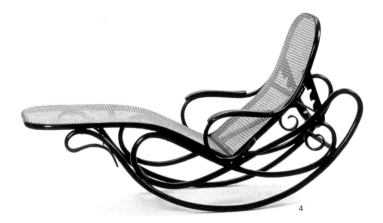

1 *No. 14* chair, 1859
2 *210R* chair, 1900
3 *S411* sofa, 1932
4 Rocking chair, 1883

Matteo **Thun**

b. 1952 **Italy**

The trendsetter. Matteo Thun says, "I do not specialize in anything." Critics would rather agree with him! But he confounds the implied criticism by his commercial success. In the light of his productivity it seems that his statement is simply a definition of the extraordinary range of his skills. Matteo Thun was born in the Southern Tyrol as Matthäus Graf Thun-Hohenstein. His catchy, fashionable designs are sometimes reminiscent of fairgrounds, like the *Hommage an Madonna* cutlery decorated with rings (1986, for WMF), the *Jacobelli* glasses covered in chains (1989, for Barovier e Toso) and the watches he designed for Swatch (1990–93). Thun concentrates on the surfaces of objects. His agenda is the fast-moving nature of the modern world. The faster fashions change, the quicker the designer changes his approach to materials. As a co-founder of Sottsass Associati, Thun learned versatility above all, and as a member of Memphis he made significant contributions to contemporary ceramics. Since 1984 he has had his own studio in Milan and he is now one of the country's most sought-after design consultants.

1 *Chad* ceramic, 1982
2 *Danubio* jug, 1982
3 *Candy* cutlery, 1998

3

1

Kurt **Thut** b. 1931 **Switzerland**

"What sells is allowed." Kurt Thut belongs to that rare species of manufacturers who design their own products. Asked about his design concept, the furniture designer has views that sound as matter-of-fact as his designs: "All you need is the idea," and "Obviously no conscious narrow-mindedness." In the late 1950s when the Swiss Design collection was initiated jointly by Kurt Thut, Hans Eichenberger, and Robert and Trix Haussmann, their timeless furniture achieved international status. Since then the Bauhaus-inspired Thut has met the constantly changing demands of the world of design with a combination of continuity, innovation and fantasy, yet always in the service of usefulness. This is as true of his early work—such as his strictly rational rotating folding table, his ascetic sofas and his table-chair combinations—as it is of his projects of the 1980s and 1990s: a single-legged, square table, adjustable scissor-beds that can take any size of mattress, or light natural beechwood cupboards whose canvas front conceals a structure of aircraft plywood. "How would you like it: postmodern, deconstructivist, or in a new simplicity?" asks Kurt Thut rhetorically, and he is sure to find the right practical answer.

1 Screen bed, 1990
2 Folding cupboard, 1998
3 Coat stand, 1999

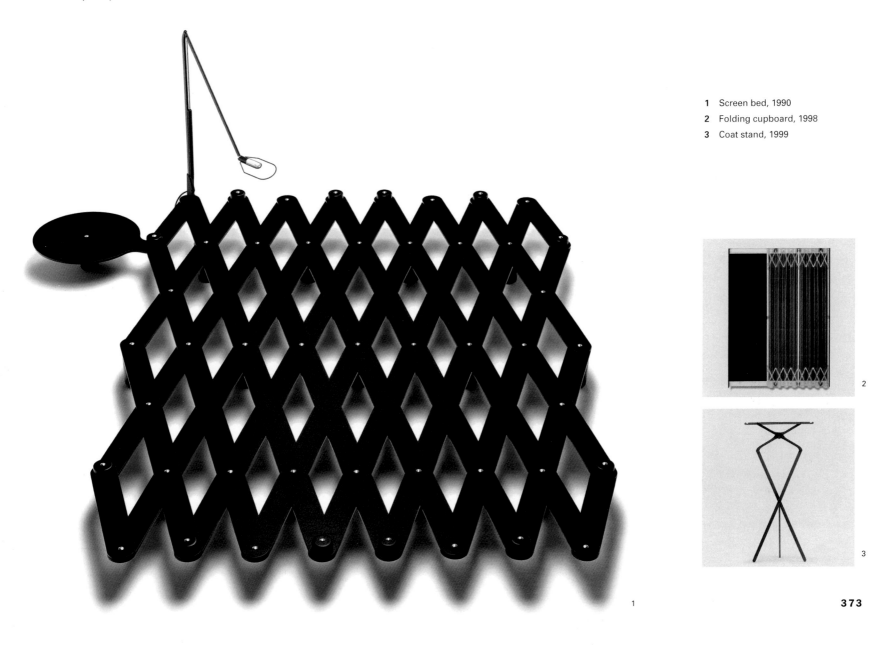

1

Louis Comfort **Tiffany**

1848–1933 **USA**

Precious glass made in the USA.
Tiffany glass is synonymous with the patented manufacturing process of lead-mounted colored glass lamps, vases, jewelry and bronzes that are today among the most sought-after collector's glass-ware of this century. Instead of joining the family business the New Yorker Louis Comfort Tiffany chose to study art. After a stay in Paris, he traveled extensively through Europe and North Africa. He was fascinated by the sumptuous colors and forms of French decorative arts and the Moorish heritage of the Mediterranean. He returned to the United States and experimented with new colors, luster, and transparency effects. This led to the patenting of lusterglass (1881) and the manufacturing of so-called carnival glass (1886), where metal chloride was sprayed onto red hot glass to produce the famous iridescent rainbow sheen. In 1894 he registered the trademark "Favrile" for his own designs. In 1902, when Louis Comfort Tiffany came into his inheritance, he was able to realize his lifetime dream: the setting up of an artists' colony on Long Island. When Tiffany died in 1933 he had made studio glass so popular in the United States that it already boasted more than 900 studios.

Bulb vase, c. 1900

Tomato

Founded 1991 **Great Britain**

Communicate quicker! Adidas, Coca-Cola, IBM, Levis, MTV, Nike, Philips, Reebok. The list of Tomato's main clients reads like a *Who's Who* of globally successful brand names. This team of graphic designers was set up in the early 1990s by Steve Baker, Dirk van Dooren, Karl Hyde, Rick Smith, Simon Taylor, John Warwicker and Graham Wood, and it has already won an impressive number of design prizes. Tomato has even rejuvenated the image of venerable institutions such as the British Broad-casting Corporation (BBC) and the television company Channel 4, mixing commerce and culture with a light hand. The group's recipe for success is to bring together creative people with many different abilities to collaborate in the ever-accelerating world of visual communications. Tomato's works are playful, direct and rough, yet sophisticated. The group's rise is proof of the regenerative ability of the British graphics scene, which has flourished throughout the nineties because of the strength of its multimedia and multi-cultural creativity. The pop group Underworld that provided the soundtrack for the successful movie *Trainspotting* is also associated with Tomato.

1   *Process: A Tomato Project*, book,
    Bangert Verlag, 1996
2   *Underworld: Second Toughest in the Infants*
    CD case, 1996

2

Masanori **Umeda**

b. 1941 **Japan and Italy**

Looking back in fun. Masanori Umeda was engaged by Memphis to contribute some of his own garish, witty creations to the group's shocking collections. He designed ceramics and furniture for this trendsetting Italian company, including the *Ginza Robot* shelf unit (1982) whose form is reminiscent of a popular toy and of Japanese science fiction characters; it is now an icon of postmodernism. Masanori Umeda used allusions to the recent past, the humor and the irregular proportions that made Memphis famous. He was one of the wave of young Japanese designers who came to Europe in the 1960s. In Italy he worked for Achille Castiglioni and later as design consultant for the Olivetti office machine company. In the mid-1980s he moved his field of activity back to Japan, this time under the company name of Umedadesign. This move broadened to include industry and environmental design. Among the products he has created since then are streetlights and bathroom fittings (both in 1989, for Iwasaki and Inax respectively), as well as some very traditional objects like the *Be-Byobu* illuminated screen made from steel and Japanese paper (1996, for Ishika Waseishi).

3

1

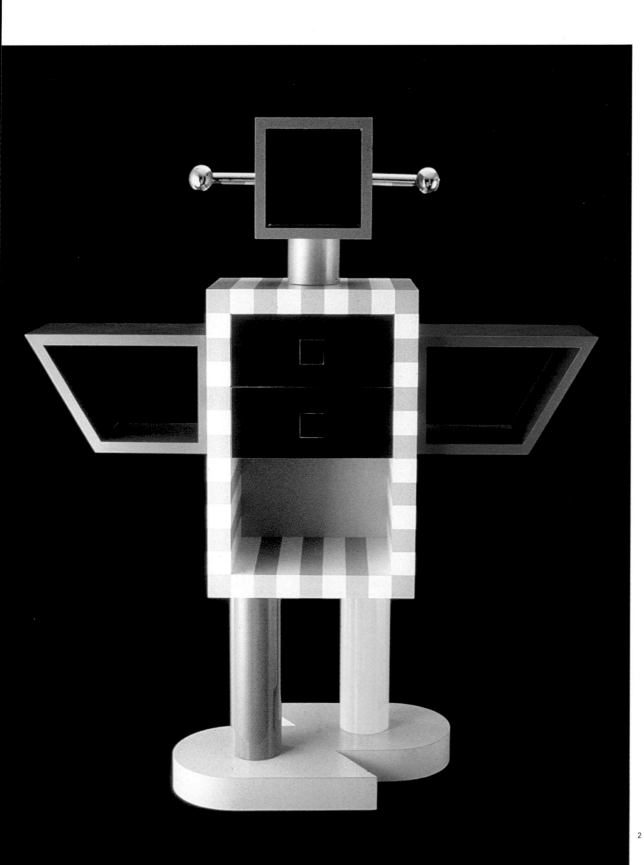

1 *Getsuen* armchair, 1990
2 *Ginza Robot* cupboard, 1982
3 *Rose* armchair, 1990
4 *Star Tray*, 1985

2

Valentino

b. 1932 **Italy and France**

Tailor of high society. In the world of
Valentino, women are seductresses
whose lascivious elegance is never too
shocking. His glamorous look with soft,
flowing lines and quantities of lace and
frills soon attracted famous names like
Jacqueline Kennedy, Farah Diba and
Elizabeth Taylor. Valentino attended
fashion classes even while he was still at
school, and he learned French in order to
realize his dream of becoming a fashion
designer in Paris. He moved to Paris
when he was only seventeen and there he
met Jean Desses and Guy Laroche. In the
1960s he returned to Italy and founded his
own couturier in Rome with his partner
Giancarlo Giammetti. Valentino's
breakthrough was his international debut
in the Palazzo Pitti in Florence in 1962.
Since then the creations with the famous
V logo have become sought after all over
the world.

1 Autumn collection, 1967
2 Spring collection, 1973
3 Spring collection, 1967
4 Autumn collection, 1981

4

381

1 *Cifra 3* desk clock, 1966
2 *Supermarket* cool box, 1958
3 *330* cool box, 1956

2

3

1

Gino **Valle** b. 1923 Italy

The rationalization of the everyday. Gino Valle once said that he does not intend to "fall in love with his objects." Indeed, his objects are not particularly exciting, yet they are landmarks that have influenced the concept of whole groups of products. His designs are inspired by his desire to combine utility with simplicity and clarity. Born in the Udine, he studied art in Venice and turned to painting before working in his father's architect's office, where he set definitive standards in product design in the 1950s and 1960s. With his household appliances for Zanussi he achieved new aesthetic standards. The cooker, washing machine and refrigerator acquired a geometric profile and were cleanly designed with well-indicated controls that caught the eye and gave the appliance its image. This gave the company a competitive advantage that was shown in its increased market share. Valle also designed some of the earliest digital timepieces. A much-copied classic is his *Cifra 3* desk clock (1966, for Solari). In addition, Gino Valle was one of the first design consultants to create an image for the company as well as for the product.

Valvomo

Founded 1993 **Finland**

The new optimism. In 1997 a couple of unknown designers who had recently set up the Valvomo studio in Finland decided to have their own stand at the Milan Furniture Fair. The positive response they attracted was even more surprising than their bold decision. The impatient heirs of Alvar Aalto exhibited "visionary articles for the age of the computer network." One of the most talked about exhibits was the *Max* computer workstation, an aerodynamic sofa for the Internet surfer. "I want to integrate the vision of the computer era into domestic design," says Ilkka Terho, who created this horizontal browser with Teppo Asikainen. Valvomo now works with companies like Artek, runs an experimental design workshop under the label Snowcrash and has produced classics in record time. Examples are the *Globlow* lamp that blows up automatically when switched on and deflates again when switched off, and the legless chaise longue *Chip*, inspired by a snowboard.

1 *Globlow* light (Asikainen, Nevalainen and Vierros), 1997

2 *Chip* chaise longue (Asikainen and Terho), 1996

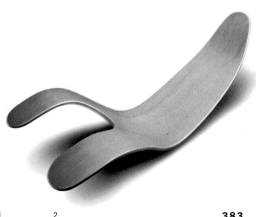

1   2   **383**

Henry van de Velde

1863–1957 **Belgium, Netherlands, Germany and Switzerland**

A European universalist. The Belgian artist, architect and theoretician Henry van de Velde studied in Antwerp and Paris and he was one of those brilliant, polyglot individuals who was a pioneer of design at the end of the nineteenth century, thus making the way clear for modern product design. Henry van de Velde was influenced by William Morris's views on art and craft, and he later became one of the leading representatives of Jugendstil. Before World War I the Grand Duke of Saxony appointed him head of the Weimar school of arts and crafts (the forerunner of the Bauhaus). He was a co-founder of the Deutscher Werkbund, an organization that quickly acquired a good reputation. The ideal of *Gesamtkunstwerk* (the total work of art) led to the need for furniture designed specifically for particular buildings or interior design projects. Henry van de Velde adopted it for the first time in his own house at Uccle, near Brussels (1895), where the chairs with their combination of rustic forms and the easy elegance of the Art Nouveau were in keeping with its very specific style. As well as designing furniture, van de Velde was very busy designing wallpaper, glass and dishes, among other things for the Meissen porcelain factory (1902). He emigrated to Switzerland during World War I, finally settling in Holland and Belgium once peace had come.

Rocking chair, c. 1904

Rudy **Vanderlans** b. 1955 **Netherlands and USA**

In the realm of the digital. In reply to questions about his design philosophy, Rudy Vanderlans's answer is short and to the point: "Effective communication." The Dutchman studied graphic art in The Hague and worked as a graphic artist before moving to the United States. He is founder and art director of a graphic arts studio, and since 1984 he has published the magazine *Emigre* that appears twice a year, the central organ of design on the Apple *Macintosh* (the computer that first came out in the same year). The new typeface developed for the magazine was designed by the Czech graphic artist Zuzanna Licko. The consistent refusal to use the new digital techniques to copy existing conventions has resulted in an avant-garde style and above all in a calculated interaction between page layout and typography whose boundaries become blurred. Vanderlans soon acquired several important clients including Esprit and Apple.

1 *Fact Twenty-Two* poster, 1980
2 *Emigre* magazine, 1998

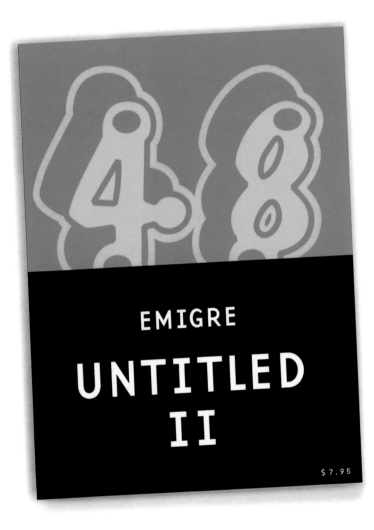

1

Paolo **Venini** 1895–1959 Italy

Dreams of glass. When Paolo Venini founded his glassworks in Murano he was not merely following a Venetian tradition. On the contrary, the academically trained lawyer introduced the concept of modern design in glassblowing that established him as a leading manufacturer of Venetian glass, and he invented new processes for manufacturing colored glass. In contrast to his rivals, his motto for decoration was "less is more," and he surprised his contemporaries with the abstract forms of his vases, lamps and carafes. But he also revived some ancient Venetian glass techniques that were no longer used. From the very beginning, Venini collaborated with internationally famous designers like Gio Ponti, Carlo Scarpa and, later, Gae Aulenti.

Fazzoletto vase, 1957

1   *Queen Anne* chair, 1984
2   *Campidoglio* tray, 1985
3   *Sheraton* chair, 1984

2

Robert **Venturi**

b. 1925 **USA**

"Less is bore." Robert Venturi's critical essays on modern architecture are perhaps even better known than his buildings and designs. His pamphlet *Complexity and Contradiction in Architecture* (1966) and his book *Learning from Las Vegas* (1978) were polemics against the absolutism of modernism (as he put it, "Less is bore"). He argued for a new eclecticism that did not shy away from the everyday iconography of advertising posters and gas stations, and thereby helped lay the foundation of postmodernism. The ideas developed by this successful architect are also reflected in his furniture and products. With these he relishes the purely decorative, the use of elements from pop culture, and an openly irreverent attitude towards the past. Among some of his most famous designs are the *Piazza* coffee and tea set (1983, for Alessi) with classical columns, and his *Queen Anne* chair (1984) made from laminated wood and plastic laminate with a synthetic leather cushion, yet stylistically reminiscent of Art Deco. The example shown is a mixture of a floral tablecloth and motifs from the artist Jasper Johns.

3

1

Gianni **Versace**  1946–97 **Italy**

Prophet of beauty. "Whatever I touch becomes fashion" was Gianni Versace's first commandment, and all his life he succeeded in putting himself and his work in the limelight. Film stars and theater personalities loved Versace's exciting designs with their daring lines, garish colors and gaudy patterns. He was also sought-after as a costume designer for the ballet and cinema. He was not afraid to experiment with unusual fabrics, as for instance with his *Heavy Metal* evening clothes, which were expensive dresses made from the same material as butcher's aprons. Normally, however, Versace's clothes were sensual, feminine, openly erotic and in addition very commercial. He described them as "works of art" that were thought garish by some and praised by others for their excellent workmanship. Versace paid little attention to this. "What is beautiful, good or bad, is for you alone to decide," he told his critics. After studying architecture he worked as a fashion buyer in Paris and London before setting up as an independent fashion designer in the 1970s. In 1978 he opened his own studio in Milan, shocking the traditional Italian fashion industry with his ostentatious lavishness. Since his death, the company has been run by his sister Donatella and his brother Santos.

3

1

1 *Wild Baroque* towel, 1986
2 Spring collection, 1993
3 *Wild Baroque* table light, 1986
4 Spring collection, 1992
5 Autumn collection, 1997
6 *Russian Dream* service, 1998

2

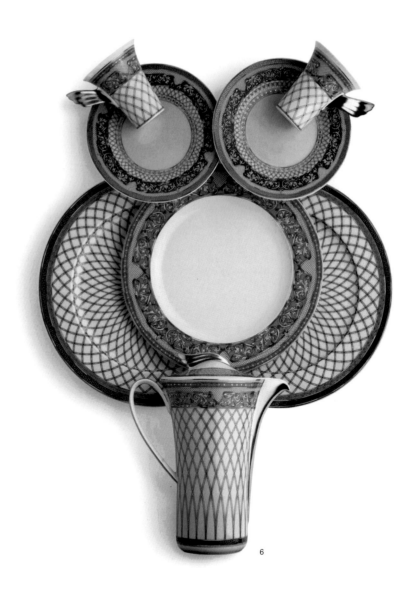

6

Lella **Vignelli,** Massimo **Vignelli** b. 1934 and 1931, **Italy and USA**

Two Italians in America. Industrial design, furniture design, graphic design, exhibition stands, showroom arrangement, corporate identity and direction signs: Massimo and Lella Vignelli are extremely versatile in their talents. There is not much that this gifted husband-and-wife team have not thought of, planned and finally executed. After completing his architectural studies in Milan and Venice, Massimo Vignelli worked for Venini (1954–57). In 1960 he founded his own studio in Milan. Five years later, Massimo and Lella Vignelli, who is also an architect, moved to New York and set up a corporate identity studio, Unimark, with other designers. In 1971 they founded their own studio, Vignelli Associates. The corporate identity they created for Knoll (1972) made them famous in the United States. But the Vignellis have also used their European origins to further their contacts with the old continent: Rosenthal, Poltrona Frau, Morphos and Acerbis, not forgetting the Guggenheim Museum in Bilbao, northern Spain, for which they developed the direction signs.

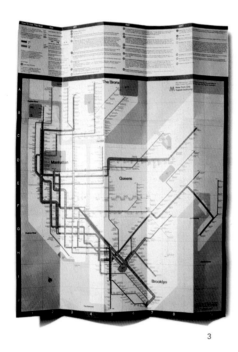

3

390

1

1 *Ciga Silverware* cutlery, 1979
2 *Saratoga* sofa, 1964
3 New York Subway plan, 1970
4 Publicity material, 1984

Arnout **Visser**

b. 1962 **Netherlands**

The school of Archimedes. Most of Arnout Visser's ideas are founded on physical or mechanical laws. For instance, he exploited the fact that oil is lighter than vinegar and that these two liquids do not mix when he designed the *Salad Sunrise* oil and vinegar carafe (1996, for DMD/Droog Design), in which the two substances are not separated by any physical barrier. Visser's other passion is glass with its transparency that allows the observer to see how an object works, like the *Archimedes* letter scales (1996, for Droog Design). He also uses glass to produce spectacular effects such as his faucet (1997, also for Droog Design), with its glass water pipes that light up red (hot) and blue (cold) when water runs through them. Visser studied in Arnhem and Milan, and since 1993 he has been working for the Foundation set up in the early 1990s. Recently he has designed ceramic ware with Erik Jan Kwakkel. In 1997, they surprised visitors to the Milan Furniture Fair with their *Functional Tiles*: tiles with radio, with writing table, with a hole for toilet paper, an opening to hang a hand towel, or acting as a drawer.

1 *Saltglass*, 1995
2 *Four Flower* vase, 1999
3 *Salad Sunrise* oil and vinegar flask, 1996

2

3

1

Burkhard **Vogtherr**

b. 1942 **Germany and France**

1 *Spin* office chair, 1995
2 Armchair, 1995
3 *Spin* office chair range, 1995

Expert in a royal discipline. Burkhard Vogtherr has always concentrated on developing the most comfortable shape for the human anatomy, whether he is designing armchairs, sofas or office chairs. The German designer who lives in Mulhouse, France, specializes in seating furniture, usually considered the greatest challenge in furniture design because it requires the solution of complex spatial problems and physical proportions. After training as a cabinetmaker, Vogtherr studied industrial design first in Kassel and then in Wuppertal. At the age of thirty, he set up as an independent designer. Since then he has been working for leading furniture manufacturers such as Arflex, Cappellini, Cor, Dietiker, Fritz Hansen and Wittmann, just to mention a few names from his list of clients. The understated style of his creations probably plays an important part in their appeal. Vogtherr's designs are based on the interpretation of simple geometric proportions, with special attention paid to comfort and enjoyment.

Wilhelm **Wagenfeld**

1900–90 **Germany**

Max und Moritz are mass-produced.
Wilhelm Wagenfeld was an industrial designer to the core, and one of the best of his generation. He became famous with his white opal glass-shaded table lamps (1924 with Karl J. Jucker, reedition by Tecnolumen) that he designed when he was at the Bauhaus, which resembled miniature street lamps. When Wagenfeld said that the most important quality of an object was "its simplicity," he was referring to useful, inexpensive, everyday objects that are pleasing at the same time. This skilled silversmith designed many such objects from metal and glass, all of which stand out for their excellent quality. In 1923 he went to study at the Bauhaus under László Moholy-Nagy in the metalwork department, of which he later became head. While many Bauhaus artists were forced to leave Germany after 1933, Wagenfeld was able to continue his work, teaching at the Berlin College of Art and elsewhere. Later, when working for the glass manufacturers Jenaer Glaswerke, he experimented with what had always been considered a cheap material, pressed glass. The ovenproof casseroles with lid (1938) became a best-seller, as did the *Kubus* stackable storage ware (1938). After World War II, Wagenfeld repeated his earlier successes, working for companies like Rosenthal and Braun. His butter dish and the *Max und Moritz* salt and pepper shakers (1952, for WMF) may now be found on half the dining tables in Germany.

1

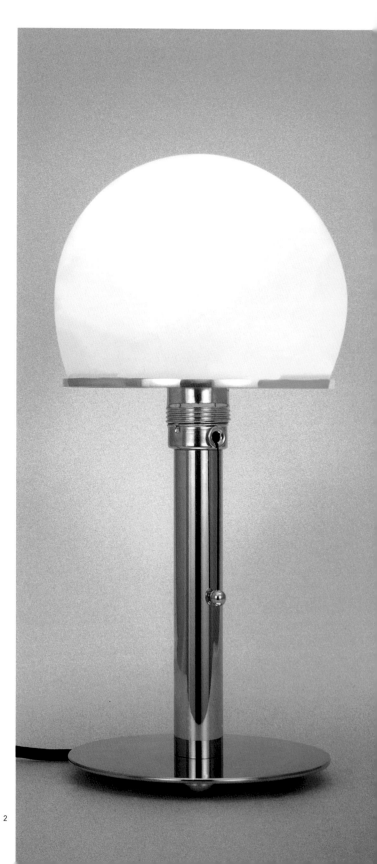

2

3

4

5

1 *Form* cutlery, 1953
2 Table lamp (with Karl J. Jucker), 1924
3 Teapot, 1932
4 *Max und Moritz* salt and pepper shakers, 1952
5 *Kubus* containers, 1938

Otto **Wagner**

1841–1918 **Austria**

Architect of the modern. When the Viennese architect Otto Wagner presented his design for the new Steinhof Church (1907), opinion was divided. The man who had been responsible for the transformation of the Austrian capital into a modern metropolis wanted to express his philosophy of architecture with this design, as he explained: "All modern creations must be appropriate to the new material and satisfy the requirements of the present; it must reflect our own better, democratic, self-conscious self and our clearly thinking being." Today the once-controversial church is considered the most important religious building of the Jugendstil movement. A believer in the synthesis of all the arts, Wagner paid attention to everything from the creation of harmonious proportions to the smallest detail of the acoustics. This resulted in him becoming a trendsetter in many fields. Whether he was designing a bridge, a bank, or a railway station (such as the Vienna Stadtbahn), small details and any furniture or other objects needed were always perfectly integrated into the project as a whole. So it was that at the turn of the century Otto Wagner designed many chairs, lamps, and pieces of silverware that clearly demonstrate his rejection of the prevailing historicism. As a teacher he inspired a whole generation of young architects and designers, including Josef Hoffmann and Joseph Maria Olbrich.

1 *Savings Bank* chair, 1904
2 *Tramway* ceiling light, 1900

2

1

Marcel **Wanders** b. 1963 **Netherlands**

Homemade high-tech. "I feel inspired by anything that is beautiful." Marcel Wanders expresses these words with spontaneity, without worrying about being branded as a plagiarist. According to the young Dutchman, our society lacks respect for the past, yet it is tradition that gives people the feeling of stability and warmth. For that reason, Marcel Wanders creates objects that are surprising yet familiar at the same time. For instance, his *Knotted Chair* (Droog Design, since 1996 from Cappellini) has the traditional chair shape and it uses the ancient craft of knotting, but executed with a material used in astronautics. For Rosenthal he has designed porcelain vases quite unlike anything else. The basic material of his *Foam* vase (1997, Droog Design/Rosenthal) is a natural sponge, which is dipped in liquid porcelain slip before being destroyed when fired in the kiln. All that remains is the filigree structure of the sponge. Marcel Wanders studied at four different art and design schools in Holland and Belgium, and he has attracted international attention through his work for Droog Design. He set up his own studio in 1995. His objects are distinguished by their poetic simplicity, the plain forms of his products conveying a rare combination of basic research, a willingness to take risks, poetry and vision.

2

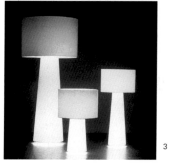
3

1 *Knotted Chair,* 1996
2 *Salt 'e peppa* salt and pepper shakers, 1996
3 *Shadow* table lights, 1998

1

Kem **Weber** 1889–1963 **Germany and USA**

Cubism for the living room. Kem Weber's Bakelite digital clocks (1934, for Lawson) were symbols of a streamlined, accelerating world. One of his best-known furniture designs is the *Airline* chair (1934), a fascinating combination of traditional craftsmanship and the modern mechanical aesthetic. *Airline* has another advantage; it can be packed flat, and it can be assembled using the simplest tools. Its design reflected a principle that clearly pointed to the future. Unlike his tubular steel furniture, *Airline* is still made by hand today. Born in Germany, Kem Weber studied at the Berlin Academy of Art and started his career as a cabinetmaker. He arrived in San Francisco in 1914 in order to organize Germany's participation in the Panama-Pacific Exhibition. With the outbreak of war he had to remain in the United States and look for work. His first job was as an interior designer in Los Angeles. He was one of the immigrants who brought European trends to America, for instance Art Deco, which he introduced to the general public and popularized by organizing exhibitions in department stores.

Airline table and chair, 1934

Josiah **Wedgwood** 1730–95 **Great Britain**

Cradle of design. By the end of the eighteenth century Wedgwood's reputation had already traveled as far as Russia, and Empress Catherine II ordered a dinner service of nearly a thousand pieces. Josiah Wedgwood was technically innovative: he developed creamware (Queen's ware), and black basalt Jasperware, a fine, unglazed fired stoneware, which he coloured in a variety of shades to provide an effective background for white reliefs. His classical designs appealed to the taste of his more prosperous customers, to whom he usually sold by catalog. Wedgwood employed artists who created prototype "models" that were then used as a basis for the development of new production lines, an early form of industrial design. In the 1930s Josiah Wedgwood V added modern tableware with simple designs to the range, including some based on designs by Keith Murray. After surviving some difficult times, the company has recently expanded and taken over the German maker Rosenthal.

1   *Portland* vase, 1789
2   Coffee set (Robert Minkin for Wedgwood), 1979
3   Vase (Keith Murray for Wedgwood), 1933

Daniel **Weil** b. 1953 **Argentina and Great Britain**

Transparent technique. Born in Buenos Aires, the architect Daniel Weil remained in London after his design studies, encouraged by the success of his range of "naked" watches, lamps and radios that made him internationally famous. Weil is fascinated much more by the technical aspects of these pieces of equipment than the casing in which they are housed. The best example of his design philosophy in the 1980s is the witty *Bag Radio*, whose case consists of clear PVC bag (1981, for Apex Inc). Together with the designer Gerard Taylor he has gone on to work for clients as varied as Alessi, Esprit, Knoll, and Great Britain's National Coal Board, always remaining faithful to his philosophy of questioning and reviewing traditional, existing concepts. Daniel Weil has since became professor of industrial design at the Royal College of Art in London and a partner at Pentagram, an internationally famous design and consultancy agency.

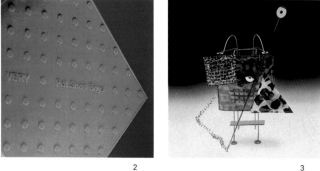

2

3

4

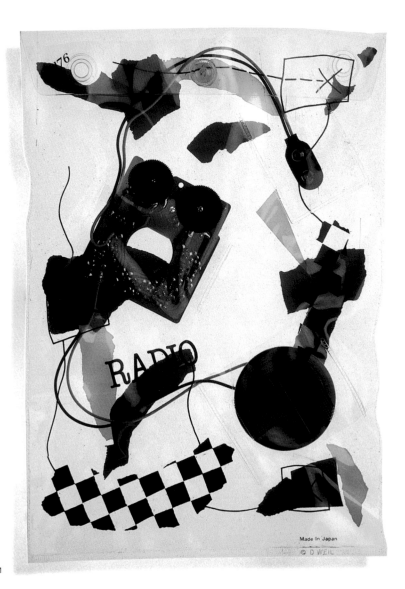

1

1 *Bag* radio, 1981
2 *Very Pet Shop Boys* album cover, 1994
3 *Cambalache*, 1982
4 Logo, c. 1985

Vivienne **Westwood** b. 1941 **Great Britain**

The Madonna of the punks. When Vivienne Westwood was awarded the OBE (Order of the British Empire) by the Queen she probably wore no panties under her tweed skirt. Her perfume *Boudoir* which she launched in 1998 smelled of "grass, bird's nests and dirty things like sex," as she said herself before the product was launched. These shocking statements are part of the image of the fashion queen whose motto is "Shock 'til you drop," a maxim to which she remained true for decades. Westwood's career began in 1970 selling printed pornographic T-shirts in the King's Road. A little later, as the Muse of the founder of the Sex Pistols, Malcolm MacLaren, she caused something of a stir with the far-out, tattered clothes she designed for the band. This simultaneously marked the birth of punk fashion and Westwood's meteoric rise and reputation as one of the most vociferous figures in the world of fashion. Her creations included a classic outfit with a long skirt at the front and hot pants at the back. Westwood herself says of her designs, "Fashion needs irony. My clothes always make me laugh."

1 Collection, 1993
2 Collection, 1999

1

2

403

Stefan **Wewerka** b. 1928 **Germany**

Environments with a deeper meaning. The conceptualist artist Stefan Wewerka claims that "one must be crooked to go straight," and the objects found in his studio include chairs without seats, crooked chairs, chairs that disappear into the wall, chairs that only consist of one half, only becoming whole again when reflected in the mirror, and parts of chairs where one part leans upon another, looking for support. This architect from Magdeburg later became an action painter, a designer, a jeweler, and a filmmaker. He began his career by building a youth hostel (1954) and he went on to develop unusual ideas for a so-called "earth-architecture." In the 1970s he was associated with the extreme avant-garde Fluxus movement that centered on Wolf Vostell, but suddenly he showed interest in industrially produced furniture and interior design. Creations like the *Einschwinger* chair (1982, for Tecta), consisting of a tube 10 feet 6 inches (3.20 m) long bent into a chair, or the multi-swiveling *Küchenbaum* all-in-one cooking unit (1984, for Tecta) are as sculptural as they are practical and they demonstrate Wewerka's own conceptual versatility that enables him to compress a maximum of function into a minimum of space.

1 *Einschwinger* chair, 1982
2 *Anlehnung* chair sculpture, 1974

1

2

Why Not

Founded 1987 **Great Britain**

Possible and impossible. Nurtured by the creative force fields of street style, the advertising industry and pop music, Why Not is a typical flower of the British culture. But in this case the stimulus came from outside. Andrew Altman, David Ellis and Howard Greenhalgh were inspired by the works of the Dutchman Gert Dumbar, who was a professor at the Royal College of Art for a short time in the mid-1980s. The group formed a studio with the descriptive name Why Not. From the beginning the intention was that, without affecting visual clarity, they should as far as possible ignore all the traditional rules of design. The trio was particularly good at making use of the opportunities offered by the Mac computer, whether for advertising campaigns, image brochures, posters or unusual books. With it they could create collage-like combinations of different typefaces, if necessary distorted or superimposed one on top of another, thus creating a completely new typographic universe.

1 Cover, 1996
2 Book, 1997

Tapio **Wirkkala**

1915–85 **Finland**

The nature man. He was the most productive of all the Finnish designers, but he spent most of his life in the woods rather than at the drawing board. The long-bearded nature-lover tackled almost every material, whether wood, metal, stone, ceramic, lights, glass, or paper. The combination of organic forms inspired by nature with traditional craftsmanship became the trademark of Wirkkala's work. He started his career working for the Finnish glass manufacturer Iittala where in 1946 he designed the *Kantarelli* mushroom vase in whose skin-thin glass very fine lines have been cut. His real breakthrough came in the 1950s with his blue *Tapio* glass goblets. He achieved international fame with the flat plywood shell that embellished the Finnish pavilion at the Milan Triennale. He designed a typical men's tool, the *Puukko* knife for the man in the wild that is still manu-factured today by the Hackman company.

3

1

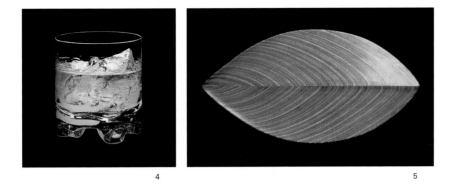

4

5

1 *Kantarelli* vase, 1946
2 *Puukko* knife, 1961
3 *Kantarelli* vase, 1946
4 *Gassia* glass, 1973
5 Plywood leaf, 1951

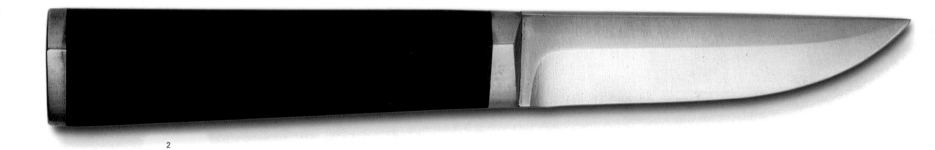

2

Frank Lloyd **Wright**

1867–1959 **USA**

Genius, the whole and the individual. Frank Lloyd Wright was undoubtedly the most important American architect of the twentieth century; he had an unrivaled grasp of the overall appearance of a building in its setting and also of the creation of a building and its contents as a total work of art, down to the smallest detail. As a child he knew he wanted to be an architect, and after his studies he worked in the offices of Louis Sullivan. The defining characteristics of Wright's furniture designs are their simplicity and geometrical forms, thus fitting in with the machine aesthetic of the time, although in practice very few pieces were produced in quantity. He integrated his furniture with the building as closely as possible, where necessary having the freestanding furniture specially made by small sub-contractors so that he could keep control. Many of his most celebrated pieces date from the turn of the century when he built a series of private houses in and around Chicago, such as the oak chairs (1900) that he designed for a dining room, whose tall, narrow, mobile backs provided a rhythmic pattern in the room. His Imperial Hotel in Tokyo was a total work of art, filled with his furniture, lamps, dishes, cutlery and carpets. Among his best-known furniture is the desk (1936) for the Johnson's Wax offices in Racine, Wisconsin. The warm red panel that fills the framework of aluminum tube harmonizes perfectly with the color of the walnut wood. The three-legged chair and the brilliant construction of the desk with its work areas arranged freely above each other are quintessential Wright.

1

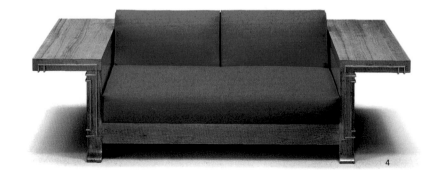

4

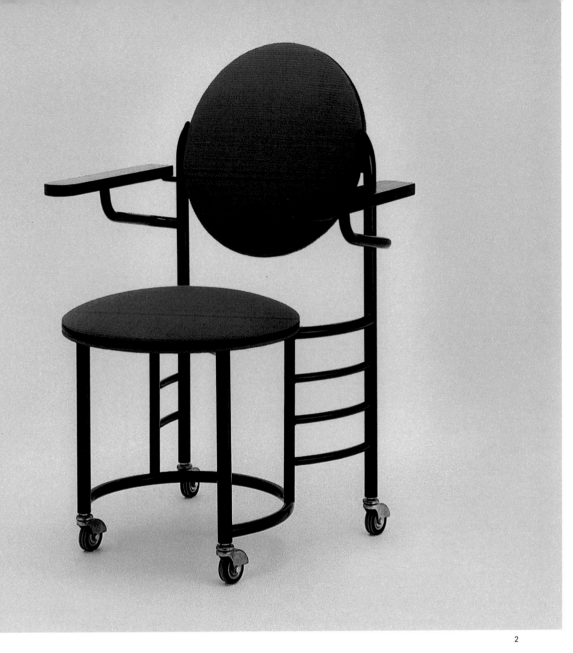

1 *Midway* chair, 1914
2 *Johnson Wax* chair, 1936
3 Table, 1908
4 *Robie* sofa, 1906
5 *Taliesin* table, 1925

3

2

5

Russel **Wright** 1904–76 **USA**

The million figure. As the promoter of Bauhaus ideas in America and one of the most successful product designers of the country, Russel Wright began by designing modern pianos, radios and furniture to suit the postwar budget of middle-class Americans, for whom imports were too expensive. The artist and stage designer then became famous as "Mr American Modern," the designer of the most widely sold tableware in the world. Because Wright preferred eating from plain, undecorated plates, he created the pioneeringly unconventional service *American Modern* in 1937. Manufacturers thought that the asymmetric shapes and unusual colors were too radical, so Wright was forced to finance the production himself. By the end of the 1950s over eight million pieces had been sold (today the figure is nearer 350 million), and there are nearly 100 imitations. *Fortune* magazine lists *American Modern* among the 100 best-selling design products of all time. Wright was enthusiastic about the synthetic thermoplastic melamine, which he used for his plastic tableware designs *Meladur* (1945) and *Residential* (1953). He collaborated with Raymond F. Loewy, Walter Dorwin Teague and Gilbert Rhode in the "American Way" interior design concept that coordinated color, form and material.

American Modern service, 1937

Yohji **Yamamoto** b. 1943 **Japan and France**

"I make clothes." Yohji Yamamoto is the head of business empire with a turnover of over $100 million. His collections have achieved cult status and are often seen on the Paris catwalk. Yet he is a quiet star who explained his approach to his work in an interview as follows: "I am not a fashion designer. I make clothes." Yamamoto sees himself as a craftsman in the traditional Japanese sense, one who first examines the materials with care before using them for the purpose he intends. But that is not the only reason why this cosmopolitan artist is considered a revolutionary among fashion designers. His designs do not reflect the ephemeral trends of fashion or the usual throw-away attitude of today. He only studied design after reading law, but by 1972 when he returned to Tokyo after a two-year stay in Paris he was designing inexpensive, easy-to-wear fashion for professional women—unlike the haute couture designers. Although he occasionally comes up with sumptuous creations, he has remained faithful to this philosophy. "Ready-to-wear clothing that everyone can buy," says Yamamoto, "is clothing that does not fit anyone perfectly. This creates the personal note."

1 Autumn collection, 1995   **2** Spring collection, 1997

Marco **Zanuso**

b. 1916 **Italy**

The embodiment of industrial design. Marco Zanuso is one of the pioneers of Italian industrial design. After World War II he was driven by intellectual curiosity and the desire to experiment, introducing international design movements to Italy where he was to make them popular among the public at large. As well as being an architect and interior designer he was also editor-in-chief of the magazine *Domus* (1946–47), editor of *Casabella* (1947–49), and co-founder and chairman of the Italian Design Association ADI (1956–59 and 1966–74). Between 1958 and 1977 while working with Richard Sapper he developed designs that permanently changed the appearance of many objects. For instance, in the *Grillo* telephone (1966, for Auso Siemens) the earpiece, mouthpiece and dial were incorporated into a single unit. Equally amazing was the little *Algol* portable television (1964 for Brionvega), and one of the first chairs made from synthetic material, a children's model *K 4999* (1964, for Kartell). Marco Zanuso worked for Italian companies in particular such as Arflex, B&B, Gavina, Olivetti, Poltrona Frau, Unifor and Kartell. Later, he concentrated more on town planning and architecture, being commissioned by companies such as Olivetti and IBM in Brazil and Argentina as well as in his homeland.

3

1

414

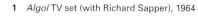

1 *Algol* TV set (with Richard Sapper), 1964
2 *Marcuso* table, 1969
3 *Grillo* telephone (with Richard Sapper), 1966
4 *Lady* armchair, 1951
5 *Martingala* armchair, 1960
6 *Celestina* chair, 1978
7 *Fourline* chair, 1967

4

5

6

7

Disegno, Dessin, Design

The *Zigzag* chair designed by Gerrit Rietveld. The *Savoy* vase designed by Alvar Aalto. The *Volkswagen* by Ferdinand Porsche. The *Grand Confort* armchair by Le Corbusier. The *Arco* standard lamp by Achille Castiglioni. The *little black dress* by Coco Chanel. "Design classics" are usually closely linked to the personality who has created them. They embody their creator's "philosophy" and individuality.

All these famous names have long been part of the pantheon of designers—but none of them would have described themselves as designers during their lifetime. They were artists, cabinetmakers, technicians, constructors, couturiers, architects and so on. Had they heard of it at all, the term "design" would have been a foreign word to them. The term which is today such a common concept became part of the international vocabulary in the second half of the twentieth century. Nonetheless, in spite of its American roots, the history of design is not exclusively American, and many countries have contributed to the development of the concept. However, America can justly claim to have invented the profession of "designer."

Disegno, Dessin, Design

Machines and myths

In the United States, the late nineteenth century heralded the beginning of a super-capitalism that not only introduced the culture of consumption but also revolutionized consumption itself. The car industry, the backbone of the new American affluent society, was the forerunner of this new culture. In 1926 General Motors created a department for "Art and Color." Turnover was increased by introducing new models more frequently, models distinguished from their predecessors by new "styling." Manufacturers in other fields, such as camera manufacturer Kodak, followed suit.

So it was that at the end of the 1920s New York saw the opening of a new kind of business whose nameplate displayed a hitherto unknown combination of words: "industrial designer." The names of Henry Dreyfuss, Norman Bel Geddes, Raymond F. Loewy, Walter Dorwin Teague and Russel Wright, who were the first heroes of the new profession, were widely known. Their backgrounds were surprisingly similar. Teague and Geddes came from advertising, as did Loewy, who had studied technology but worked as a layout artist. Dreyfuss, Geddes and Wright (who knew each other personally) had worked as stage designers on Broadway. America's first designers were "commercial artists," and so were skilled craftsmen with visual convictions.

When the consumer paradise was suddenly destroyed by the Great Depression that hit the West in the early 1930s, hopes for recovery were pinned on self-made designers such as Raymond Loewy, a virtuoso of publicity and already a cult figure in his own lifetime. He convinced America that he could turn around whole industries, and his miracle cure was streamlining. Whether they were radios, vacuum cleaners or locomotives, all kinds of products were housed in smoothly formed casings. Loewy designed a streamlined refrigerator for the chain store Sears and sales doubled in the course of a year. The master of elegant streamlining had taken an angular, cupboard-shaped object with visible hinges and long, thin legs, and converted it into a smooth white block. Loewy's much-copied monolith was quick and easy to manufacture because of its

reduced number of parts. It became an icon of the American way of life, reflecting the triumph of machines over time and space, as the car had done.

In its early days, industrial design combined commercially motivated pragmatism with a highly developed talent for theatricality. It came to affect almost the entire inventory of consumer society, creating many legendary artifacts, and after 1945 its influence spread to Europe and Japan. In 1950, on returning from a trip to America during which he met the country's design elite, the Swede Sigvard Bernadotte set up an industrial design office in Sweden, the first enterprise to be named outside America. Two years later, the French-born Loewy set up an industrial design office in Paris. However, he did not want to use the American term in his own

2

country and he called his firm *Compagnie de l'Esthétique Industrielle* ("Company for the Industrial Aesthetic").

Opposing worlds

The concept of design was also reimported to Great Britain, the country it had originally come from. In English the word *design* (derived from the French *dessin*, which is itself derived from the Italian *disegno*) has a wide range of related meanings, such as *idea*, *sketch*, *outline*, *pattern*, *diagram* and *drawing*. It refers not only to the construction of a product in a technical sense, but also to its decoration. Thus the word *design* can refer to the development which preceded the product or to the product resulting from this development. As if this

were not confusing enough, the versatile abstract word has acquired many other meanings in the course of its history.

It is well known that the first factories were built in England, that it was the first country with capitalists and a proletariat. It was also the country that produced the first designers, and they too were the product of steam and iron. Already in the early phases of industrialization, manufacturers entrusted the design (meaning the appearance) of their products to specialists. In 1840, some 500 such draftsmen were employed in Manchester, the center of the textile industry. Artists were commissioned to perform this preliminary work because it required drawing skills and dealt with matters of style. Thus the emergence of the designer was a result of the division of labor. The key to understanding the designer's position in the company lies in that fact. Because the designer's professional emancipation was a consequence of the factory system, it also meant that the work of design was originally quite separate from the rest of the manufacturing process: the designer was not involved in production and could not make any decisions on that subject. The history of design reflects the contradiction arising from the abstract nature of the designer's work and the tangible impact of the final product. The designer is a hybrid, living in contradictory worlds. England is an excellent example of this, being a country where art and industry developed from directions that were also geographically opposed. The artists studying at the Royal Academy in London belonged to the aristocratic gentlemen's culture of the South. In contrast, the newly rich manufacturers of the industrial North represented the unpleasant face of a world dominated by money.

One of the first businessmen to take the advice of the new experts was the English china manufacturer Josiah Wedgwood. His company became famous for its innovative production and management methods. He exhibited his products in "showrooms" and used catalogs to sell his wares. At the end of the eighteenth century, Wedgwood employed several artists, including the renowned sculptor and connoisseur of antiquity John Flaxman.

It was the use of Neo-Classical elements from painting and architecture on vases and tableware that made Wedgwood famous all over the world. The reference to the supposedly eternal value of ancient art satisfied the yearning for permanence at a time when nothing remained as it was. Wedgwood was responsible for introducing the very first "design classics" to the market.

But Wedgwood was the exception. On the whole it was the deficiencies of existing designs that led to the encouragement of a sense of art as a means of improving them. The *Journal of Design*, the first magazine to include the word "design" in its title, began publication in London in the mid-nineteenth century. Henry Cole, its energetic publisher, used the magazine to express his disapproval of the "lapse of taste in modern design." Industry had raised production levels to figures counted in millions, but it had also created an "anything goes" mentality, with an indiscriminate use of period styles and a strong liking for ornamentation. Machinery was British, but fashion and taste came from France, where armchairs were decorated like ladies' hats and where—since the Empire design—and decoration had developed into an art. The bourgeois drawing room was like a theatrical stage set.

It was then that design critic Henry Cole had the idea of creating a vast exhibition in which the products of all countries could be compared. This idea was welcomed by Prince Albert, Queen Victoria's art-loving husband, and it resulted in the Great Exhibition of 1851. (Its profits led in turn to the foundation of the Victoria and Albert Museum, the archetype of all design museums.)

In reality, this first experiment in reforming design from above was not particularly successful in its intended purpose. Like many professional visitors to the Great Exhibition, the German-born architect Gottfried Semper was disappointed by the majority of the exhibits. He summed up his thoughts in his "practical aesthetic" in which he predicted a "new art" that would accept the rules of mechanization, and which would be based on "pure forms." This fundamental approach to design was so prophetic that most of his contemporaries were dumbfounded by it.

Rebellion of the Romantic artist

Richard Sapper has said that "having an idea is something that cannot be learnt anywhere," and he certainly knows what he is talking about. Giorgio Vasari, the father of art history, believed that it was *disegno*—the instinctive creative approach—that distinguished the artist from the craftsman. He held that an artist had just this single extra skill, that of inspiration, which he called *disegno;* and after several linguistic geographical detours this has become the word "designer." Vasari's distinction corresponded to a hierarchy that penalized the association with the profane and practical by downgrading it, so that the creation of everyday objects was seen as a lesser calling. But the situation

3

is actually more complicated: historically, there is no doubt that a close relationship exists between designer and artist. There have always been "border crossings" in both directions; today, an excellent example is found in the complex work of Alessandro Mendini. There have also been many attempts to enhance the reputation of the designer. In 1995, an exhibition of chairs created by famous designers was entitled "100 Masterpieces," as if the exhibits were works of art rather than everyday objects.

In fact, the designer clearly straddles the dividing line drawn by Vasari. This unclear position has resulted in a wide range of "compound disciplines," such as applied arts, decorative art, arts and crafts, commercial art and industrial art, terms that all

clearly express their intermediate status. Similar terms are used in other languages, and from this overlapping of meanings it follows that attempts at defining the differences between the various disciplines would not be particularly instructive. The reason why the Konstslöjdmuseet in Gothenberg, the Museum für Angewandte Kunst in Cologne, the Kunstindustrimuseum in Copenhagen, and the Musée des Arts Décoratifs in Paris are called by these almost identical names can only be explained by their history.

The designer's ambiguous intermediate position has given rise to many debates and identity crises, and it has also contributed to the fact that the profession of designer has taken such a long time to become established academically. (In this and other aspects, it is very much like psychology.) But what does it actually mean that a country like Italy, which boasts so many excellent designers, did not offer any professional training until quite recently? Is it not possible that one of the greatest strengths of design lies in this very openness? The position of design as a platform for cross-fertilization between disciplines is invaluable, as is apparent from the range of fascinating personalities who are designers and their unusual biographies.

The trend towards unorthodoxy

This tendency began—again in Britain—in the second half of the nineteenth century. A group of artists gathered around the versatile artist William Morris, a self-taught man who produced amazing designs in many fields. He was involved in painting, writing, poetry, cabinetmaking, tapestry weaving and embroidery. Later he also became a printer, and the handmade books he designed, and produced in very small editions, were reminiscent of medieval manuscripts. Morris was an early socialist and a passionate opponent of existing conditions. He saw machinery as the main cause for all the evils of his day. His ideal was the preindustrial society in which life and work were still interwoven, as they had been in the European Middle Ages. Named the Arts and Crafts movement after one of its exhibitions, it soon became firmly established, with the creation of "Guilds" and artists' colonies. Morris sold much of his work but to his disappointment it had to be priced at a level that only the well-off could afford. However, his theory of alienation caused by industry unleashed a Romantic rebellion and (like Karl Marx) his anticapitalist vision spread internationally. *The Studio*, the mouthpiece of the movement, became compulsory reading in Europe and the United States for all artists weary of industrial civilization.

The Arts and Crafts movement sought to re-instate the lost unity of mental and physical work, and to remove Vasari's fatal distinction between fine arts and applied arts. In reality this proved impossible and the situation was in fact made even more complicated by the creation of this new intermediate category, Arts and Crafts. But it set in motion the search for the authentic, true values that were to be found in simple, rural settings. Craft methods were revived throughout Europe, frequently inspired by strong national feelings. Museums of Arts and Crafts were created, to which schools were often attached, thus providing training in design. The results of the British reform initiative were the rehabilitation and transfiguration of craftsmanship, and a climate favoring the alteration of dominant conventions. These were excellent conditions for a new generation of designers who were truly innovative. This included designers such as Josef Hoffmann, Charles Rennie Mackintosh, Henry van de Velde, Frank Lloyd Wright, and—last but not least—Paul Poiret, the first avant-garde fashion designer. However, like the Arts and Crafts movement, their work still failed to confront the problem of industry.

The triumph of good design

The Bauhaus would be "a new brotherhood of craftsmen without the class division that seeks to construct a haughty wall between craftsmen and artists." This noble aim comes from the manifesto drawn up by Walter Gropius for the Bauhaus, a document that still reflected the spirit of the Arts and Crafts movement as well as the revolutionary passion of the postwar years. But the initial dismantling of walls was no easy task. Artists like Johannes Itten left the project when the pragmatic Walter Gropius showed concern for the interests of

outside customers, for instance, in an order for chairs placed by a municipal theater. According to the renegade artist, this restricted artistic freedom in a way that was completely unacceptable.

Walter Gropius succeeded in giving the project an international angle by attracting talented artists such as Hungarian László Moholy-Nagy and Austrian Herbert Bayer. Holland also contributed to the project through the artists' movement De Stijl, which had already introduced constructivist ideas into architecture. When the group's chief theorist Theo van Doesburg was guest lecturer at the Bauhaus, speaking on the subject of the "Fundamental concepts of a new radical design," the spark ignited. Marcel Breuer was inspired by the furniture of his Dutch colleague Gerrit Rietveld to

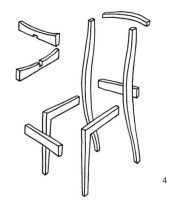

4

produce similar spatial constructions. People now spoke of "industrial form-giving," a combination of words that deliberately distanced itself from commercial or applied art and corresponded to the Dutch term "Vorm geving." The fact that the Bauhaus developed into a kind of laboratory for experimentation with form played a fundamental part in this development. It became more generally accepted that industrial production (as was also encouraged by the Deutsche Werkbund) and minimalism of form (as had been predicted by Gottfried Semper) should be welcomed. This led to an attempt to develop universally valid forms for everyday objects through reduction and rejection of decoration. In some cases this was evidently successful, leading to a large number of modern

"classics," such as the "Bauhaus light" by Wilhelm Wagenfeld. But in the long term the attempt was bound to fail because the supremacy of pure form was ultimately defeated by changing tastes. Nor could abstraction meet the difficult challenge of the last great objectives, the overturning of Vasari's verdict on the lesser status of the craftsman, and the ending of the division between designer and maker in modern industry. The close links that appeared to exist with industry were in practice quite fortuitous. The largest client, the carpet manufacturer Rasch, came into contact with the Bauhaus only because the owner's daughter happened to study there.

But progress was made and it had a name: functionalism. Modern industrial design developed on both sides of the Atlantic, but from opposite directions. The Bauhaus was the academic counterpart of pragmatic American design. It is quite understandable that the word "functionalism" was only learned from the Bauhaus designers when they moved in droves to the United States.

It was after World War II that the longest-lived "ism" in the history of design reached the general public. The key year was 1954, when the Design in Scandinavia exhibition opened. The idea was the brainchild of the editor-in-chief of *House Beautiful*, the interior decorating magazine and America's leading propagator of good taste. It was probably the most successful design campaign of all time, leading to a further series of exhibitions on the same theme. These traveled the country so that no significant region of it was left out. Until then artists such as Arne Jacobsen, Bruno Mathsson, and their colleagues would never have thought of calling themselves designers; they saw themselves as architects, artists or craftsmen. It was only when the label "Scandinavian design" was invented that these suddenly much sought-after Scandinavians became "designers," and the other, older definitions slowly disappeared.

The Scandinavian craftsmanship that was the subject of the exhibition incorporated qualities which in America became synonymous with "good design." When the Museum of Modern Art began to popularize this concept, the definitive "classic" style of functionalism that had originated in

Scandinavia spread to the best living rooms everywhere. The new terminology was used in countries that had discovered the trading advantages of exporting beautiful, expensive objects to the United States. For instance, in Denmark, people spoke of "Danish Design" and in Italy of *bel disegno*. "Design" in the sense it is used today was introduced in the 1950s. It reflected the trend towards international marketing, as well as the policy of enlightened "good design" that is now vigorously pursued by the design councils founded in many countries after the American example. The slogan of the Design Council of the USA emphasizes the twin points: "Good design and good business."

In the realm of freedom

When the Memphis group first introduced their angular, slanting objects in 1981, the public was at first amazed, but then reacted as if it had long been expecting this kind of audacious design. It is true that there were some angry critics at first, but in the end a consensus was reached. Like punk in pop music, Memphis swept away the established yet worn-out verities of the history of design like a thunderstorm clearing the atmosphere. The assumption that functional design was here forever was finally eradicated. The desire for superficiality and a restrained eclecticism emerged once more. Although ultimately it was about the "great design swindle," Memphis also marked a turning point that had been expected for some time. It had been hinted at by the plastic pop designs of the 1960s, with works by artists such as Gaetano Pesce. He was a renegade who revived the pleasure principle but in particular espoused the protest movement of "radical design," which degraded the ideology of functionalism and "good design." Although it looked like it at the time, this was neither the end of capitalism nor of design. On the contrary, the liberal decade of the 1960s was very favorable to design. Nonconformism and pop culture created the right conditions for a completely new dimension: consumption linked to lifestyle, a situation that developed with the leisure and disco culture of the 1970s, and which continued in the post-Memphis

era. Design became synonymous with lifestyle, and the designer became the ideal profession of the pop-video generation. At the same time, advertisers developed the idea of promoting design as a cult and selling that "philosophy," a phenomenon perfectly symbolized by Philippe Starck. The new jargon now distinguishes between everyday products and "designer objects," as if products without labels had not been designed. Design became a fetish, both as a concept and as an object, especially when it was Italian. This is clearly demonstrated by Alessi, the makers of household goods who in the 1980s became *the* design company. What has made Italy the leading design nation in the world is the abundance of creative artists and their close links with enterprising

5

businessmen, exemplified by Alberto Alessi with Memphis, and Ernesto Gismondi, the head of Artemide. Alessi explains that "a designer must have taste, but he must also be able to break the rules that we will try and impose upon him in our capacity as industrial partner."

In the topsy-turvy world of the late twentieth century, the concept of avant-garde has become an economic principle. A country where this is government policy is Great Britain. In the 1980s, it was decided to nominate "creative industry" as a new driving force in the economy. It is true that the contribution of British design to the gross national product is marginal. Nonetheless there is a flourishing export of trends, for instance in fashion by rebel designer Vivienne Westwood, and in

furniture design with the new sobriety introduced by Jasper Morrison.

London is the pop capital where underground movements, media and markets have long lived in happy symbiosis and the road from street style to superstore has never been so short. Thus it is also a center of communication design. Truths are not proclaimed. Here professional piracy of style has been perfected to a fine art. Another example of a successful export is the "designer-maker." These are individuals with bohemian tendencies who create one-off pieces by hand, often producing remarkable objects. Such a designer is the furniture maker Ron Arad, whose dislike of industry was notorious until he succeeded in giving it an innovative push. In view of such alliances, it appears that on the eve of the

next millennium, the words of Josef Frank, the forefather of all postmodernists dating back to the time of the Bauhaus, turn out to be true: "The style we use is unimportant. What the modern movement has given us is freedom."

Bernd Polster

1 Porsche *356 Speedster*, Ferdinand A. Porsche, 1958
2 *Dadada* stool, Philippe Starck, 1993
3 *Savoy* vase, Alvar Aalto, 1936
4 Ply chair (sketch), Jasper Morrison, 1989
5 Book: *The End of Print*, David Carson, 1995

Before the fusion of art and industry. The design and social reformer **William Morris** proclaimed the virtues of **Arts and Crafts**, that were eagerly appreciated throughout the world. Everywhere artists sought to emulate the British example, often with innovative results. Historicism was replaced by **Art Nouveau (Jugendstil)** at about the turn of the century. It was a period notable for strong artistic personalities such as **Antoni Gaudí, Charles Rennie Mackintosh, Henry van de Velde, Otto Wagner,** and **Frank Lloyd Wright**, who all created an impressive "Gesamtkunstwerk" ("complete works of art"), designing both setting and contents. **Peter Behrens**, co-founder of the Deutsche Werkbund, promoted the connection between art and industrial machinery. His lamps and fans for AEG were among the earliest and best-designed industrial artifacts. The slogan of the time was "Beautiful everyday objects for everyone!"

The Paris Universal Exposition includes arts, crafts, and industry, with **Eliel Saarinen**'s Finnish Pavilion, works by **René Lalique**, and the Art Nouveau pavilion of the industrialist Siegfried Bing.

Antoní Gaudí designs the Casa Calvet.

Secessionist exhibition held in Vienna.

Ferdinand Zeppelin's first airship, *LZ1*.

Henry van de Velde designs pieces for the Meissen porcelain factory.

The International Exhibition of Arts and Crafts held in Turin marks the climax of the Liberty style (Jugendstil). It includes furniture by **Carlo Bugatti** and **Charles Rennie Mackintosh**.

Arts and Crafts designer C. R. Ashbee founds the Guild of Handicraft

Louis Comfort Tiffany takes control of his family company.

The silversmith **Georg Jensen** opens a shop in Copenhagen. (1)

The English House by Herman Muthesius is published.

Paul Poiret frees women from the corset.

Wiener Werkstätte shows geometrical cutlery at the "Table Settings" exhibition.

Otto Wagner's Post Office savings bank, Vienna. (2)

Sitzmaschine by **Josef Hoffmann**. (4)

Mass transportation begins with the *Model T* Ford.

Start of the "Round the World" automobile race in New York.

Cellophane transparent film appears on the market.

1900 | 1901 | 1902 | 1903 | 1904 | 1905 | 1906 | 1907 | 1908 | 1909

Frank Lloyd Wright publishes his manifesto *The Art and Craft of the Machine*.

Inspired by **William Morris**, the Swedish artists Carl and Karin Larsson create an idealized style of life in the country.

The London furniture company Heals sells pieces in the Arts and Crafts style.

Wiener Werkstätte founded.

Margarethe Steiff makes the first Teddy bear.

In Chicago the twelve-storey Schlesinger and Meyer department store by Louis Sullivan is a prototype of modern design.

Richard Riemerschmid's machine furniture.

In New York Elsie de Wolfe offers an interior design service.

First streamlined train in France.

Albert Einstein's *General Theory of Relativity*.

The Deutsche Werkbund is founded to encourage a policy of design in industry.

Peter Behrens designs modern products such as electric kettles and fans for AEG, as well as carrying out the first overall "Corporate Identity" program. (3)

The electric toaster is invented in the USA.

Publication of the Futurist manifesto.

Herman Hollerith invents the punched card tabulator.

Movie production begins in California.

The world is reconstructed. Trailblazing design ideas emerged from the studios of **avant-garde** artists and architects. In Paris, the capital of the avant-garde, Cubist paintings were first exhibited, and the fashion rebel **Paul Poiret** produced designs inspired by children's art. While Europe disintegrated in the inferno of World War I, capitalism developed rapidly in America. As a result of the war, traditional conventions went to the wind and new radical movements were built on the ruins of the old order. Among these were **De Stijl**, the group of Dutch artists that included the cabinetmaker and architect **Gerrit Rietveld**, and the **Wkhutemas schools** in revolutionary Russia where artists like **El Lissitzky** and **Alexander Rodtschenko** were seeking to create a better world. The most successful of these experiments was the **Bauhaus**, a meeting point of international innovation and a laboratory for creations in which form rigidly followed function.

Richard Riemerschmid exhibits at the Autumn Salon in Paris.

Architectual scandal in Vienna triggered by the modernist **Adolf Loos**, who considers decoration a crime. (1)

Werkbund Exhibition with more than one thousand exhibits tours the United States.

Franklin Gothic typeface by **Morris Fuller Benton**. (3)

Sinking of the *Titanic*.

First heat-resistant dishes of Pyrex glass.

Deutsche Werkbund Exhibition in Cologne: argument between Hermann Muthesius and **Henry van de Velde** on the question of the standardization.

American Institute of Graphic Arts set up.

Outbreak of World War I.

The Dadaist Manifesto is published in Zurich.

British troops use the tank.

Development of an artificial hand for amputated soldiers.

Gerrit Rietveld's *Red-Blue* chair is a prototype of constructivist furniture. (2)

Revolution in Germany at the end of World War I.

1910 1911 1912 1913 1914 1915 1916 1917 1918 1919

Josef Hoffmann completes the Palais Stoclet in Brussels.

First Cubist exhibition in Paris.

Fagus factory in Berlin designed by **Walter Gropius** and Adolf Meyer.

Eileen Gray exhibits lacquer furniture in Paris.

In Prague Jodef Gocár designs a Cubist sofa.

Prototype of the *Leica* miniature camera by Oscar Barnack.

First filling station in the USA.

Henry Ford introduces the assembly line for automobile production.

Citroën founded.

First autobahn (AVUS) in Berlin.

The London Underground (subway) introduces its own type design.

"Successful Design Types" exhibition from Austria and Germany is held in London.

The British Design and Industries Association is set up, following the model of the Deutsche Werkbund.

Tank wristwatch by **Louis Cartier**.

Theo van Doesburg and Piet Mondrian set up De Stijl.

"Hemutställningen" ("Home-living exhibition") in Stockholm displays beautiful, individual items for the house.

First exhibition of American design at the Metropolitan Museum of Art in New York.

First supermarket in the USA.

Russian Revolution.

The Bauhaus is founded in Weimar and develops into a school of functionalism.

Fiat's Lingotto factory opens in Turin.

Foundation of the Art Directors Club in New York.

Raymond F. Loewy arrives in New York.

A

Models of modernism. Between the two World Wars, **functionalism** in Central Europe became a reforming movement that shocked through its very plainness. Life had to be simplified with rectilinear architecture, rational kitchen units, and plain typefaces devoid of serifs and decoration. The tubular chair became the symbol of the new functionalism, a form tried by countless designers including **Marcel Breuer**, **Le Corbusier**, **Giuseppe Terragni**, **Gunnar Asplund**, and **Warren McArthur**. At the same time, France developed a different style, the fashionable **Art Deco** modern movement. This was the style of the "Jazz Age," perfectly expressed by **Jacques-Émile Ruhlmann** and **Kem Weber**. In the United States, the land of the skyscrapers and prosperity, the first "industrial design" companies were created. The concept spread so that the profession became recognized and established. **Harley Earl** introduced "styling" to the American car industry and made the annual introduction of a new model into a national ritual.

Wilhelm Wagenfeld's table lamp ("Bauhaus lamp").

Aino Marsio and Alvar Aalto get married.

Kaare Klint sets up a furniture school in Copenhagen.

"Form without Ornament" exhibition by the Deutsche Werkbund in Stuttgart.

Mart Stam constructs the original cantilever chair, using steel gas pipe.

General Motors sets up the "Art and Color Section" and Harley Earl becomes the first automobile designer there.

Container Corporation of America develops cardboard packaging.

Paul Renner designs the functional typeface *Futura*. (2)

The magazine *Domus* commences publication.

"Art and Industry" exhibition held at Macy's in New York.

Plexiglas (Perspex) available.

Wkhutemas schools established in Moscow.

El Lissitzky designs poster for the Russia-Polish struggle.

The bobbed haircut becomes the fashion.

Paul Jaray's streamlined car patented.

Reinforced concrete is used for shell construction.

Department store chains spread throughout America.

1920 1921 1922 1923 1924 1925 1926 1927 1928 1929

Chanel *No. 5* perfume comes on the market. (3)

Maurice Marinot produces modern art glass.

The Alessi houseware company is founded.

There are over 14 million telephones connected in the USA.

Jean Prouvé opens a metal workshop. (1)

Jazz and flappers become fashionable.

First refrigerator for private use.

Marcel Breuer's *Wassily* tubular steel chair becomes the icon of the Bauhaus.

Ferdinand Kramer's knock-down furniture.

"Exposition des Arts Décoratifs" in Paris, with many pieces in the Art Deco style, glass by Edward Hald, Poul Henningsen's *PH* light and Le Corbusier's Pavillon de l'Ésprit Nouveau (Pavilion of the New Spirit).

Cranbrook Academy of Art founded in Michigan with Eliel Saarinen as director.

The Bauhaus moves to new premises at Dessau.

The Deutsche Werkbund initiates the Weißenhof housing development in Stuttgart, bringing together European avant-garde architects and designers.

Herbert Bayer completes the *Universal* typeface.

Cassina furniture company founded.

Art Deco exhibition held at Macy's in New York.

Barcelona chair designed by Ludwig Mies van der Rohe for the German pavilion at the "Exposición Internacional" in Barcelona.

Museum of Modern Art founded in New York.

First Cologne furniture fair.

First commissions for Raymond F. Loewy and Henry Dreyfuss. Industrial design becomes established in the USA.

Streamlined visions. The collapse of the world economy threw America into deep economic depression and hopes for recovery came to be pinned on industrial designers. Men such as **Henry Dreyfuss, Raymond F. Loewy, Walter Dorwin Teague** and **Russel Wright** were revered like heroes. Their miracle cure was dynamic streamlining, which not only promoted sales but also promised a future; it was applied to every kind of product, from pencil sharpeners to refrigerators and locomotives. The style was celebrated at the 1939 New York World's Fair. During the 1930s many emigrant designers left National Socialist Germany for the USA, among them **Herbert Bayer, Walter Gropius, Ludwig Mies van der Rohe** and **László Moholy-Nagy.** They brought **functionalism** with them. This movement soon became known as the International Style, and it even acquired an effective advertising department in the form of New York's Museum of Modern Art.

El Lissitzky's dismantleable plywood chair.

"Stockholm Exhibition" by **Gunnar Asplund** brings functionalism to Scandinavia.

Art Center College of Design founded in Los Angeles.

"Modern Architecture" exhibition at the Museum of Modern Art, New York brings functionalism to America (International Style)

The book *Horizons* by Norman Bel Geddes is a tribute to streamlining.

Raymond F. Loewy designs the streamlined *Coldspot Super Six* refrigerator.

Eve chair by **Bruno Mathsson.**

Nuccio Bertone joins his family's coachbuilding company.

Erco lighting company founded.

Guiseppe Terragni designs the Casa del Fascio in rationalist style.

Nylon produced by Du Pont.

Hoover *One-Fifty* vacuum cleaner by **Henry Dreyfuss.**

Walter Dorwin Teague's Kodak *Bantam Special* is an early compact camera. (2)

Royal Designers for Industry (RDI) founded in London.

Inauguration of the Hoover Dam on the Colorado.

Prototype of the *Volkswagen.*

Hans Coray wins a competition with his *Landi* aluminum chair.

Marcel Breuer, Walter Gropius, Ludwig Mies van der Rohe, and **Ferdinand Kramer** emigrate to the USA.

With **Herbert Bayer,** Walter Gropius organizes a Bauhaus exhibition at the Museum of Modern Art.

The 20th Century Ltd. luxury train designed by Henry Dreyfuss runs between New York and Chicago. (3)

1930 1931 1932 1933 1934 1935 1936 1937 1938 1939

1931

Alvar Aalto's *Paimio* armchair with "organic" form. (1)

Den Permanente design gallery opens in Copenhagen.

Empire State Building in New York.

1932

1933

First Milan Triennale.

The Bauhaus is closed down by the National Socialists.

Useless Machines by **Bruno Munari.**

Adolf Hitler comes to power.

1934

1935

The streamlined Douglas *DC-3* designed by Walter Dorwin Teague.

First magnetic sound recorder made by AEG.

Laurens Hammond's electronic organ.

1936

1937

American Modern service by **Russel Wright.**

Josef Frank creates "Swedish Modern" at the Exposition Universelle, Paris.

László Moholy-Nagy sets up the "New Bauhaus" in Chicago.

First Xerox photocopier.

1938

1939

Prototype of the Citroën *2CV.*

Hans Knoll sets up his furniture company in New York.

Gino Sarfatti founds the Arteluce lighting company in Milan.

New York World's Fair.

World War II begins.

Temporary solutions. During World War II, design benefited from some unexpected developments. In Denmark, for instance, a new generation of imaginative, resourceful designers came into being under German occupation. In Great Britain, a program of functional "Utility" furniture was developed out of necessity. The order of the day was "Low Cost Furniture," and this was also the title of a postwar exhibition at the Museum of Modern Art that included young designers like **Hans J. Wegner** and **Marco Zanuso**. During the war **Charles** and **Ray Eames** developed the shell chair made from molded plywood, an innovative technique derived from military research that caught the imagination of designers like nothing before it. A new movement was closely connected with this technique, the playful, romantic, "organic design" represented by names such as **Alvar Aalto**, **Grete Jalk**, **Finn Juhl**, **Bruno Mathsson** and **Carlo Mollino**, which became the style of the 1950s.

Kantarelli vases by **Tapio Wirkkala**.

"Britain Can Make It" exhibition in London promotes good product design.

Vespa motor scooter developed by Corradino d'Ascanio.

First Levittown, consisting of mass-produced prefabricated houses, in the USA.

Louis Réard invents the bikini.

Cappellini furniture company founded.

Olivetti *Lexikon 80* typewriter.

Sixten Sason's Hasselblad camera. (1: prototype)

Akari lighting range from string and paper designed by **Isamu Noguchi**.

The *Land Rover* introduced.

"Organic Design in Home Furnishings" exhibition at the Museum of Modern Art, New York. **Charles Eames** and **Eero Saarinen** win the competition with a chair made of molded plywood.

First sketches for the *Jeep*.

The British Government stops deliveries of wood to the furniture industry.

Ferdinand Kramer designs *Knock-Down* furniture in the USA.

The British Government sets up the Utility Furniture scheme, run by a Committee under **Gordon Russell**.

The first *V2* rocket flight takes place at Peenemünde.

Council of Industrial Design (today the Design Council) set up in Britain on the American model.

Messerschmitt *Me 262* jet aircraft.

The first deportations of Jews to Auschwitz.

1940 1941 1942 1943 1944 1945 1946 1947 1948 1949

New package for Lucky Strike by **Raymond F. Loewy**. (2)

In California, **Charles** and **Ray Eames** experiment with plywood. (3)

Wurlitzer Model *850* jukebox.

Foundation of the American Society of Industrial Designers.

Norman Bel Geddes works on psychological warfare equipment for the US government.

The first nuclear reactor goes into operation at Oak Ridge.

George Nelson's *Storage Wall*.

Tupperware comes to the market

Finn Juhl's *Teak Chair*.

Harvard's *Mark 1* mainframe computer.

World War II ends.

The first postwar American car is the Studebaker *Champion* designed by **Raymond F. Loewy**.

Christian Dior invents the "New Look."

Salvatore Ferragamo designs an "invisible" ladies' sandal.

Kaj Franck's *Kilta* service. (4)

Round Chair by **Hans J. Wegner**.

Plastic furniture manufacturer Kartell founded.

Tail fins appear for the first time on the Cadillac.

Naturally Nordic. The School of Design in Ulm was an attempt to continue and promote the democratic traditions of the Bauhaus. It became one of the most important influences of the postwar period, associated with important designers such as **Otl Aicher**, **Max Bill** and **Hans Gugelot**. This Cold War era saw an apparently never-ending increase of prosperity in Europe. Here too, there were now cars for all: the Citroën *2CV* by **Flaminio Bertoni**, the *Volkswagen* by **Ferdinand Porsche**, the Fiat *500* by Dante Giacosa and the Morris *Mini* by **Alec Issigonis**. The force field of the period's design history was represented by the triangle formed of Italy, Scandinavia and the USA. Scandinavian designs were regularly awarded prizes at the Milan Triennale, where designers like **Tapio Wirkkala** and **Timo Sarpaneva** became celebrated stars. Pieces such as **Henning Koppel's** *Fish Dish* and **Hans J. Wegner's** *Round Chair* became cult objects. Since then the enthusiasm for everything Nordic and "natural," and the demand for "good design," have become ubiquitous in the living rooms of the middle classes.

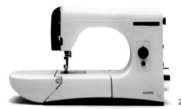

Ulmer stool by **Max Bill**.

Porsche *356* speedster. (4)

"Good Design" exhibition at the Museum of Modern Art, New York (four others follow).

Myren ("Ant") chair by **Arne Jacobsen** becomes the quintessence of industrial chairs. (1)

Harry Bertoia's *Diamond Chair* of metal wire.

London artists form the Independent Group.

Greyhound bus by **Raymond F. Loewy**.

The Lego construction toy first appears.

"Compasso d'Oro" becomes the most important Italian design prize.

The "Design in Scandinavia" exhibition in the USA releases a wave of modern design.

Braun *Phonosuper* radiogram by **Hans Gugelot** and **Dieter Rams**.

George Nelson's *Marshmallow* sofa.

Alfa Romeo *Giulietta Spider* designed by **Pinin Farina**.

Popular success of rock'n'roll.

Eero Saarinen's TWA terminal at Kennedy Airport, New York, is the quintessence of 1950s architecture.

Sella bicycle saddle chair by **Achille Castiglioni**.

J. K.Galbraith's book *The Affluent Society* is published.

Atomium at the Brussels "Universal Expo".

1950

1951 1952 1953 1954 1955 1956 1957 1958 1959

Shell chair program of **Charles** and **Ray Eames**.

First design conference in Aspen, USA.

The Festival of Britain in London shows modern products such as **Ernest Race's** *Antelope* chair.

Rat for Formgebung (German Design Council) set up in the Federal Republic of Germany.

The first Chevrolet *Corvette* goes into volume production.

Teaching at the Ulm Design School begins.

Osvaldo Borsani founds the Tecno furniture company.

Citroen *DS 19* by **Flaminio Bertoni** inspires both laymen and specialists.

Saul Bass creates the first creative title sequence and integrated marketing strategy for the film *The Man with the Golden Arm*. (3)

Mary Quant opens her boutique Bazaar in London's Kings Road.

Superleggera chair by **Gio Ponti** for Cassina.

Univers typeface by **Adrian Frutiger**.

Mirella sewing machine by **Marcello Nizzoli**. (2)

"Interbau" in Berlin exhibits modern architecture and "Gute Form".

Yves Saint Laurent appointed to Dior.

Sputnik orbits the earth.

The Morris *Mini* designed by **Alec Issigonis** is the first modern small car.

Frank Lloyd Wright's Guggenheim Museum opens in New York.

The plastic tube hula-hoop becomes a craze.

Shocking colors and "pop" enterprises. Archizoom, Studio 65, **Superstudio**, UFO: Creators of crazy exhibitions and utopian designs that were mass-produced in Italy, these groups were part of a rebellion later defined as "**Radical Design**," or "**Anti-Design**." By an irony of history, they heralded Italy's leading role in the world of design. There was an abundance of great designs that rejected all the established concepts of furnishing, like the *Blow* plastic armchair by **De Pas, d'Urbino**, and **Lomazzi**. Others who made important contributions to the bold, often colorful world of "Pop Design" were the Finnish designer **Eero Aarnio** and the Danish experimental artist **Verner Panton**. In the field of audio equipment, Bang & Olufsen, Braun and Brionvega entered a kind of competition for the most innovative creations. One of the reasons why Italian design was so successful was the alliance of creative rebels and happy-go-lucky risk-taking entrepreneurs. This merging of counter-culture and business was reflected in the work of **Mario Bellini, Joe Colombo, Ettore Sottsass** and **Marco Zanuso**. The same situation applied in Great Britain, where **Mary Quant** and **Terence Conran** opened their first "lifestyle" boutiques and turned pop culture into an industry.

2

World Design Conference in Tokyo.

World-wide "twist" craze.

The book *The Measure of Man* by **Henry Dreyfuss** published.

Braun produces the *Sixtant* electric shaver by **Hans Gugelot** and the *T 1000* world radio receiver by **Dieter Rams**. (3)

Polyprop chair by **Robin Day**.

Karl Lagerfeld designs furs for Fendi.

Elio Fiorucci becomes a fashion designer.

Posters by **Yusaku Kamekura** for the Tokyo Olympic Games.

Terence Conran's first Habitat shop opens in London.

Rudi Gernreich's topless bathing suit is a media event.

New York World's Fair.

RR 125 radio-phonograph by **Achille Castiglioni**.

Mary Quant and André Courrège simultaneously invent the mini-skirt.

The groups **Archizoom** and **Superstudio** establish "Radical Design."

In Cologne **Verner Panton** exhibits "Visiona," his plastic living environnment.

Driade furniture company set up.

Worldwide student protests against the war in Vietnam.

1960   1961   1962   1963   1964   1965   1966   1967   1968   1969

1961

IBM *Selectric* typewriter by **Eliot Noyes**. (2)

First Milan furniture fair.

Archigram architecture group set up in London.

The Beatles appear for the first time in the British charts.

Building of the Berlin Wall.

1963

Eero Aarnio's synthetic resin *Ball* armchair. (1)

Action Office by Hermann Miller.

President John F. Kennedy assassinated.

1965

Jacob Jensen designs the *Beolit 600* portable receiver for Bang & Olufsen.

Cassina begins the *I Maestri* series of reeditions of classic modern pieces.

Mobil introduces modular *Pegasus* filling station designed by **Eliot Noyes**.

Gaetano Pesce publishes his *Manifesto on Elastic Architecture*.

Ikea opens its first furniture store in Stockholm.

1967

Verner Panton's plastic cantilever chair.

Blow chair by **De Pas, D'Urbino** and **Lomazzi**.

Pipistrello light by **Gae Aulenti**.

NSU *Ro 80*. designed by **Claus Luthe**

1969

Sacco beanbag chair by **Gatti, Paolini and Teodoro**. (4)

Il Monumento Continuo by **Superstudio**.

Kenzo boutique opens in Paris.

Sony color video recorder.

Moon landing.

3

4

Between crisis and creative confusion. The intoxicating freedom of the 1960s was followed by a morning-after mood, particularly in the aftermath of the oil crises of 1973 and 1979. The new trends ranged from the intellectual guidance of Victor Papanek, commending a philosophy of awareness in design, to the "No Future" movement of the British punk revolt, with its anarchic emblem designed by **Jamie Reid**. The "small is beautiful" attitude was also evident in the world of car design, where **Giorgetto Giugiaro** created the VW Golf, the most successful model of all time. A side effect of the continuing crisis was the final separation of industrial design from arts and crafts, which for a time became identified with alternative lifestyles. The new sense of responsibility led to original, ecological, ergonomic approaches, exemplified by Sweden's **Maria Benktzon**'s designs for the handicapped. It was a decade when international mega-agencies such as **Pentagram** were created, especially in Great Britain. In the world of fashion, American designers launched the concept of leisure fashion such as the T-shirt, the track suit and **Calvin Klein**'s "designer jeans."

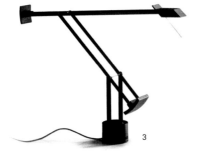

Tizio halogen light by **Richard Sapper**. (3)

Valentine typewriter for Olivetti by **Perry A. King** and **Ettore Sottsass**.

Side 2 cabinet by **Shiro Kuramata**.

Kompan's spring seesaw conquers the playgrounds of the world.

Frank Gehry's *Easy Edge* chair range made of laminated cardboard.

"Italy: The New Domestic Landscape" exhibition at the Museum of Modern Art, New York.

Design for the Real World by Victor Papanek is published.

Pentagram design agency established in London.

Otl Aicher develops the corporate image of the Munich Olympic Games.

VW *Golf* by **Giorgetto Giugiaro**. (1)

Giorgio Armani shows his first men's fashion collection.

Sears Tower in Chicago is the tallest building of the world.

Cab chair by **Mario Bellini**.

The subversive designer group Alchimia is set up in Milan.

Punk festival in London.

Richard Sapper's espresso machine for Alessi.

Alessandro Mendini's Re-Design projects, for example the *Proust* armchair. (2)

New Wave fashion.

1970   1971   1972   1973   1974   1975   1976   1977   1978   1979

1971

Serpentone snake seat by **Cini Boeri**.

"Let it rock" boutique opened by Malcolm McLaren and **Vivienne Westwood**.

Joe Colombo dies.

1973

Milton Glaser's NY sticker.

The T-shirt, which can be printed with any slogan, spreads throughout the world.

Triptrap baby's high chair by **Peter Opsvik**.

Energy crisis caused by the Arab oil embargo.

Vietnam war ends.

1975

Erik Magnussen's cylindrical vacuum flask for Stelton.

Fiorucci makes fashion fun.

Design Management Institute founded in Boston.

1977

Atollo table lamp by **Vico Magistretti**.

Jamie Reid designs punk graphics for the Sex Pistols (4), who are styled by Vivienne Westwood.

John Makepeace sets up a college for cabinetmaking and furniture design.

Centre Georges Pompidou in Paris.

1979

Sony brings out the *Walkman.*

Alchimia's *Bau.Haus* Collection.

Alberto Meda returns to his Milan studio.

When design trends overflowed. Under the leadership of **Ettore Sottsass** and in the spirit of **Alessandro Mendini**, the Memphis group finally shattered the hope that paradise was furnished with "good design." This eclectic gathering of artists ranging from **Hans Hollein** and **Shiro Kuramata** to **Javier Mariscal** and **Oscar Tusquets Blanca** continued the tradition of postmodern blasphemy. Meanwhile the West came to enjoy luxury again, especially the hedonistic "Young Urban Professionals" (yuppies), who saw design as an expression of their up-to-dateness. An amusing kettle, created for Alessi by **Michael Graves**, became the symbol of the period. "Designer fashion" now also concentrated on underwear, sold in shops that were themselves created by designers. Inner cities changed their appearance, as did shopping malls and filling stations, some of which were completely redesigned by **Saul Bass**. **Ingo Maurer**'s *YaYaHo* suspended lighting system, **Bill Moggeridge**'s *Grid Compass* laptop, Apple's *Macintosh* computer and **Frank Gehry**'s *Cross Check* wickerwork furniture were all products that questioned the "commanding" role of mechanization, positioning them among the pioneering creations of the decade.

Toshiyuki Kita's *Wink* armchair.

Frontier Fashion designs by **Ralph Lauren**.

Lucius Burckhardt's article "Design ist unsichtbar" ("Design is invisible") appears.

MTV goes on the air.

The television series "Dallas" achieves a worldwide audience of 300 million.

Grid Compass laptop computer by **Bill Moggeridge**.

Stiletto's *Consumer's Rest* chair marks the new German protest design. (2)

Domus Academy set up in Milan.

Frogdesign opens a branch office in California.

Apple's *Macintosh* launched.

La Conica espresso machine by **Aldo Rossi**. (3)

Rudy Vanderlans and Zuzanna Licko co-found Emigre. (4)

Yayaho lighting system by **Ingo Maurer**.

John Galliano opens his own fashion house.

Jasper Morrison opens a studio in London with designers following the new simplicity.

Christian Lacroix shows his first couture collection.

Swatch *Jelly Fish* wristwatch.

TGV high-speed train by **Roger Tallon**.

"Design for Independent Living" exhibition at the Museum of Modern Art, New York, showing designs for the disabled.

1980

1981
The Memphis group (including **Ettore Sottsass, Michele de Lucchi, Andrea Branzi, Michael Graves, Shiro Kuramata, Javier Mariscal**) introduces post-modernism in design.

Daniel Weil's *Bag Radio* in a transparent plastic pouch.

Ron Arad sets up his **One Off** studio.

Neville Brody become art director of *The Face*.

1982

1983
Alessi's *Program 6*.

Ted plastic chair by **Niels Gammelgaard** for Ikea.

The track suit becomes popular.

Karl Lagerfeld moves to Chanel.

1984

1985
Bird Kettle 9093 by **Michael Graves** for Alessi, the archetype of fun design.

ICE high-speed train by **Alexander Neumeister**.

1986

1987
Tolomeo table lamp by **Michele De Lucchi**.

Gaetano Pesce's *I Feltri* armchair. (1)

Casino by **Pentagon** at the art show "Documenta 8".

European Design Prize introduced.

Fiat takes over Alfa Romeo.

1988

1989
David Carson becomes art director of the magazine *Beach Culture*.

Jasper Morrison's *Plychair* for Vitra.

Madza *MX-5* marks the revival the sports car.

Berlin Wall comes down.

Trends in the global village. Two clearly recognizable trends became apparent. On the one hand there was neo-objectivity, represented by **Jasper Morrison**, while on the other hand there was the complete opposite, reflected by the baroque lushness of **Borek Sipek**. In the absence of historical perspective, it will only become clear later whether the stylistic Babylon of the 1990s is larger than before, or whether it is simply an optical illusion. Yet another question is whether the world has finally become a cultural melting pot as a result of the globalization of corporate design. What is certain is that some designers have succeeded in irritating viewers with their creations, some of which use digital manipulation techniques. The American graphic artist **David Carson** distorts and mixes typefaces and layouts on the computer, creating a much-imitated "deconstructivist" style. Similarly the fashion designer **John Galliano** constantly offends the world of haute couture, only to be paid vast sums for doing so. **Ron Arad** recycles rubbish and is hailed as the messiah of furniture design. Lastly, the 1990s have seen a completely unexpected revival in the field of car design, which is looking towards the future while at the same time reflecting a decidedly nostalgic tendency.

New Beetle by **J Mays**. (4)

Audi *TT Coupé* by **Peter Schreyer**.

Damien Hirst and **Jonathan Barnbrook**'s theme restaurant *Pharmacy* opens in London.

Peter Saville joins Pentagram.

Spike Lee opens a chain store for street and leisure fashion.

Torn jeans become fashionable.

Erco *Quinta* heater range by **Knud Holscher**.

The Brionvega audio company is wound up.

Seville Universal Expo.

Ron Arad's *Bookworm* bookshelf. (1)

Sheet iron chair *200* by **Mats Theselius** for Källemo.

Mobil plastic tube car by **Antonio Citterio**.

Nokia *Communicator*.

Lufthansa terminal by **Hartmut Esslinger**'s Frogdesign.

Tom Dixon becomes art director of Habitat.

Richard Meier is architect of the Getty Center in Los Angeles.

1990

1991

Frank Gehry *Cross-Check* chair of woven wood.

Bubu stool by **Philippe Starck**. (3)

Ericsson digital mobile telephone.

1992

Enzo Mari becomes chief designer of the Royal Prussian Porcelain factory.

New foam trainers by Nike.

The Dyson *DC01* vacuum cleaner is launched.

Gaultier's *Hasidim* collection.

Alexander McQueen opens his own fashion house.

1993

1994

Olavi Lindén's *Handy ax* for Fiskars.

The Inflate group projects light over London.

"Mutant Materials in Contemporary Design" exhibition at the Museum of Modern Art.

Calvin Klein withdraws advertising using children.

Ikea buys Habitat.

1995

1996

Fantastic Plastic Elastic chair by **Ron Arad**.

Vico Duet chair by **Vico Magistretti**.

Valvomo shows design for the Internet age at the Milan Furniture Fair.

Hackman's *Tools* kitchen range.

Andrée Putman sets up a company under her name.

Royal Copenhagen takes over Orrefors.

Gianni Versace murdered.

1997

1998

Apple *iMac* computer. (2)

Armchair *40/80* by **Achille Castiglioni** and Ferruccio Laviani.

Glass collection *Relations* by littala

Lighthouse Museum opens in Glasgow.

Daimler merges with Chrysler. Exxon takes over Mobil.

1999

Design museums

Centre Georges Pompidou
Rue Beaubourg
Paris, France

**Cooper Hewitt Design Museum,
Smithonian Institution**
2 E. 91st St. / 5th Ave
New York, USA

Design Museum
Butler's Wharf
London, UK

**Det Danske Kunstindustrie-
museum**
Bredgade 68
Copenhagen, Denmark

Kunstmuseum Trapholt
Aeblehaven 23
Kolding, Denmark

Lighthouse
22 King Street
Glasgow, UK

Metropolitan Museum of Art
5th Ave. / 82nd St.
New York, USA

Musee des Arts Décoratifs
107 rue de Rivoli
Paris, France

Museum für Angewante Kunst
An der Rechtschule
Cologne, Germany

Museum für Angewante Kunst
Stubenring 5
Vienna, Austria

Museum für Gestaltung
Im Schwarzenbach 6
Basel, Switzerland

Museum für Gestaltung
Ausstellungsstraße 60
Zürich, Switzerland

Museum für Kunsthandwerk
Schaumaikai 17
Frankfurt / Main, Germany

**Museum für Kunst und
Gewerbe**
Steintorplatz 1
Hamburg, Germany

Museum of Modern Art
11 W. 53rd St.
New York, USA

Neue Sammlung
Prinzregentenstr.3
Munich, Germany

Nordiska Museet
Djurgardsvägen 6-16
Stockholm, Sweden

Oslo Kunstindustrimuseet
St. Olavsgate, Oslo, Norway

Röhsska Konstslöjdmuseet
Vasagatan 37-39
Gothenberg, Sweden

Taideteollisuusmuseo
Korkeavuorenkatu 23
Helsinki, Finland

**Umeleckoprumyslove
muzeum**
17. listopadu 2
Prague, Czech Republic

Victoria & Albert Museum
Cromwell Road,
South Kensington
London, UK

**Vestlandske Kunstindustri-
museum**
Nordahl Brunsgate 9
Bergen, Norway

Vitra Design Museum
Charles-Eames-Straße 1
Weil am Rhein, Germany

Design institutes

**Agence pour la Promotion de
la Création Industrielle A.P.C.I.**
3 rue de Crillon
Paris, France

**Associazione per il Disegno
Industriale ADI**
Via Bramante 29
Milan, Italy

**Belgisch Instituut voor Design
BDI**
Heizel Esplanade
Brussels, Belgium

Dansk Design Council DDC
H.C. Andersens Bd. 18
Copenhagen, Denmark

Design Exchange DX
234 Bay Street
Toronto, Canada

Design Forum Finnland
Fabianinkatu 10
Helsinki, Finland

**Design Institute of Australia
DIA**
50 Burwood Road
Hawthorn, Victoria, Australia

**Federation and Center
São Paulo State**
Av. Paulista, 1313-5th floor
São Paulo, Brazil

**Fudacio BCD
Centre de Disseny**
Av. Diagonal 452-454
Barcelona. Spain

**Fundacion Centro de Diseno
Industriale de Madrid**
Serrano 208
Madrid, Spain

Föreningen Svensk Form
Renstiernas gata 12
Stockholm, Sweden

French Institute of Design
10 rue Jaques Bingen
Paris, France

**Institut de Design Montreal
IDM**
360 rue St. Paul East, Suite 300
Montreal, Canada

**International Council of
Societies of Industrial Design**
Yrjönkatu 11 E
Helsinki, Finland

**International Design Center
New York**
30-20 Thomsom Avenue
Long Island City, USA

**Irish Trade Board Design and
Product Development**
Strand Road
Dublin, Ireland

Japan Design Foundation
3-1-800 Umeda 1 chome
Osaka 530, Japan

**Japan Industrial Design
Promotion Organisation**
2-4-1 Hamamatsu-cho
Tokyo, Japan

**Korea Institute of
Industrial Design**
128-8 Yunkun-dong
Seoul, Korea

Norsk Form
Uranienborgveien 2
Oslo, Norway

**Österreichisches Institut
für Formgebung**
St. Ulrichsplatz 4
Vienna, Austria

Rat für Formgebung
Lundwig-Erhard-Anlage 1
Frankfurt / Main, Germany

**The American Center
for Design**
325 Huron Street
Chicago, USA

The Design Council
34 Bow Street
London, UK

Triennale
Via Alemagna 6, Palazzo
dell'Arte
Milan, Italy

Vormgevings Instituut
Kaizergracht 609
Amsterdam, Netherlands

Photo credits:

A&B: 74/1; Archivio ADI: 414/3; 415/4; AEG-Archiv, Nürnberg: 37/2,3; Archive Aldo Ballo: 75/6; 219/2; 264/1; 237/1,2; 293/1; 332/2; 333/5; 415/2; Bangert Verlag: 66/1; 375/1; Bauhaus- Archiv, Berlin: 35/2; 37/1; 54/1; 251/1,2; Belesia, Milan: 62/2; Bella & Ruggeri: 237/3; Bitetto-Chimenti: 262/2,3; Bosch-Archiv, Stuttgart: 43/1; Torsten Bröhan: 134/1; Beppe Caggi: 398/3; Danish Design Council: 42/2,3; 50/ 1,2,3; 158/1; 172/1; 173/2,3; 175/1; 185/2; 189/1; 203/1,2; 221/4; 245/1,2,3; 283/2,5,6; Christie's Images, London: 228/1; 319/1,2; Carine d'Orlac de Polignac: 70/1,3,4; 71/5; Chanel: 76/2; Benjamin Grätz and Nikos Choudetsanakis: 16/1; C. Cournut, 67/1; British Design Council, Brighton:299/1,2; British Design Council, Manchester: 58/3,4; 91/1; 99/1; 132/2; 147/5; 217/5; 257/1; 261/1; 301/1; 259/3; 320/1,2; 361/1; Design Forum Finland, Helsinki: 190; 406/1,3; 407/5; Thomas Dix: 104/2; 170/1; 266/1; F. DuMoulin / Java: 70/2; 71/6; Patrik Enquist: 80/1,2,3; Erco, Lüdenscheid: 364 /2,3; Fulvio Ferrari, Torino: 65/2; 84/1,2,3; 244/1; 253/5; 287/1; 293/4; Graziano Ferrari: 254/2; Joachim Fliegner (Wilhelm Wagenfeld Stiftung), Bremen: 395/5; General Motors Photo Archives, 106/1,2,3; Gutenberg Museum, Mainz: 207/1; Hans Hansen: 54/1; 78/1; 79/5; 105/3,4,5,6; 136/1; 137/3,4; 241/4; 356/1; 357/8; Hille International: 91/1; Henry Dreyfuss Associates: 100/2; 101/3,4,5,6,7; Issey Miyake: 1999: 248/1,2; Andreas Jung / Galerie Ulrich Fiedler, Köln: 15/3,4,5; 161/2; 221/6; 335/2,3; 414/1; IBM, Stuttgart: 306/1; Timo Kirgeleinen: 407/2; Christophe Kicherer: 23/3; Archiv Michael Koetzle, 119/2; Karl Lagerfeld, Paris: 196/1; Per Larsson: 157/2; Tom Linglau, Cologne: 404/2; Los Angeles Modern Auctions: 398/1; 410/1; François Maillard: 181/1,3; John Makepeace Ltd.: 222/1,2,3; Loew's Agentur, Munich: 186/1,2; Manufactum, Waltrop: 95/1; 273/2,6; Masera: 31/3; 47/1; 74/2; 133/1; 362/1,2; 368/2; Musée de la Mode et du Costume, Collection UFAC, Paris: 291/1,2; Museum für Gestaltung, Zürich: 34/1; 68/1; 69/2,3; 179/1; 233/1; 316/1; 319/1; 347/2; Museum für Kunst und Gewerbe, Hamburg: 374/1; Museum für Kunsthandwerk, Frankfurt / Main: 384/1; MoMA, New York: 347/1; Die Neue Sammlung, Munich: 8; 57/1,2; 82/1; 198/1; 211/2; 272/1,3; 311/1,2; 366 /1,2,3; Neumeister Design, Munich: 268/1; Paschall/Taylor: 148/3,4; Pininfarina Studi & Ricerche: 110/1; 111/2,3,4; Polo Ralph Lauren, New York/Paris: 199/3; PPR Harder, Munich: 197/1,2,3; Marino Ramazzotti: 75/4; 93/2; 353/3; Ramazzotti & Stucchi: 93/3;227/5; 368/1; Rat für Formgebung, Frankfurt am Main: 47/2; Raymond Loewy Foundation: 210/1,3,4,5,6,7; Rooks Photography, 104/1; Phil Schaafsma: 105/5; Bernhard Schaub, 285/2; Axel Siebmann, Hamburg: 27/1,2; 96/1,2; 135/1,2; 199/1,2; 254/1; 263/1,2; 300/1,2; 389/2,4,5; 412/1,2; Sipa Press, Paris: 142/1,4,5; 143/2,3,6; 23971,2; Chris Frazer Smith, London: 62/1,3; Sotheby's, London: 63/1,2; Svenskt Tenn, Stockholm: 124/1,3,4; 125/2,5,6; Walter Dorwin Teague Associates: 367/4; William Taylor: 148/1; Sylvain Thomas: 132/1,2,3; Gianni Viviani, 118/1,2,3; Vitra, Birsfelden: 267/2, 6; Deidi von Schaewen: 77/1,2; 223/2; 298/1,2; Kris Willner: 382/1; Franz Wittmann Werkstätten, Etsdorf/Kamp: 162/1,2; 162/3,4; Nigel Young: 121/1; Miro Zagnoli: 136/1; 193/3.

Photographs and illustrations that are not listed separately are reprinted by courtesy of the designers and companies. Unless otherwise indicated, the copyrights are with the respective designers and companies. In a few cases it was not possible to identify the copyright holders. Legitimate claims will be settled according to customary agreements.

Special thanks to the following companies and museums:

Alessi, Alias, Artemide, Audi, Cappellini, Cassina, ClassiCon, Daimler Chrysler, Driade, Erco, Ecart, Fredericia, Fritz Hansen, Honeywell Inc., littala, Georg Jensen, Knoll International, Los Angeles Modern Auctions, Herman Miller, Néotu, Orrefors, Pininfarina, Rosenthal, Tecnolumen, Tecta, Thonet, Vitra, Volkswagen, Wittmann, Woka, Zanotta

Museum für Gestaltung, Zürich; Museum für Kunsthandwerk, Frankfurt am Main; Vitra Design Museum, Weil am Rhein

Thank you: Vivien Antwi, Aubrey Lawrence, Michael Schönberger, Gert Schröder, Jeremy Stout

Assistance:
Tim Elsner, Donatella Cacciola, Steve Cox, Hildegard Hake, Susanne Kaps, Janina Kossmann, Anita Mayer, Heike Tekampe and Thomas Donga, Astrid van der Auwera, June Ueno, Oliver Wolf